Gullible's Travels:

From Diaper Rash to Kissing Frogs

My Life's Stories — Book One

by
Deanna Purcell Pendleton

authorHOUSE®

AuthorHouse™
1663 Liberty Drive, Suite 200
Bloomington, IN 47403
www.authorhouse.com
Phone: 1-800-839-8640

First published by AuthorHouse 8/3/2007

ISBN: 978-1-4343-3154-0

Printed in the United States of America
Bloomington, Indiana

This book is printed on acid-free paper.

DEDICATION

I would like to dedicate my first book to my grandchildren: Timothy, Emma, Connor, and Cadan Dickson—especially to Tim, because it is he who really got me started putting my stories down on paper for posterity. I'd also like to thank my sons, Shawn and Dan, and their wives, Edna and Cara, who spent hours with me—listening, commenting, editing, and generally helping me work through the creative process. Finally, special thanks to my husband, George, for listening to each story after it was written and for taking over most of the household chores while I wrote.

PREFACE

In my beginning, God created my father, John William Purcell, and my mother, Aeneita Irene Clark Purcell. I was their first child, Deanna Aeneita Purcell, born on February 18, 1938. My one sibling, John Darrell Purcell, joined us on November 15, 1940. Life was good back then . . .

As I think back on my life, I am sometimes overwhelmed by the memories of my childhood. What a grand and wonderful time it was. I am also saddened that I was unable to give my two boys the same kind of childhood I enjoyed. Even with the terrible events of WWII, the simplicity of life I enjoyed in those days can never be recaptured.

I know times change and each of us is formed by the events that take place in our lives. Still, I look at the way life is today, and tightness grips my throat. Life has changed so much. My grandchildren will never experience that *life*: neither the simple life of my childhood, nor will life be even as uncomplicated as it was for their own parents, my sons, Shawn and Dan. Technology is supposed to make things better, easier for people. But sitting here now as a 67 year old woman, I look at all the advancements that have been made since my birth; and I can't help but wish that I could do away with most of them and take my grandchildren back to that simple life of my childhood.

Yes, we had our war—World War II. And we got hot without air conditioning. And we had polio and other diseases that have now almost been eradicated. And a lot of people were living at borderline poverty as recognized today—even if we didn't know it then.

We hadn't heard of *free love* then, and most girls didn't get pregnant before they got married. If they did, they got married right away and most of those marriages lasted anyway. They didn't just *live* with the father of one child and then, *on a whim,* move on to another father and another child. In most families, the children knew that they all had the same father. Most girls wore bras for modesty and wouldn't have participated in a *wet tee-shirt contest* if you had paid them. And *ladies* or not, women didn't get tattoos! Tattoos were an *indiscretion of youth* made by males who were in the navy or some other branch of the service. So much has changed!

Back then, people seemed to be a whole lot friendlier. They helped each other. If somebody was *down and out* or there was a major illness in a family, the whole town banded together to help them. And you didn't label people by the clothes they wore—even if they were made of flour sacks—because, at one time or another, almost everybody wore clothes made from flour sacks, too. You didn't have to worry that you only wore your *good shoes* to church on Sunday because everybody saved their shoes for Sunday. Certainly no one had $100 Nikes to wear, let alone steal.

Safety wasn't an issue. You didn't have to lock doors, and you really only slept with the screen door *hooked* at night so it wouldn't make that knocking sound if the wind picked up. And you didn't have to worry if you left all your windows open at night. It's not like anyone was going to crawl in; there wasn't anything to take. And besides, you'd suffocate from the heat in the summer if they weren't open.

Back then, everything seemed to smell and taste better. Clothes smelled better when you put them on after taking them off the clothesline. Nothing was quite like ice cream made from ice right out of the ice house—even if it was usually just vanilla flavored (made with Watkins Vanilla). And Mama's fried chicken was always the best on the 4th of July, even if you were assigned the job of shooing away the flies at the picnic table—and you knew how many times those flies got past you.

Thanksgiving and Christmas Dinner at Grandma's, with all the family and relatives (people you only saw once a year), was an unforgettable event. Those 10 and 25-cent presents were so much more exciting than the much more expensive ones we trade today. Riding in the rumble seat of Grandpa's car and letting the wind blow my hair was certainly much more satisfying than having it plastered down with hair spray and still having to roll up the window like I do now. Grinding up bologna and pickles for sandwiches made them taste much better than any fast food you can purchase. Yes, we lived a more simple life, but I'd go back to it in a minute—well, except for maybe the flies and living without air conditioning.

This book is intended to be the first in a series of My Life's Stories. I expect to have at least four books because I have a lot of stories to tell. I will try to keep them consistent with different phases of my life— separated into approximate 20-year segments. This is *Book One* consisting of stories about the events and people who affected my first 18+ years of life—from birth through my high school years.

My son Shawn suggested the title for the series—***Gullible's Travels***—because he says I'm "so open and trusting" that he doesn't know anyone as "gullible" as I am. And, because these stories are about my travels in my journey through life, the title seemed rather appropriate. Again, this first book is entitled ***Gullible's Travels—From Diaper Rash to Kissing Frogs.***

All of these stories are as I remember them. I have tried to present an honest representation of the people and places mentioned. It is certainly not my intention to be unkind in what I say or how I depict anyone living or dead. I look back on these memories with great fondness. So please forgive me if I unintentionally say anything hurtful. It is my hope that you will get as much enjoyment from reading these stories as I have had in first living, and then writing them. And if all goes well, I hope you, too, will look forward to Books Two, Three, and Four.

December 28, 2005

TABLE OF CONTENTS

1.

MEMORIES OF MARSHAL CLARK

Horton, Kansas, is my hometown, but I couldn't go back *home* now. I've become too acclimated to the *good life* of the city—all the conveniences just a short drive away. But I often look back at my beginnings and think what a marvelous thing it was to grow up in a small town.

As I smile to myself and relax in my recliner, I mull over memories of my childhood, thinking quite often of that small town and the fateful day that drastically changed my relationship with my beloved grandfather, Marshal Clark, and began my path leading away from Horton.

Horton is located at the south end of Brown County, in Northeast Kansas, fifty some miles northeast of Topeka and about the same distance southwest of St. Joseph, Missouri. Being a major railroad hub back in the 1920's, Horton, with its population estimated at over fifteen thousand, was predicted to become a second Chicago. However, by the time I grew up in the forties and fifties, Horton was on a steady downhill trek, gradually becoming a shadow of its earlier existence (with a population of just under three thousand).

My parents were both products of the Great Depression. Even though my father had a successful Radio, Television and Appliance Store in Horton for over thirty years, neither he nor my mother ever forgot life during the Depression. My father had graduated from high school in

1926 and my mother in 1929. Over and over I heard stories of my father working for the WPA and hauling concrete in a wheelbarrow for 10-12 hours a day to repair the dam at Mission Lake, on the northeast side of Horton. Daddy was paid 50 cents a day for his efforts. His story always ended with "and I thanked God that I had a job." Most of my parents' siblings and relatives had endured the same kind of struggle. It affected them the rest of their lives.

There is always the exception, however. This was my grandfather, W. L. Clark (Winifred Littleton Clark). *Lit* as he was known to friends and relatives, and *Marshal Clark* as he was known to the citizens of Horton, my grandfather was a man of character. When he died in 1952, he had been Chief of Police for the City of Horton and a Brown County Deputy Sheriff for over thirty years. *Grandpa* had job security even during the depression. "People don't change and crime doesn't stop," was one of his quotes.

Although he wasn't a big *churchgoer*, his job made him the guardian angel and moral icon for the family. Because of his steady employment, he ended up being the *money* behind each of his children during the depression years. Although they had been dating since Mom was 16 (1927), my mother and father put off getting married until 1936 because they felt they didn't have the resources to strike out on their own. Even after they married and until I was three years old, they continued to live in an apartment they had fixed in two upstairs rooms of my grandparents' home.

It wasn't until the 1980's that I learned that Grandpa never earned over $150 a month during his years of service for the city. That *lofty sum* wasn't achieved until the very end of his service in the late forties and fifties just before he died in 1952. He got a few dollars extra to act as a Brown County or Atchison County Deputy Sheriff, but considering the number of times he laid his life on the line; it hardly seems like just compensation.

According to my mother, my grandfather was particularly fond of babies, and each of us, my three older cousins (Junior, Duane, and Roger) and I, took turns being the *baby* to be held and carried by Grandpa as he walked around the yard in the evening. Whether just talking or stopping to admire the flowers, or some rocks, or the bumble bees, Grandpa always gave a *grand* tour. My brother Darrell and my cousin Kathleen were born later and didn't get in on all the carrying around. As we grew, the four older grandchildren were taught how to catch and hold a butterfly without causing damage to its wings—so that after observing it, we could allow it to fly free. But the others, *the old boy babies*, outgrew Grandpa's favor because they got dirty and smelly, sassed or said bad words, or didn't hold butterflies with a gentle hand. I *always listened* to Grandpa and *followed his directions well*. At least, Grandpa never disagreed when I said so. And when I was too old to carry, Grandpa continued to walk around the yard with me, holding my hand and telling me his stories.

In the winter when it was too cold to go outside, he would sit in his oversized wooden rocker with the fancy carving on the back. He'd pull his chair up closer to the wood heating stove in the *parlor* where he would rock for hours—just listening to his upright Philco radio with the big yellow-lighted dial. He would hold me on his lap, and I would take his ivory comb or brush and pull his hair down over his eyes—parting it and combing it in amusing fashions. Sometimes, Grandpa would hold the mirror from Grandma's dresser. He would laugh and make faces at me in the mirror, and then we would both laugh together.

As it got close to Christmas, Grandpa liked to play a particular *game* with whatever grandchildren happened to be at his house when he came home from work. He called this game *Hokey-Pokey*. First, he'd go directly to his room to hang up his overcoat and change out of his uniform. Next, he'd come in and sit in his rocking chair like any other day. But soon he'd stop his rocking and would put his right hand index finger up to his mouth. "Shush! Shush, kids!" he'd say. "Did you hear that noise? I think I saw that old Mr. Claus slinking around behind Cook's Variety Store this afternoon. He had a notebook with him. I think he was checking on you kids."

"Oh, Grandpa, do you think he's outside now," we'd say in almost unison.

"I'll bet he's up on the roof right now—trying to get down the chimney in the closet. Tell you what . . . you kids be real quiet, and I'll go see if I can catch him." Then Grandpa would walk into his bedroom, and we would all get in a line and tiptoe as we followed him. Next, Grandpa would open the closet door, rush in, and close the door behind him while we tumbled over and against each other trying to sit on the bed or some-where on the floor—but always away from that closet door.

Soon we would hear a lot of moving, bumping, and mumbling and the sound of arguing and fighting. We'd hear Grandpa saying, "Hey, you old man! You're not going to get back up that chimney without leaving me some of that. You're in for a real fight now . . . Hokey-Pokey! Diddle Dee Dum! If you've got any candy, give me some!"

Momentarily, Grandpa would emerge from the closet with candy for each of us. Or sometimes it would be English walnuts, or apples, or oranges. But each time he would be wiping his brow and would say, "He sure was tough tonight. I really had a tussle with him. I had to really *hokey-pokey* him to get treats from him tonight." Then we en-joyed the best time of all as we sat around Grandpa's chair while he passed out candy, cracked walnuts, or peeled oranges or apples for all of us to share.

Grandpa always went to bed by eight each evening. He used to say he had gotten used to *going to bed with the chickens* during his early years when he was a farmer, but it was really because he had to get up between 4 and 4:30 AM so he could have a leisurely breakfast, read the paper, and still get to work by 6 AM. There was just my grandfather and one other policeman to handle the job seven days a week/twenty-four hours a day. A fellow by the name of Rollie Wallingford was the other policeman during most of this time. There were a couple of other fel-lows Grandpa had deputized; but they only came in occasionally so Grandpa could get his one week's vacation a year, or if something big was going on—like the annual Tri-County Fair.

Because of his schedule, Grandpa had to miss our school programs. One of these was the Christmas program when I was in the first grade. Mama made me a floor length, white, flannel gown and cardboard silver wings for the solo I sang as the angel that appeared at the manger an-nouncing the birth of the Christ child. Even though I stood in front of his rocker more than a dozen times to practice, Grandpa never complained. I'd be singing "Away in a manger, no crib for a bed. The little Lord Jesus lay down His sweet head . . ." while gesturing as though the Christ child was in the manger in front of him, but he never seemed to get tired of hearing his "Little Angel" sing. Tears would well up in his eyes, and he'd hug me and pull me up onto his lap. Then we'd laugh, and I'd pat

4

his red cheeks and lean against him enjoying the faint smell of tobacco. The smell had almost a flavor to it and wasn't at all unpleasant to me because it was *Grandpa's smell.*

Grandpa always had rosy, red cheeks. He said it was from the years of being out in the weather, both when he was a farmer and later as he walked about acting as *guardian angel* over the town of Horton. Grandpa did not smoke cigarettes or cigars, but occasionally he would smoke a pipe or chew tobacco when he walked his beat.

———————

Since it only happened so rarely, it was always quite an event if Grandpa took time off from work. One of those *events* happened when I had just turned seven. It was in the spring, and my first grade class was going to make our First Communion.

By the time the big day arrived, my *Mama* (Grandpa's daughter) had spent weeks shopping for the material to make me a beautiful white taffeta slip with white roses designed into the material. To go with the taffeta slip, she made an elegant, white, see-through, silk organdy ruffled dress. She had sat for days at her new electric sewing machine until the dress and slip were just perfect. She had purchased my veil at Einbender's in St. Joe and had spent time weaving pieces of my Grandma Campion's orange-blossom wedding wreath together as a headpiece on my veil. My outfit was complete with my white lacy anklets, my little white gloves, and my black patent leather shoes. When First Communion Day arrived, I was dressed and oh-so beautiful!

Daddy pulled our 1938 Gray Chevy Sedan around to the front of the house. We had washed it the previous day and brushed off all the seats and the floor. My little brother, Darrell, opened the front car door on the passenger side and jumped into the front seat next to my father. Grandpa Clark opened the back passenger door for Grandma and me, then climbed into the front passenger seat and shut the front door. The men were ready.

Mama was dressed in her Easter dress and coat that she had made and worn for the first time on Easter Sunday just the week before. The coat was a gray-blue, and it matched her gray straw hat with the blue grosgrain ribbon and veil. Grandma Clark was also dressed for the occasion in her deep blue, print dress, her good brooch, her dress-up black tie shoes, and black hat with a veil. Mama went around the car, opened up the back door on the driver's side, and climbed into the back seat behind Daddy. Grandma scooted into the car behind Grandpa and then moved to the middle seat. I got into the car last, sitting directly behind Grandpa. Grandma helped me by lifting up my skirt as I sat down so that I wouldn't sit on it and wrinkle it. I pulled the back door closed. We were all ready to go.

Now, as luck would have it, it was already getting warm that morning—so one of the first things we did after getting into the car was to roll down the windows. As we drove north the seven blocks to St. Leo's Church, it seemed extraordinarily quiet—the only sounds being the gentle rustle of leaves, the sound of a few birds singing, and the gentle *purr* of Daddy's well-tuned Chevy. From off in the distance, I began to hear the bells ringing at the Methodist Church—the sound growing louder as we approached. Spring had arrived in all its beauty. And as we passed by all the yards, the trees and bushes were in full bloom. Wherever I looked, tulips and daffodils in shades of red, purple, pink, and yellow could be seen. Driving along deliberately but cautiously, we passed people dressed in their finest as they exited their cars and crossed the street in front of the Methodist Church.

Looking further on down the road, St. Leo's Catholic Church was within sight. I remember we had just begun discussing where the First Communicants were to assemble when Grandpa leaned out the window and spit out the tobacco he had in his mouth. And, in that split second, my life changed. I looked with disbelief at the front of my dress. It now had big brown spots that were not only on the outer dress, but were sinking through the sheer material to the taffeta slip.

I started screeching, "Grandpa killed my dress! He spit *toe-backy* juice all over me!" I began to cry hysterically.

Everybody was initially in shock. Then Grandpa turned to look back over the seat. "Oh, glory be to God," he said. "What did I do?"

I continued to screech at the top of my lungs. Mama leaned across Grandma to look at my dress. I buried my head into Grandma's shoulder and continued to bawl.

Momentarily, Mama seemed confused. She spoke in a low moaning tone as she carefully examined my dress. "Oh, no. Oh, no! What are we going to do?" Then she pulled herself together and began barking orders. "Johnnie," she said to my father. "Take us home quick! Let's see if we can get this out. We can't do anything from here. We've got to get home!"

Daddy brought the car to a complete stop. He looked back over his shoulder into the back seat. His lips were parted as though he was about to say something, but no words came out. At Mama's command, he pulled around the corner at 13th street and then backed up to head home.

Almost quietly, Grandpa asked, "Did that much come in? Can't you wipe it off?"

"Wipe it off!" Mama said. "It went through the top layer and now it's on her taffeta slip. It can't be wiped off. We'll have to try to wash it out. And I'm not sure we can do that. Tobacco stains!"

"We don't have time, do we?" Daddy asked. "We're going to be late."

As we got out of the car, Mama continued to yell orders. "Johnnie, you go on up and pick up your mother and drop her off at the church. Then come back and pick us up."

Mama had already run up the steps to the porch and was unlocking the door. Grandpa got out of the car and opened the back door for me. He looked like a hunched up old man who had aged twenty years in just the last 10 minutes. "I'm sorry, honey," he said. "I'm just an old bull in a China shop. I should have known better than to try to go to church."

Mama came back down the front steps and virtually dragged me into the house. I was still crying as she pulled off my dress and slip and retreated into the bathroom. Grandma had come into the house with us. Mama yelled at her, "Mom, will you put up the ironing board for me and set the iron on 'low'." Grandma Clark set up the wooden ironing board and Mama's new Sunbeam iron. A few moments later, Mama appeared with the dress and slip in hand.

I was still sniffling and crying. "For heaven's sake, stop crying, Deanna, or your nose and cheeks will have big red blotches that will show more than the spots on your dress. Mom, please take her and wash her face while I finish up here."

I don't know how my mother managed the miracle, but within five minutes I was back in my slip and dress and out at the curb waiting for

Daddy. There were no tell-tale stains left from the tobacco. There was also no Grandpa. He had decided to stay at home. But I did get to my First Communion on time.

———————————

But, of course, that's not the end of the story. In a split second, something was lost. My relationship with my Grandpa was never the same after that day. Sure, Grandpa still loved me, but it was as though he had slammed the door closed to his heart. We had conversations, but there were no more personal stories, no more offers to climb on his lap, and no more opportunities to rock for hours listening to him talk about long discarded hopes and dreams.

At first I thought that my cousin Kathleen, who was born four years after me, was taking my place with Grandpa; and I was jealous. But as I watched his relationship with the other grandchildren, including Kathleen, I saw this wasn't so. Grandpa was remote from everybody after that. It was as though something in Grandpa had died that day.

Our relationship remained pretty much the same for the next seven years until 1952. I knew something was wrong, but I couldn't figure out how to make it right. Then, one summer night, as I lay at the foot of my bed trying to capture any breath of air coming in my window, I suddenly heard a great deal of noise coming from my grandparents' house next door. I pressed my face against the screen as I tried to see into Grandpa's room directly across from my window. I could tell that something was also going on at the front of the house. I called out to my mother, but it was my father who came into my bedroom. Daddy said that Mama had gone next door, that Grandpa had died, and the doctor was there with Mama and Grandma. He told me to lie down and try to go back to sleep.

I lay down by the window again, but I was unable to sleep—watching and listening. Soon my gown and pillow were wet from the tears that I quietly shed. In silence prayer, I talked with God and tried to bargain with Him for just one more day to make things right with Grandpa—one more chance to tell him how much I loved him. But morning came and Grandpa was gone forever.

I realize now that it's affected me for the rest of my life. Some might consider it a loss of innocence. I see it as that and more. I lost a *good part* of my *home* that day.

2.

THE PREACHER AND SHORTY WALKER

Now, my Grandpa Clark was pretty much the eyes and ears of the community in his position as Chief of Police for the small town of Horton. And as I've mentioned, he held that position for 30 years until shortly before his death in 1952. Grandpa lived to see the birth of six grandchildren—four by my mother's older sister, Aunt DeVere (Hays), and two by my mother, Aeneita (Purcell). He loved all his grandchildren; but I like to think I was his favorite. I was the one who consistently walked around with him each spring and summer evening just to smell the flowers and listen to his stories.

One story that I clearly remember Grandpa telling me was about a circuit-riding preacher who frequently came to Horton during the 1920's and early 1930's. "He would ride-in on the seat of a big buckboard wagon drawn by two huge, dark horses," Grandpa said. "No one ever knew when the preacher was coming; he'd just seem to swoop in." Grandpa called him "the *Salvation Army* in Horton before there was one." The rest of the town knew him as *Preacher Pendleton*. He'd preach Salvation at his meetings and would accept cash or donations (chickens, produce, old clothes, etc.). Then he'd ride out again, taking his Bible and donations to the next stop on his circuit.

Preacher Pendleton would usually appear on a nice sunny day in the spring or fall of the year. He would arrive at the main intersection of the town, tie up his horses at the hitching post in front of the Bank, and then walk up and down both sides of the street— crossing where they met at

Four Corners, the main intersection. At that time, the town was laid out in the form of a cross with *Four Corners* at its center—one block to the west, one block to the east, two blocks to the north, and three blocks to the south. He would cover the town in a day, soliciting people to attend his prayer meeting that night.

By all accounts, Horton was quite a place in *the 20's* when the Rock Island Railroad was the main employer and the big old round house for engine repair was active. Horton's population was informally reported as being around 15,000 for a short time. But, unfortunately, like most everything else in Horton that started before the Depression, *things* just seemed to go downhill from there.

So Horton, in *the 20's*, had become the *Good Ol' Days* to Grandpa, and as I've said Grandpa just loved to tell stories about the Good Ol' Days—this one in particular. Still, with *source material* on 15,000 people, it might seem a bit odd that one man's story would be so memorable. Well, that's okay because the real story involved another major participant, Shorty Walker. This story is about how the two met one fateful day—a *Clash of Titans*.

Grandpa described Preacher Pendleton as "part preacher and part snake oil salesman," but he quickly added that "there wasn't a more interesting character or more likeable man who passed through Horton than Burgess E. Pendleton." Grandpa always took up the story where *Preacher* arrives in town and parks his wagon in front of the Bank. Then he'd walk across Central to the west and start down the street on the North side, then the South side and so forth, crisscrossing Four Corners until he had visited each shop.

Preacher Pendleton was dressed pretty much like the typical country preacher of the time. His clothes showed signs of wear. Often, he showed up with patches on his pants which were dark wool held up by a pair of wide elastic suspenders. He wore dark, laced boots with homemade repairs showing at the heels and toes. Sometimes, layers of newspaper showed through holes in the soles. His shirt had been white once, but even with lye soap washings, it bore a strong resemblance to grey. When he left the buckboard wagon, he took off a vest that looked like it might have been made of skins, and replaced it with a dark wool jacket that had probably matched the trousers before all the patching. At his neck, instead of a tie, he wore a thin black ribbon tied in a simple, but dignified bow.

As Preacher Pendleton went into each shop or store, he made sure he made direct eye-to-eye and hand-to-hand contact with the owner—letting him know that he was in town, where he was planning to hold his meeting, and just what kind of preaching was going to take place that night. Preacher always made sure he carried his Bible with him; and as he went into the store, he would always transfer the Bible from his right hand to his left in order to shake hands with the proprietor. That way, he sent a message to the proprietor: "You, Sir, are important to me—second only to God and His Word."

Preacher would always laugh and carry on until he flat out got a donation on the spot, or at least an *affirmative agreement* to his invitation to *come to Meeting* that night. Meetings with Preacher were always quite a lively and enjoyable spectacle. He was quite a musician, considering it was rumored that he was self-taught. He carried his fiddle, banjo, squeeze box, and juice harp along with him; and he knew the music to all the hymns that might be requested. Although it was clear (especially from the way he chastised the crowd during his sermons) that he had a powerful voice, he didn't try to lead the singing himself. He had identified several ladies from local Horton Churches who were reputed to have the most gifted singing voices in town, and they would vie for the opportunity to lead the songs as Preacher played. In between his visits, these same women would also collect old suits and other clothing, pots and pans, and other items that Preacher would toss up into his wagon and carry off with him when he left town. They looked upon their diligence in collecting these items as potentially leading to their reward—an opportunity to lead the singing at Preacher's next Meeting.

Now, one fine spring day, just after Preacher came to town, he found he had almost completed his visits to all the merchants when the Hand of God began to set the stage for this might clash. Preacher had one last merchant to see, a merchant just two blocks south of Four Corners on the West side of the street. This was the Feed and Grain store of a *Mr. Walker*, a respectable businessman already of considerable age, and his adult son, *Shorty*.

The name *Shorty* was, of course, well deserved as *Shorty* was several inches less than 5 feet tall. Shorty, like his father, always wore a dark shirt and bib overalls—complete with a red rag hanging out of the back pocket. This red rag was used for several purposes—as a handkerchief, a rag to wipe dirt or oil, or lastly, as a *danger* flag to tie onto an item too long for the bed of a wagon. And while Mr. Walker seemed to be able to keep track of what the last use of his red rag had been, it was frequently reported that Shorty had been seen with residue on his brow from a *forgotten* previous use of the red rag.

Although very well liked, Shorty was known to be *different*. Nobody ever went further to define it. "He's quite a case," they'd say, or "There just ain't nobody like Shorty . . . He's one of a kind." Shorty was reported to be as *strong as an ox,* as he spent most of his days loading and unloading wagons. When he wasn't working, Shorty had a menagerie of animals in the fenced backyard behind the feed and grain store. The back lot of the property bordered on the land owned and operated by the Rock Island Railroad. The railroad roundhouse for repairing engines was located on this other property. Like many of the merchants of the times, the Walker's home was on the second floor above the store.

Before entering the store, Preacher took a folded, off-white handkerchief out of his back pocket and used it to wipe off his brow. The day had turned out warmer than expected, and Preacher had been walking and talking a long time. The top of his head, with his thinning hair, seemed to have formed little beads of sweat, so he used the handkerchief to wipe it off, too. Preacher's bushy mustache twitched back and forth, and he seemed a little more nervous than usual. But he set his jaw and lower lip in a determined look and entered the Walker establishment.

Mr. Walker was one of the few holdouts in the community. One way or another, Preacher had been able to bargain, negotiate, or plain *out horse trade* everyone else to get them to donate up front or attend the Meeting. There were even a number of the Catholics or Lutherans who would give something, but Mr. Walker was a confirmed *non-believer*. He was determined that neither Preacher nor his Bible would have any effect on him.

"Good afternoon, Mr. Walker," said Preacher. "How are you on this beautiful day?"

"It looks like a storm is going to blow up out of the Southwest. Are you sure you've been thumping your Bible right, or is the weather going to blow away your Meeting tonight?" responded Mr. Walker.

"I believe we'll be just fine, Mr. Walker. But I'll be watching the Southwest as you suggest," said Preacher.

"Be you a buyin' or a tradin' today, Preacher?" Mr. Walker inquired.

"I guess I'll be doing a little trading," responded the Preacher. "So tell me . . . What might I have, Mr. Walker, that would get you to my Meeting tonight? I believe that if'n you will only come to the Lord, He will save your immortal soul. Now that's got to be worth something to you—say, a couple of bushels of grain for the horses?"

Mr. Walker threw his head back and roared with laughter. Witnesses said that he laughed so hard that tears came to his eyes. When he was finished, he coughed a few times, cleared his throat, and then went to the door to spit. At the time, spitting was something akin to an art form—worthy of a detailed description   It's said Mr. Walker's *toe-backy* traveled in a perfect arch a distance of four feet across the wooden sidewalk before it landed with a gentle *splat* in the street. Mr. Walker believed he had the Preacher just where he wanted him. He could finally work *the plan* that he had been telling his good ol' boy friends about for months—since Preacher's last visit.

"Well, then" said Walker. "I got a challenge for you, Preacher. I know that you believe in your God and the layin' on of the hands and all that, but I'm not askin' you to *lay on hands.* I want to see you use your *head* for somethin' instead."

Now, Walker's Feed and Grain was the *local hangout* for any farmers who might be waiting for their wives to finish shopping and for old men who just wanted to play checkers. The floor boards around the potbellied wood stove were scarred and scuffed from chair legs and boots. Although they hadn't been told to do so as nothing had been prearranged, it was obvious what must be done. Four men bolted from their chairs and out the front door. The town had to be warned! The gauntlet was being thrown down.

"I've got a challenge for you, Preacher, and if'n you win, my boy Shorty and me will be your prizes. And I won't even dicker with you about the grain for the horses—you'll get that, too. If'n you win, we'll both be there right up front slappin' our knees and dancin' to the sound of your music tonight. Now, do you accept my challenge, Preacher?"

The Preacher took his handkerchief out and wiped his brow again. "I certainly like the sound of your offer, Mr. Walker. But I'm not sure I've heard your challenge. You're not trying to get me set up for a wrestling match with the devil, are you?" asked Preacher.

"Well, he certainly can be a wild one, and he has been called quite a number of names in his time, but for all his faults, I truly don't believe Shorty is the devil."

A bit taken aback by this last statement, Preacher paused, then asked, "You want me to wrestle Shorty?"

"No, Preacher, you got me wrong. It's not wrestling I'm talking about," said Mr. Walker. "I want you to *butt heads* with Shorty. You see, my Shorty thinks he's the head butting *cham-peen* in these parts. He challenges people all the time, but he ain't never had to butt heads with you."

Mr. Walker took another chaw of tobacco, swished it around in his mouth to make a good wad, and then continued. "Everybody says that you're a hard headed so and so, Preacher. And I want Shorty to stop this infernal challenging people to *head butting!* So I figured, with the Lord on your side, you can beat Shorty and make him stop."

Oh, how Mr. Walker worked and cajoled Preacher. Eventually, he convinced Preacher that he would be doing a good deed to take the challenge, and thus stop Shorty from hurting himself and others. But most of all, Preacher told himself that by doing this, he would be bringing Mr. Walker and Shorty to the Lord. How could the Preacher resist all that— and the two bushels of grain for the horses on top of it all?

"And just exactly where would this here contest take place?" asked the Preacher.

"Why, right here," said Mr. Walker. "We'll do it right here—right straight away."

"Well, then," said the Preacher. "I guess we've got us a wager." With that, he transferred his Bible from his right hand to his left hand, and the two men, Preacher and Mr. Walker, shook hands on their wager.

The minute they clasped hands, the hooting and hollering and clapping of those assembled commenced. Only then did the Preacher become aware of the large number of men that had been gathering at the

Walker establishment. As broker for the upcoming event, Mr. Walker took a victory lap around the room—raking in the bets while shaking outstretched hands and getting the fuzz on his head roughed up as he passed through the crowd. It's said the back slapping could be heard all the way out into the street where an even larger crowd was already gathering. There was quite a bit of pushing and shoving already as men jostled for position to get a better place from which to watch.

Preacher was finally getting the idea that this had been some kind of setup, but he couldn't quite figure it out. Shorty was just a stubby, little fellow, perhaps a bit wider than most, who kind of wobbled back and forth when he walked. What was the big deal?

Mr. Walker went to the back of the store and called Shorty. Within a short spell of time, he came in and walked to the front of the store. "Shorty," said his father. "It is such a fine day out. If'n I was to say to you that you could stop your work and do just about anything in the world you wanted, what would you want to do?"

"Butt heads!" said Shorty. "I'd wanta' butt heads!" Shorty was obviously excited. He started to stamp his right foot and began acting more and more like a bull getting ready to charge.

"Well, Shorty. You're a gonna' get what you want today. You and Preacher are gonna' to have a head-butting contest," said Mr. Walker.

Preacher's eyes opened wide. What was going on? What had he gotten himself into?

———————————

By the time Preacher, Shorty, and Mr. Walker stepped out into the street, it looked like the whole male population of Horton had assembled for the contest. Notably, among the crowd, was Mr. Fete, there with his journal, also taking bets. And so, too, was Mr. Christ, with a big basket of concessions from his store across the street. A couple of boys who worked at the Lumber Company after school had run over to the round house to tell the shop workers. They were on their way back yelling at the top of their lungs, "Don't start until we all get there!"

Preacher was seen to stumble slightly as he stepped off the wooden walk and into the street below. Several hands reached out to steady him and keep him from falling. He still had his Bible in his hand and some thought they heard him mumble, "Help me, Lord. What manner of foolishness have I gotten myself into now?"

Mr. Walker laid out the rules for the contest. The double front doors of the Feed and Grain Store had been propped open, and both men were to step back six steps from the point where the sidewalk and the street abutted. Shorty would be just inside the store to start and would run to the East. The Preacher would start out in the street running toward the West. They were to run with their heads down and meet at the point where street and sidewalk met, the sidewalk being about a step higher than the street. It was explained to the Preacher that it had to be done this way to allow for the height difference between the Preacher and Shorty. Otherwise, Shorty would make contact with the Preacher's chest or neck and the Preacher would miss Shorty's head altogether.

Shorty knew the rules already and quickly stepped off his six steps. From just inside the store he could be seen stamping and scraping his foot on the floor like he was trying to get traction. And the sounds alone were enough to send shivers through his competitor. Shorty snorted and growled and hooted and howled. There isn't an animal in the world that has ever sounded more fierce.

Preacher took his place six paces into the street. Mr. Norris, the banker, looked by far the most civilized of the leering horde. Preacher kissed his Bible and handed it to Mr. Norris. "Would you please hold my Bible until this is over?" he said. Mr. Norris took the Bible from Preacher's hand and nodded an affirmative.

Preacher turned toward the waiting Shorty, lowered his head, and mumbled an audible prayer, "Stay with me, oh Lord. Forgive my pride and transgressions."

And with that, Mr. Walker announced, "Get ready! . . . Set! . . . Go!"

Both Preacher and Shorty ran as fast as they could without hesitation. The crowd went totally silent. As if pre-ordained, they met in a full-speed crash at the appointed juncture of the street and sidewalk. The only sound heard was *likened* to the sound made when a ripe watermelon is *accidentally* dropped on concrete. *Pop!*

[*Grandpa usually made this noise by putting his right index finger into the left side of his mouth, huffing up a big batch of air, and then popping his finger out of his mouth for emphasis. Now each time I hear that sound, I think of the two men colliding.*]

Now, the Preacher was definitely in trouble. He had a large gash and the top of his head was bleeding. His knees buckled under him, and he just seemed to glide down to the brick pavement of the street below him. The crowd gasped in unison as Shorty wobbled around in a circle several times and then just sat down on the sidewalk, dropped backward, and fell unconscious. Both contestants were out; it was a draw!

Doc Crawford, one of the local veterinarians, jumped out of his buggy where he had parked over in front of the Christ Grocery Store. He brought his bag and proceeded to clean up Preacher's wound. Preacher started to *'come to'* just as Doc was sewing up his head with what appeared to be fishing line. Mr. Walker, who was tending to Shorty, announced to the crowd that, while he appeared to be *fine,* this was the first time a *human competitor* had ever knocked Shorty out.

As soon as Preacher had come around, Mr. Walker came over and shook his hand. Then everybody took turns shaking Preacher's hand. When it was his turn, Mr. Norris gave him back his Bible. "Yes sir, Preacher. The Lord must have truly been with you for you to be able to put Shorty down. No one else has been able to do it; and there's no one left, *man or animal*, that wants to try."

"I owe you an apology, Reverend Pendleton," said Mr. Walker. "And I'm a big enough man to admit it when I'm wrong. Shorty and *me* will be at your Meeting tonight—along with those two bushels for your horses."

The Preacher reached out to take Mr. Walker's arm as Walker helped the Preacher to his feet. "I'll be happy to see you and Shorty at Meeting, but there's something I've got to know. A few of these folks have alluded to something I don't understand. How did all of this *head-butting with Shorty* get started?" he asked.

"Well, Preacher," replied Mr. Walker, "Shorty never has much fitted in well with people. But even when he was just a young'un, he got along fine with animals. And, it's a fact that he always hankered to be around goats more'un anything else. So when he was a little fellar, I fenced in the back there yonder behind the store and got him some goats. Twern't long afore he was a buttin' heads with one Billy and then another. As he got older and he would *cow tow* the most recent Billy, I'd have to get him a new one over and over—causein' he would chase that Billy until that Billy'd do most anything to get itself over the fence. I don't think that there's a Billy in the tri-county area that doesn't run when he sees Shorty coming. So I'm a guessin' now in hindsight that it twern't really fair to you—him having all that experience, as it twere."

And with that, Mr. Walker walked over to Shorty who had sat up and was rubbing the sore spot on his head. "Can you get up, Boy?" Mr. Walker said. "We got some work to do before Meeting tonight."

People started to arrive an hour before the designated time for Meeting. The crowd was even larger than the one that had witnessed the head butting contest. Wives and children were all there to get a look at the *reigning hero*. Everyone wanted to see the man who had butted heads with Shorty Walker and *lived to tell* about it. And the *laying on of the hands* was a big part of this momentous event. Everybody wanted to see and touch Preacher's head. True to his word, Mr. Walker had brought Shorty and the bushels, and they sat at the front of the crowd. Shorty even took around the collect basket for Preacher, and it was reported that he had to come back to empty it three times before he'd made his way completely through the crowd.

The music that night reached to the Heavens. Preacher seemed to be inspired. Never before had he played his instruments so well. And it should be noted that the ladies of the town teamed up in their singing that night instead of vying for top billing. The sermon itself was a dandy with lots of fire and brimstone. And no one seemed to notice, or mind, that, in addition to the usual punctuation thrown in by the crowd, "Amen, Brother," Shorty Walker could be heard adding his own exclamations, "Baaaa! . . . Baaaa! . . . Baaaa! Baaaa! Baaaa!" The Lord works in mysterious ways!

When Grandpa told this story, I could visualize it all happening. I can't vouch for the truth in every statement since I wasn't there, but I can still visualize Grandpa's version in my mind's eye yet today. Hopefully, if I've done the story *justice,* you will be able to visualize it happening, too. Grandpa would have been pleased.

Oh, there is one final point I should clarify; it may be something you're wondering about. *Pendleton* is my married name. Now, it certainly wasn't something that anyone would have considered as a possibility way back when Grandpa Clark was telling me this story. (In fact, I hadn't even been born when the events of this story took place.) And it wasn't something I considered until years later, long after Grandpa was gone. I had met and married my husband, George Pendleton, by then. In fact, I had read him the first draft of this story when he told me that his great grandfather, Burgess E. Pendleton, was a traveling preacher. Boing! The connection was made.

How about that? The Lord truly does work in mysterious ways!

3.

POLIO

When I was a small child, Mama said I caught every virus and disease that happened to be going around. Grandma Clark said that was because my cousins, *the Hays boys*, always had the sniffles, bad coughs, or the latest contagious disease. The Hays boys were always over at Grandma's house, and they visited with us so much that it would have been impossible to keep me isolated from all the germs they carried. Where Mama had always tried to protect me, the Hays boys got to live a life that I often envied—a pseudo *Tom Sawyer-Huckleberry Finn* type of existence. I thought that type of freedom had to be wonderful.

Now, the beginning of this story started well before my third birthday. In September of 1940, my cousin Junior (Al Hays, Jr., or Junior, as he was known to us during our childhood years) was 8 years old when he started complaining about having a stiff neck and was running a temperature. He also said he was feeling *achy* all over and, in general, just felt tired all the time. For a child who had always had a lot of energy before and had never wanted to stop playing or go inside at night, this suggested something horribly wrong. Mama said, "All he wanted to do was lay on Grandma's couch."

Then the rest of us started feeling sickly. My parents and I were living at Grandma's house then. This was at a time when Grandma and Grandpa Clark still lived in the big two-story house on 5th street, and Mama and Daddy were still living in the small apartment on the second floor. Junior's brothers, Roger and Duane, started showing some of the same symptoms, and I was also running a temperature and felt *achy* all over. Mama was pregnant and expecting my brother, Darrell, at the time. Darrell was born a couple months later, on November 15, 1940.

Grandma was really most concerned with Junior. His symptoms were the most pronounced, and he seemed to be getting worse by the minute. That September afternoon, Grandma called Dr. L. C. Edmonds. Doctors still made house calls at the time. *Dr. L.C.*, as he was known, came down to the house about an hour later. Almost immediately he recognized the problem: Polio!

Within minutes, Dr. L.C. had called for an ambulance to take Junior to the University of Kansas Hospital in Kansas City, Kansas. Dr. L.C. took the harsh, brusque attitude that he always did when he was worried, and so he told Aunt DeVere and Uncle Alfred that Junior had to get to the hospital right away. He called ahead and made arrangements because he knew that there was no way to take care of him in the Horton Hospital. After they had left for Kansas City, Dr. L. C. told Grandpa that he really didn't expect Junior to live long enough to get there.

But Junior wouldn't give in. Even though he had the bulbar type of poliomyelitis (Polio) and this was the most dangerous kind, he seemed to will himself through it all. As Mama said in her memoirs, "He had the worse case to develop in the Midwest that year. It was the severe type that develops at the base of the skull in the back of the neck. He was given a blood transfusion and placed in a respirator or *Iron Lung*. He was in the Iron Lung for six weeks or longer." It was quite a long time before he showed any sign of improvement; yet, he fought his way through it.

The rest of *us kids* were sick for awhile, but we didn't ever develop the same symptoms that Junior had. We had more flu-like symptoms with lots of aches and pains. Grandma used to say that nothing kept Duane and Roger down for long, however. So, true to form, it wasn't long before the two of them were out and about running to and fro. I, on the other hand, was still having lots of pain in my legs.

Grandma rubbed my legs with alcohol and wrapped them in hot towels. She said that I got to the point where I didn't want to stand or walk—although I had been walking for about two and a half years at the time. Dr. L. C. was contacted and told Grandma to just keep doing what she was doing and to watch to see if complications developed. He said that I might have had a lighter case of polio—the muscular type. On the other hand, he thought it might just be a reaction to Mama having another baby, and that maybe I was just trying to get attention.

October and November of 1940 was a busy time. Darrell was born on November 15 and Junior, who had another birthday while still in the Iron Lung, came home around Thanksgiving. Still, Grandma would rub my legs when she had time during the day and put on the hot towels, and Mama or Daddy would rub my legs and continue the treatment before I went to sleep at night.

When the weather would allow, Grandpa Clark carried me or took me around in my wagon. I remember we would go out for walks around the yard or up and down 5th Street as the mood would strike us. Grandpa always tried to get me to walk at least a part of the way on my own. By the following summer when my parents had moved with Grandma and Grandpa to the *bungalow* on Sixth Street and 1st Avenue East, I was walking all the way on my own. Grandpa always talked to me and told me stories when we went for walks, and as I've mentioned, I remember most of these stories even today.

Now, Junior amazed the doctors with his recovery, so much so that he later went on to become an athlete in high school and joined the Air Force immediately after graduation. He had always been interested in Electronics, and he had worked in my father's store repairing radios when he was in high school. My parents were always so proud of his accomplishments when he went on to college, got several degrees, and worked for several aircraft manufacturers in California as a senior scientist and sonar expert. It's difficult for me to think of him as anything other than *Junior*, but everybody else calls him *Al*—Alfred W. Hays, Jr.

As for me, the doctors may have suspected, but they never confirmed, that I had polio. From that time, my legs always ached a great deal. My leg muscles were never strong, and I couldn't walk or stand for long periods of time even as a child and teenager. My legs were never very straight either. But at 67, it is hard to say whether any of my present condition, which requires me to use a walker, had anything to do with polio. I had an auto accident in 1981 which injured my feet and legs, and I also am plagued with arthritis. Post-Polio Syndrome, too? Who can say?

There was one immediate effect of polio to which I can attest. In Horton, like in many towns and cities across the United States, there were many kids who never got the opportunity to learn how to swim. A lot of cities across the country set up rules during that time period that prohibited anyone under 16 or 18 years of age from being allowed to go swimming, especially in public pools. At that time, the only pool in Horton was both down by and fed by Mission Lake. Now, to be fair, it probably wasn't the cleanest pool. But, even though improvements were made and I grew older, my parents still feared polio well into my high school years. Because of it, I was never allowed to go swimming. As a result, instead of *fearing polio*, I have developed and maintain *a fear of water*. The summer my two boys were eight and five, I saw to it that they took swimming lessons. I certainly didn't want to pass down my *fear*.

In addition to lost opportunity, fear of polio also drove strange behavior. Since polio was also thought to be passed through contact *wherever large groups of people congregated*, parents tried to keep kids away from anyplace where there were crowds—such as going to large cities to shop or going to the circus. My Mama always seemed to carry things to the extreme. She thought germs could be passed on through anything and everything that anyone else touched—even newspapers. I can remember her getting out the old pump bug sprayer and giving the *Horton Headlight* and *Kansas City Star* a big zap each time they arrived. If I close my eyes and take a deep breath, I can still smell the strong odor of bug spray in the morning at the breakfast table as Daddy sat reading the paper. Overall, however, I think breathing the fumes probably did us more harm than anything else we might've otherwise been exposed to at breakfast.

So, for those of you who don't remember, polio was a dreaded word from about 1940 until mid-1950. Parents lived in fear of their children getting it because there was no known cure at the time—only bed rest and isolation could do any good. Polio was also known as Infantile Paralysis; and it sent parents into a panic if their children would start complaining of stiff necks, having a fever, or just feeling out of sorts and very tired. Even our great president of that era, Franklin Delano Roosevelt, who led us out of the Depression and through World War II, did so having been crippled by polio. In possibly his most famous quote, FDR said, "The only thing we have to fear is Fear itself." Had I been his speechwriter, I might've pointed out that failure to follow his sound advice only leads to more and more *crippling* fear—like Mama's fear.

Parents were given hope in the early 1950's when Dr. Jonas Salk developed a polio vaccine, and later felt a little peace of mind when Dr. Albert Sabin developed an oral vaccine that was given on sugar cubes. By the time I graduated from high school in 1956, the threat of polio was pretty much over. Now, we have other things like Avian Flu to worry about. In any case, we should always be prepared to fight the good fight, ask for help when we need it, keep hope alive, and pray for a little peace of mind.

———————

I don't want to downplay the polio my cousin Al had in any way by comparing my *polio* with his. He almost died. I did not. He has accomplished so much and has come so far for someone whose young life could have been taken away at such a young age. No one ever firmly diagnosed me as having polio. I just know that my legs have always been misshapen, and I have lived with the aches and pains I felt in them for my entire life. Overall, I am just thankful for scientists like Dr. Jonas Salk and Dr. Albert Sabin.

Personal Note: Now, if we could just get our nation's leaders to take new diseases like the Avian Flu more seriously, we might get a few more smart young scientists busy working on a cure before we have a major pandemic on our hands. I wasn't around for the flu pandemic of 1918, but reading about it now is enough to make a person realize that we don't want *a sequel* to that drama.

4.

MY EARLIEST MEMORY

I can still recall a number of *flashes* of memory of miscellaneous events that happened during the first few years of my life. My cousin Roger is a part of many of them. This was still at a time when Mama, Daddy, and I lived in the upstairs apartment at Grandpa's house on 5th street.

I remember Grandma taking her sofa scarf with the fringe on it off the back of the couch and wrapping me in it. Then she attached colored chicken feathers to a piece of material and made me a headband. Roger had a holster and gun set and a cowboy hat. I wasn't sure why, but we chased each other all over the front and back yards. He'd hit his hip as he pretended to break into a gallop and would make horse sounds. I was always the one who got shot and had to lay on the ground *dead*. I must have been only 2 or 3 at the time.

I also had a doll, doll buggy, and table and chair set. I liked to do *tea parties,* but Roger didn't like playing that way. Sometimes Mrs. Gullickson and her daughter Joyce would come down the street walking 'baby Ila' (Mrs. Gullickson's younger daughter) in her buggy. Occasionally, they would stop so Ila and I could play together while Grandma and Mrs. Gullickson would sit and talk—watching us from the stone retaining wall in front of the house.

Another *flash* memory is that of Mrs. Rice, our next door neighbor. I'd take my doll and buggy and would push it up to their front porch. Mrs. Rice would help carry it up through her front door, and then I'd walk pushing it through the house and out the back door. I'd do this over and over again until she finally had to go into the house and close the doors. I must have been a real pain. Of course, Grandma would be watching the whole time, and she and Mrs. Rice were very good friends. So maybe the two of them decided when *enough was* enough. All of the events above must have happened before I was three years old because we moved when I was three.

The first *real memory* I have that is more than just a *flash* happened when I was just two months short of my fourth birthday. I remember this event because of the effect it had on the adults in my life. Never before had I seen so many of the adults I loved become so upset, agitated, and angry. Even today I can picture it in my mind's eye just as if it were all happening again for the first time.

I remember Mama and Daddy had left after church that Sunday morning. They had gone across the street from Grandma and Grandpa's house. They were working on *our new house*—which was really two three-room houses that Daddy had hauled to the empty lot he purchased on the *southeast* corner of 6th Street and 1st Avenue East. With a crew of men, he had worked for several days to get the two houses up on concrete blocks. Then he had the Winklebauer brothers, Leonard and Al, connect them as one unit. After completing the electrical wiring in several of the rooms, Daddy was trying to do the plastering himself, with Mama overseeing his work. She had more of an artist's eye, and I imagine she did most of the critiquing and smoothing of walls to make sure they came out straight and even.

Although our family (Mama, Daddy, Darrell, and I) had all lived with Grandma and Grandpa Clark for several years (Mama and Daddy since '36), we had only lived with them in their little bungalow, located on the *southwest* corner of 6th and 1st Avenue East, since the past summer. Grandpa had sold the big house on 5th Street to Uncle Alfred and Aunt DeVere. They had three boys and a new baby girl, Kathleen, who had been born several weeks earlier—so they really needed that extra space.

So there we were, all living in a two bedroom bungalow while Daddy spent his evenings and weekends trying to get our new home in shape so we could move into it.

Now, as I've mentioned, Grandpa worked his job as Chief of Police seven days a week. As usual, he had gone up to the city offices and jail at 6 AM. After a little paper work, he had made his rounds visiting all of the buildings in the downtown area—checking to see if doors were locked, etc. About noon, as was his usual practice on a quiet Sunday, he walked the two blocks back home and sat down in his rocking chair to read the Sunday paper before lunch. (Or as it was known in most small towns back then, *Sunday Dinner*. In small towns you didn't have *lunch*. Your three meals were breakfast, dinner, and supper—in that order.)

Grandpa leaned over and turned on the big Philco radio. As he listened to it, he rocked back and forth. KFEQ in St. Joe was doing the news and stock reports. It started with the local news, and then at 12:30, the world report was broadcast from the national affiliate. I was on the floor playing with my dolls. Grandma was in the kitchen keeping tabs on the two big roasting hens in the oven. Mama had prepared them before leaving with Daddy. In the meantime, Grandma had been making homemade noodles. Having set them out on a table on the sun porch to dry, she was just waiting for the oven to do its job so she could get all the good juices off the hens and finish them up. Since her kitchen was tiny, she brought a bowl of potatoes out to the dining room table and sat there peeling and dicing them into chunks to boil for mashed potatoes. Then she put them into a pan and took them back into the kitchen.

The local news was just about over. Suddenly, Grandpa heard something on the radio that made him jump to his feet. He started yelling and walking around hurriedly, back and forth across the floor. I had to grab up my Betsey Wetsey doll because he had already stepped on her once, and she had stayed flat for awhile. I got up and ran to Grandma because I was afraid he was going to step on me next. Grandma got up and hurriedly went into the living room. "What's going on, Lit?" she said. "What's happening?"

Grandpa was upset as he tried to tell Grandma what had happened, but I didn't know what the words meant. I couldn't figure out why they were so agitated. About that time, Darrell started crying in the bedroom, so Grandma went in to pick him up and bring him into the living room.

Suddenly, the front door swung open. In came my cousins Roger, Duane, and Junior (Al, Jr.). They were all expected for dinner, along with Aunt DeVere, Uncle Alfred, and new baby Kathleen. That was pretty much a tradition at that time. We always got together for holidays and even most Sundays. Mama and Grandma would make just about everything else, but Uncle Alfred would always bring some kind of salad. He was the best salad maker that I have ever known.

My cousins were about an hour early, but it didn't take long to determine that they hadn't come to eat. Apparently, Uncle Alfred had heard the news as well. They said that their Dad was upsetting their Mom, and that she was cursing and crying when they left. Aunt DeVere *just knew* that, in some way, this was going to mean that Uncle Alfred was going to get killed.

The boys were all trying to talk at one time so very little was making any sense. At that point, Mama and Daddy came in. Daddy had taken a radio with them over to the house to try out the new electrical outlets he had installed in three of the six rooms. The radio had been on, and they had heard the noon news as well.

Voices were loud and everybody was talking at once. Mama went in to take the chickens out of the oven. She said they should *be good and done* as they should have been taken out about 15 minutes earlier. Grandma, carrying Darrell, followed her yelling, "Check the potatoes to see if they have boiled dry."

Aunt DeVere, carrying baby Kathleen, threw open the living room door. It hit Roger on the shoulder, and he fell on the floor crying. Uncle Alfred came in and picked him up, putting him on his shoulders so that his head almost touched the ceiling. I took my doll and ran into the bedroom where I jumped on the feather bed and put my hands over my ears. I felt the vibration as the front door came open and then slammed shut. Looking out the window, I saw Grandpa putting on his uniform jacket as he got into Daddy's '38 Chevy. Daddy went around the car, got into the driver's seat, and they drove off.

The noise seemed to be tapering off in the living room. Grandma sent the boys to play outside. Uncle Alfred went back to their house to finish the salad and bring it back. Aunt DeVere sat thinking and *blinking one eye* as she rocked back and forth in Grandpa's rocker—while holding the baby. Mama was feeding Darrell a bottle. In the kitchen, Grandma was dropping noodles into the hot chicken broth.

About an hour later, everybody but the babies got seated at Grandma's big dining table. Grandpa and Daddy had gotten news off the Police radio at the City Hall and had talked with the Brown County Sheriff. They had made several passes through town and found that the whole town was stirred up over the news; but, like my family, no one knew what to do other than wait and listen to the radio. In fact, they were told to go back to their radios because President Franklin Delano Roosevelt was going to speak sometime that afternoon or evening.

It was a rather quiet and somber afternoon. All the adults sat listening to the radio. The boys played and ruff-housed outside and nobody seemed to pay much attention to them. Mama and Daddy didn't seem to worry that they were getting off schedule by not spending time working on our house. And, after Sunday Dinner, for the first and only time that I remember, there were leftovers—Grandma's chicken and homemade noodles.

That Sunday was December 7, 1941, and the event Grandpa had heard about was the bombing of Pearl Harbor!

As it turned out, Uncle Alfred and my Daddy were both declared 4-F and neither was accepted by the draft board. I can't remember why Uncle Alfred was 4-F; but my Daddy had been kicked in the chest by a cow when he was a boy. After that, he had a slightly sunken chest on the left side by his heart. And, even then (1941), he had signs of heart problems.

Still Daddy managed to do his part. He was considered one of the best radio men around. He also knew Morse Code from when he was a telegrapher for the railroad. Not long after the war started, Daddy was contacted by SAC headquarters in Omaha. From then on, he would drive from Horton to Omaha two or three nights a week for most of the war—teaching radio repair and Morse Code. He also was a very active *ham* radio operator. On several occasions, he was asked to pass messages on to and from guerilla fighters in New Guinea.

Since he had to drive between 300 and 450 extra miles per week, the Air Force saw to it that we got extra gas stamps. I still have some of them that were leftover in one of his little treasure boxes he kept—along with his pearl-handled knives.

When I think back on the events of that Sunday, now fully aware of their historical significance, it is still the people (my family) and the profound effect it had on them that has held this memory in my mind and heart. None of them was fully aware of what this would mean to them in the long term, but each of them knew that this was not an insignificant incident. Each felt fear and a loss of security.

Today, people talk about where they were on September 11, 2001. Before that, it was the Challenger and the assassinations of Bobby Kennedy, Martin Luther King, or John Kennedy that impacted people to where they could tell you exactly where they were and what they were doing when they first heard about the tragedy. Before that, it was the Vietnam War, the Korean War and World War II. Most families have lost someone to one or more of these events. Yet, the list grows terribly, tragically longer. And, yes, you still remember when you first heard or saw . . . and you still feel the pain, the sorrow, the loss . . . and the regret for what might have been. But mostly, you remember the people.

It's the people; it's the families that pull together...and love survives!

5.

A RIDE IN THE RUMBLE SEAT

I told you about my beloved Grandpa Clark and how he carried me around showing me flowers and butterflies and rocks, etc., and telling me stories. But he wasn't the only grandfather that I had the privilege to know. Although the other one disappeared from my life when I was only five, I loved him just the same. This was my Grandpa Campion.

Grandpa Campion was William (Will) Campion. He was my Daddy's stepfather. Daddy's birth father, James Purcell, died in 1915 when Daddy was only seven years old. It wasn't until several years ago that I learned that Grandma married Will Campion in 1918. He had always held such a minute part of the story the boys (my dad and his two brothers, James and Joe) told about their lives growing up that I was shocked to learn that *Grandpa Campion* was in their lives for so long. Considering how much of his time he spent trying to help and support Grandma in rearing her three sons, he's never received the credit he's due. Since Grandpa Campion died in 1943, he and Grandma were actually married for 25 years— much longer than Grandma was married to James Purcell (12 years) before he died.

Sometime in the *late 70's*, I came across a photograph of Grandma and Grandpa Campion. It brought back memories of Grandpa. I remembered him being a soft-spoken man who always smelled of pipe tobacco. In fact, I remember him holding me on his lap, while sitting in his rocking chair. I told Daddy that I was confused, however, because I kept visualizing us as being down in a cave at the time. Daddy explained to me that it was most likely because we were down in the cellar of Grandma's house. To get to the cellar, one had to go to the south side of the house, just outside the screened-in porch, and open two big doors that folded open on hinges to the left and right.

Daddy said the cellar had always been Grandpa's retreat—even when Daddy and his brothers were still children. The cellar had a dirt floor, and Grandpa had a large, oval, *rag rug* that Grandma had made to set his rocker on. There, he could sit and think while smoking his pipe—and not have to be bothered by the noise of the boys or a very talkative, demanding wife. Daddy said that although Grandpa had given Grandma money to pay all the bills from the time they were married in 1918 until the time he died, Grandma never let him forget that Grandpa Purcell had been the one to buy the house for her and her children. In fact, he didn't even sleep in the bedroom with Grandma. Grandpa Campion slept on the daybed on the west side of the huge kitchen/hearth room.

Grandpa was not allowed to keep most of his belongings in the house. Most everything he had was relegated to the big red barn behind and west of the house, the garage to the south of the house, or out on his farm. He kept his clothes in the oak armoire that was on the north wall of the kitchen/hearth room, and all his boots and shoes were left on the north porch. Grandma said that this was because he was not a good role model for the boys and because he came home smelling like horses, which may have been because Grandpa had property just outside town where he raised and trained horses. He took these trained horses to Leavenworth to sell to the U.S. Army at the Fort. He was the major supplier of horses for the cavalry stationed at Fort Leavenworth from about 1910 until the 1930's.

When Daddy was a boy, Grandpa also owned some land just north of their house at the end of Euclid Avenue. This land was approximately where the current Horton Hospital and the retirement homes of Arbor Knoll are located. Daddy said they always kept a cow in the barn behind their house so they would have fresh milk. It was Daddy's job in the summer to take that cow up to the pasture in the morning and bring it back at night. He said that, sometimes, he would try to ride some of the horses that Grandpa had broken and pastured separate from the others on the land just west of Horton.

"Poor Mr. Campion," said Mama, who had been listening silently as I spoke with my father. "The poor man never had a life with Grandma Campion. She was the meanest woman I ever met."

"Now, Neta," my Daddy responded. "I don't want to hear you speaking ill of my mother. She did what she had to do for us boys. Dad Campion just knew that we always came first with her. She never tried to hide that."

I remembered the time when I was about twenty-one and I was asked to drive Grandma over to the church every Saturday afternoon so she could prepare flower arrangements for the altars. During one of these trips, I asked her how she had met and married Grandpa Campion. I remember her story . . .

During those early years after they had moved from Purcell to Horton, she and Grandpa Purcell had been very active in the Knight's of Columbus and the Altar Society. Grandpa had pledged $5,000 for the new church—St. Leo's Church as it exists today. Before the church was built, services were held in the building that I knew as St. Leo's Grade School, which was just next door to where they built the church. (That building was torn down a number of years ago, and the empty lot has now been turned into the church parking lot.)

After Grandpa Purcell died, Grandma felt it was her responsibility to pay off their $5,000 pledge. This, of course, was a huge sum or money for that time period. She had no income—other than from a couple of farms that her deceased husband James had purchased when he was Vice President at the Bank of Horton. But these farms were very heavily mortgaged. Grandma said that she tried working with the share croppers who lived on the farms, but they tried to cheat her since she was a woman and because women didn't have the same rights then that they later got. She said she knew that it would be difficult just to pay off the mortgages and meet the obligation to the church. There would be nothing left to support her and the children. Therefore, she knew that she would have to find another husband soon—because she certainly wasn't going back to work as somebody's *hired girl* (maid).

So one day at an Altar Society Meeting where everybody was sitting around stitching a quilt, one of the women was talking about being courted by William Campion, whose wife had died several years earlier. This woman said that Will and his wife never had children so she thought he would be the ideal father to help raise her daughter. Besides, the woman felt that he was probably the best prospect for a widow lady for many miles around since he seemed to be doing well with all his business ventures and the property he owned. The woman said that she expected Mr. Campion to propose within a short time.

Grandma had never liked this woman. In fact, their dislike for one another was quite well known. Grandma told me she had said to herself, "Well, old girl, I think I'll just put a stop to that proposal; and, if he would be the ideal father to help raise your daughter, it would be even better if he were around to help raise my three sons."

Grandma said that, at first, she thought the woman was speaking of Jim Campion, who had the ice house and jitney service in Horton between Central Avenue and 1st Avenue East on 9th Street. She later learned that Jim was married, and it was his brother about whom her nemesis was speaking. This was when she was doing the ground work for her plot to *steal away* the man courting her nemesis.

After she hired Jim to take her to one of the farms in his jitney, she learned that it was really Will that she needed to meet and impress. Then, under the pretense of wanting to buy a gentle horse for the boys, she had Jim send Will by to see her. Grandma was a good looking woman in her thirties at that time. She had obviously *led the horse to water*, and within a short time he was apparently dying for a drink. It wasn't long before Will married Grandma, and the boys had a stepfather to take care of them.

I asked Daddy if the boys were treated well by Grandpa Campion. Daddy said he liked Grandpa and called him "Dad," but James and Joe never got along very well with him. He said that Grandma didn't seem to want them to get along well or get very close to him; and sometimes, she set up situations where the boys were expected to choose her and stand up with her against him. He said that James started having a number of verbal battles with Grandpa when he was in the seventh and eighth grades, and that is why James ended up going to boarding school at St. Benedict's at that time. Of course, it was at that same time that Grandma had decided that James would become a priest.

Joe started playing little pranks on Grandpa but never got punished. Grandma seemed to encourage them. After Joe was in high school and until he joined the Army, he had gotten to where he was drinking quite a bit. Grandma would get into arguments with him and would then call Grandpa upstairs to discipline Joe. Daddy said this often ended with Grandpa and Joe fighting each other and rolling around on the kitchen or parlor floor. (I can remember my Grandpa Clark, Chief of Police in Horton, telling me about the time he was called up to Grandma Campion's house to break up a fight between Grandpa Campion and Joe. I remember Grandpa Clark telling me that *Mrs. Campion* had been swinging a broom and hitting the both of them all the while yelling, "Don't you hurt him, Will!")

My Daddy was supposed to be the ornery, unruly, undisciplined one of the three sons. He was the one who got into all the fights at school. He was the one who always got in trouble with his mother. He was the one she cut all the switches for when the boys were growing up. Both James and Joe agreed that my father was always the one who got into trouble. But when I asked Daddy about Grandpa Campion, he said that Grandpa was a really good guy, a real role model, a man who tried, but was not allowed, to be a real father to the boys. He said that unlike his brothers, he felt like he had lost a father when Grandpa Campion died in 1943.

So what do I remember about Grandpa Campion other than his smelling like pipe tobacco and him sitting in his rocker next to the furnace in the cellar? I remember him showing me his spurs that he wore on his boots when he was breaking horses. I remember the sweat stains on his Stetson hat next to the hat band. I remember him talking about my Daddy riding his horses bareback, but not telling Grandma because she would have been *powerful mad.* I remember him showing me a big scar on his leg where he said a horse had tried to scrape him off his back by riding too close to a tree. I remember the horse collars and bridles that he still had in the garage south of the house, and how he had told me about putting a bit in a horse's mouth so it was done correctly or it could hurt the horse. But most of all, I remember his old coupe with the rumble seat.

For those of you who don't know or remember, a rumble seat was kind of like a small trunk that opened up on the back of a small coupe. I really don't know if it was truly intended to be used for additional people to ride in, but it was just the right size for Darrell and me. Grandpa would lift me up to put me in, and then he would put Darrell in. Then he would drive south on Euclid Avenue and west on 15th until he came to a dirt road. He would put his foot down on the gas and to a young child it felt like what the astronauts must feel like on blast off. The dust from the road would swirl off behind us just like the smoke from Grandpa's pipe. What a glorious feeling of excitement and pleasure!

Then, one day, Grandpa was gone. No one really explained it to me that I remember. I'm sure I didn't get to go to the funeral. The cellar doors remained closed. At first I would run up on the rough boards of the doors and kick my heels trying to call Grandpa to open the doors and let me in. All I got for my efforts were a few splinters in my bottom when I turned, sat down, and slid down the cellar doors. So began my isolation. For years and years and years, there was nothing to do on the many week nights, and always on Sundays, when we would go up to Grandma's so Daddy could listen to her stories about the problems she was having with her most recent sharecropper. There was nothing to do but sit on the *dufold* (an early type of sofa sleeper) in Grandma's parlor and play little games with my eyes. As I stared at Grandma from across the room, I watched her *fade off into space* as she sat there rocking in her rocking chair. There she goes! Pow! Straight to the moon!

I sure missed not having Grandpa there.

6.

GOING TO GRANDMA'S FARMS

I was still a very young child when I decided that "I didn't like going to the farm." My Grandma Campion, my father's mother, had three farms which were worked by renters or share-crop farmers. Grandma provided the land, the house, and the seed. The share cropper and his family provided the farm implements and the labor. Both the share cropper and my Grandma shared in the monetary results of the effort when the crops were harvested and sold.

During the growing season, from the spring through the fall, at least a weekly trip (sometimes more) to one of Grandma's farms was mandatory. Since Grandma didn't drive, Daddy usually left work during the afternoon to take her. Otherwise, we had to make a Sunday afternoon trip. Occasionally, Daddy was relieved of this time consuming task by my Uncle James and his family, who drove over from St. Joseph, Missouri, several Sundays a month. But, more often than not, it was poor Daddy who got roped into the weekly visit to the farm. Grandma had him tied to it.

The visits to the Netawaka farm were not too unpleasant, as they required that my Daddy drive straight out K-20, across the Kickapoo Indian Reservation to where it currently intersects with 75 Highway going north and south—a trip of about 12 miles. This, I was told, was always Grandma's *best farm*. But at some time during the early 1950's, improvements were made to widen 75 Highway into a four-lane divided highway, and the highway was rerouted so that it went right through

Grandma's property. The 160 acre farm was sliced, dissected, and basically *destroyed* in the name of *progress.*

The other two farms were located down by Effingham within several miles of each other, but they were a greater distance from our home in Horton. It took about an hour's driving time to get there and about five or six hours there once we arrived. An afternoon's trip going to one (or both) of those farms meant getting home at 8 or 9 o'clock at night.

Now you may be asking yourself, "What on earth took so long?" You've heard Barbara Mandrell and George Jones in their duet sing, "I was Country when Country wasn't cool." Well, Grandma was a *Bull Shooter* before they invented the term *Shooting the Bull.* She was a talker! Talk . . . Talk . . . Talk . . . or as we called it, *Bull Shooting* for short. I guess I come from a whole line of *Bull Shooters.* Grandma could sure do it. I know that my Father was accused of it, and I'm sure that more than just my kids accuse me of it. I don't see signs of it in my sons yet, but maybe I don't keep quiet long enough to let it take hold and *fester.* Anyway, it seems to be a generational thing— handed down parent to child—never quite letting it die out. Maybe I should get my sons T-shirts emblazoned with the words *Bull Shooter in Training.* I'm sure they'd love it! Well, maybe just one for my grandson, Timmy.

Of course, I wasn't the only one in the family to carry on this tradition. My cousin Terry got it from his father, too. He can *shoot the bull* with the best of them. My father was actually proud of his nephew's abilities when he was just a teenager. I wonder how many of Terry's sons are *carriers.*

But, enough of that. Let's get back to Grandma's farms and my reasons for deciding early on that I didn't like going there. I guess I'd have to admit that it all had to do with the amount of *talking* that always took place. There was a steady *yackety-yak* all the way down to the farm. Then my mother, little brother, and I would have to wait for hours in the car while more *yackety-yak* went on with the farmer, the farmer's wife, the man at the grain elevator, the man at the seed store, etc. Sometimes, Grandma and Daddy would disappear completely from our view; but as sure as there are stars up in the sky, we knew that the *yackety-yak* was still going on (and just about as plentiful as those stars).

It didn't take but a few trips for us to learn what the wait was going to be like. It was a *powerful, painful* experience—the kind that leaves a psychic imprint on the fabric of the Universe. In fact, it's been said that on a warm afternoon in Northeast Kansas, the sounds and echoes heard emerging from the car, as we sat there sweltering in the heat, can still be heard floating in the *Ether:* "I'm hot." "Can't we just get out of the car?" "Are they coming yet?" "I have to go to the bathroom." "My legs hurt." "Make Darrell stop pinching me." "I'm hungry." "I'm thirsty." "When are they going to come back to the car?" "Stop hitting!" "Stop pinching!" "Mama!" "Deanna is hitting me again." "I really have to go to the bathroom now." "I want to go home." "I really want something to drink." "I'm going to wet my pants—now!" "Why are they just standing there?" "I did go before we left." *"I can't go there!"* "There are bees around that nasty place and I can't get the door open." "What do you mean, pee in a can?" I think you probably get the picture.

Finally, Grandma and Daddy would come back to the car, and we'd all rejoice. Soon we'd be on our way back home. What??? (My mind would scream.) No, Grandma! Not again. Not those dreaded words, "Johnnie, let's just stop by a minute and see if Elsie is at home." Please, Daddy, just this one time tell Grandma, "No!" He never did!

––––––––––––

Elsie lived on a farm not far from Grandma's farms at Effingham. She was the daughter of Grandma's deceased older sister. I know that now; but at the time, I didn't know who this person was or why Grandma wanted to stop by to see her. I also know now that Elsie had once been the *hope* for success for a woman in my Grandma's family—in the 1930's she had actually attended college to get one of those *permanent* teaching certificates they issued back then. Elsie even taught school at a country school for a few years. But knowing this now certainly doesn't taint the memory I have of *my first visit* with Elsie.

The farm where Elsie lived seemed to be laid out similar to other farms I had seen. I was probably about 5 years old at the time and hadn't paid too much attention to other farms except Grandma's farms where the houses looked pretty much like the ones in town. A visit to Elsie's place was entirely different.

The farm was down a dirt road with deep ruts from vehicles traveling on it when it was wet and muddy. On that day, the air was hot and the road was dusty. As we approached the property, there was this large, overgrown brushy area where a shabby, unpainted barn could be seen peeking out from behind the scraggy trees and brush. Just past this, was a rusty metal gate that opened into a large circle drive with a huge tree stuck right down in the middle of the circle. The ruts in the circle drive were even deeper than those on the road.

As our car approached the gate and Daddy drove into the yard, two large dogs ran out from under the porch—circling the car and barking frantically. When Daddy stopped beside the huge tree, one of the dogs jumped up on the side of the car, putting his huge paws all over the glass as Daddy tried frantically to roll up the window. Daddy cursed at him, but the dog must have been used to cursing because he took his time, as he seemed to drag his paws down the side of the door—making a scratching sound all the way to the ground. Daddy kept saying, "*Sonofabitch! Sonofabitch!*" and I guessed that, since this was a dog he was talking about, he was right by all accounts.

Both dogs appeared to be mutts, but they looked to me as big as Shetland Ponies. The one that had jumped up on the door had sores on his body and places where it must have already healed, but no fur had grown back. His ears were bleeding and the sores were infested with flies. I never knew either dog's name, but I'll call this one Ol' Scratch. The other dog was much more patient, but just as mangy. It just stood there by Mama's car door waiting for something to happen. I'll call him Cujo—for no apparent reason. Now, about that time, Ol' Scratch came around to Mama's side; and just as if he had tried to take a *bone* away from the other dog, suddenly Cujo attacked. There was snarling, growling, snapping of teeth, and the fur literally flew around the car as everybody tried to lean up and forward and around to try to see what was happening outside the windows as the dogs fought around and around and sometimes *under* the car, while Daddy kept up with his mantra, "*Sonofabitch! Sonofabitch!*"

I didn't notice that a woman and two boys had come out onto the back porch. The boys didn't seem concerned about the dogs' snapping teeth. The woman yelled, "Donnie and Ronnie, get those dogs away from the car!" Each boy took a dog as they pulled them apart using whatever they could grab hold of—since neither dog was wearing a collar. Tail, ears, scruff of neck—whatever was available—it became a handle to remove the dogs. Several kicks later, the dogs were forced back to the underworld beneath the porch, and it was safe to open the car doors.

Only after I was out of the car did I notice that the back porch was only a flat deck set up on concrete blocks so that it was all open underneath. A rusty wagon and some other kids' toys could be seen under the porch along with the dogs. Further back, I thought I saw another pair of eyes peering out, but that could've just been a child's imagination. The thought of going up onto that porch gave me goose bumps on my sweaty arms.

Across from the house, about 50 yards away, was the aforementioned barn with a fenced-in area—the pig lot. I remember thinking *how big* those pigs were and *how dark* the mud was in the pig lot. I don't know whether it smelled that bad all the time, but the smell that day was atrocious. Mama used to tell people, "Deanna has a weak stomach." And when we got out of the car, her first words were, "Now, Deanna, don't gag!" Of course, this just made me think about it. Mama gave me a handkerchief that she had taken out of her purse to put over my nose to breathe. The handkerchief had *Blue Magic* perfume on it—giving me the overall aroma of *Blue Magic Pig Lot.*

After Elsie introduced Darrell and me to Donald and Ronald, the twin boy animal tamers, she invited us into the house. Mama was carrying Darrell so it was clear that he was going in, but as I stepped between the piles of dog bones and *dog doo*, to try to follow them, I got the distinct impression that Elsie planned on me staying outside with the boys. Not me! Even at age five, I knew that these were kids I didn't want to play with. "Wait for me!" I yelled, as I cautiously walked in front of the gleaming eyes lurking beneath the porch. Once I was beyond that, I practically ran as I climbed up on the three wobbly concrete blocks leading up to the wooden porch.

The twins were somewhere around seven or eight years old. At that time, I just thought they were Elsie's kids. Later, I learned that they were her stepchildren. She had only been married to *Gus* for a few years. He had been a widower with four children when he met Elsie. She was the school teacher at the one room country school house attended by his two older daughters. I guess he must have slicked up and courted her properly—good enough at least to where an unmarried spinster teacher past thirty would think that marrying and taking on a ready-made family was the thing to do.

Now Elsie was *mother* to those two dirty, barefoot, ragamuffins in overalls, with no shoes, no shirts, and *bowl* haircuts starting to grow out over their ears. The boys poked each other and rolled wrestling on the ground, seemingly unconcerned about the *dog doo* just inches away. They reminded me so much of the dogs that they had just separated that I began to wonder, "Who was training whom?"

As the adults opened the kitchen door and walked in, I scrambled to try to keep up. The screen was torn in a jagged diagonal. Before I could open the door, another large dog exited the kitchen through the gaping hole in the screen. As soon as he had come through, I used the same hole for my entrance. Grandma yelled at me, "Deanna, don't come in that way; you'll make it worse." I just ran over to stand by Mama who was already seated in a chair at the kitchen table, still holding my brother. I looked back at the screen door. I wondered why Grandma had yelled at me. I was just sure that, given an opportunity, if they weren't penned up over by the barn, those huge grey pigs with black spots could've gotten through the hole in that screen door. They probably would have tried, too, if it would have gotten them away from that horrible smell.

Darrell was squirming and wanting to get down off Mama's lap, but she wouldn't let him. I leaned against Mama and felt that she, like me, was moist with perspiration. It was hot in Elsie's kitchen. "I'm hot," I said. Grandma handed me a piece of cardboard with a tongue depressor attached and told me to *fan* myself if I was hot. She had another one and was fanning herself in a dainty-like fashion. When I tried it that way, it didn't seem to stir up enough wind to cool anything. So, I just decided to ignore the beads of sweat running down the back of my neck, arms, and legs. I looked around the kitchen. There wasn't an electric fan anywhere to be found. Later, I learned that they didn't have electricity—no lights! And I didn't see an ice box either. No refrigerator, and there wasn't even an ice box. That meant no ice at all! That was really roughing it!

Grandma asked, "Where's Gus?" Elsie said that he was upstairs with a bad headache. This was something else I learned over the years. Gus having a headache was code for "Gus is getting drunk, is drunk, or is just getting over being drunk." I don't think I ever saw him more than once, and that was just a fluke. We happened to get there that time while he was still out in the yard. But, of course, he had to go upstairs straight away because of his headache.

Elsie said, "I'd take you into the parlor, but the boys are so rough, they've almost torn up the furniture in there. I think you'll be more comfortable in here." About that time, two girls came into the kitchen and said "hello." They were about 10 to 12 years old. They both looked like they needed baths and their hair was tangled and knotted. The sleeves were torn out of their dresses, but I don't think it was a fashion statement.

If the kitchen was in better shape than the parlor, then the parlor must have been really awful. A big wood heating stove was in the corner of the kitchen. It had the flat metal plates on it so it was used for cooking, too. There were shelves along one wall and the paint was peeling off. There were no doors, even though Grandma referred to them as cabinets. Glass jars, old pots, and several dishes seemed to be piled around in random groupings.

At one end of the room closest to the stove, there was a counter with a small pump built in and a huge, round, metal pan filled with dirty dishes next to it. Grandma jumped up and walked quickly to the pump. She said, "I guess I don't need to prime it." After that, she grabbed a big metal cup that was attached to the pump by heavy twine, moved the pump handle up and down several times, and water started running into the cup. Grandma put the cup up to her mouth and took a big drink. "Aah," she said, as though thoroughly satisfied. "There's just nothing quite as sweet as well water." She held the cup out to us. "Anyone else want some water?"

I was thirsty, but I didn't want to drink out of the same old dirty cup that I knew those boys' lips had touched. And I could envision the *mysterious Gus* taking a big swig of *headache juice* out of it. Grandma looked around as we all shook our heads. Then she threw the remaining water into this big bucket that she called a *slop jar*. Used water, fruit and vegetable peels, and food scraps all went into the jar and were later used to *slop* the pigs. I think some of the horrible smell may have been coming from the slop jar and not just the pig lot.

I continued to look around as Grandma came back to sit at the table. There was a steady buzz of talking going on, but I was more concerned with what was under the oil-cloth table covering that Elsie had thrown back over the contents of the table to *make a clear spot* in front of my Daddy and Grandma. I lifted it up by the one corner on the side that had been thrown back toward Mama. All I could see was more dirty, stinky dishes. As Mama reached out and grabbed me, she dug her fingernails into the top of my hand. She always did that when she wasn't pleased with what I was doing. That was her way of telling me to *stop*, without saying a word.

Mama did a lot of that pinching when we were up at Grandma Campion's, too. I couldn't seem to do anything right at her house either. If I wasn't sitting on Grandma's *dufold* with my legs stuck straight out in front of me, staring at Grandma as she rocked back and forth, I was perceived as *causing trouble*. To pass the time, I had learned this little trick with my eyes where, if I stared just right, I could make Grandma appear to slide back into space and then move back forward again. An optical illusion? I'm not sure, but I did a lot of crazy things with my mind back then to try to deal with the boredom. Maybe it was all that pinching!

Anyway, Grandma got up again. She walked over to the stove, lifted the top off a pan with a dish towel, and then proceeded to pick at the contents of the pan with a fork. Then, she took a dirty plate that was there on the counter and picked out a piece of chicken for herself. "Anybody want a piece of chicken?" she asked. "Elsie makes the best fried chicken." I wanted to gag.

I thought Daddy was going to say *yes* at first, but when he saw Mama reach out her hand digging her fingernails into me, he said, "No, thank you."

I yelled, "I don't want any either." Then I twisted away from Mama so she couldn't hurt me again. I wrinkled my nose at her as I inched myself toward Daddy. Anything more and I would've been in real trouble.

Darrell was getting hot and starting to fuss. He wanted to get down on the floor, but Mama wouldn't let him. "Go ahead and let him get down," Elsie said. "There isn't anything that he can hurt if he gets into it."

Mama said something about Darrell just being at that stage where everything went into his mouth and his little eyes being able to spot marbles or coins or things that he could choke on. She wouldn't let him down so he just continued to fuss and fidget, but she never dug her fingernails into him. (Actually, it's more likely that she wouldn't let him down because the floor was filthy. I don't think she was worried about "marbles or coins or things he could choke on." I think it was the chicken bones with flies and the indefinable little piles of something behind the stove. I wanted to go investigate, but one pile over in the corner appeared to be moving.)

I went over and leaned against Daddy's leg. From there, I could get a good look at Elsie. I had noticed that when she stood up she was taller than Grandma or Mama. She may have even been slightly taller than Daddy. I imagined that she was what Grandma previously referred to as a "big-boned woman." Elsie appeared to be a lot older than Mama, but not quite as old as Grandma. She had her hair pulled back straight and rolled into a little bun in back. A wisp of hair had gone its own way up front, and Elsie kept pushing it back behind her ear.

Elsie's hair was gray/black and looked like it needed to be washed. Her eyebrows grew extremely thick and simply cried out to be plucked. And, unlike Mama, she didn't have on a speck of makeup.

However, like the girls who, by then, had departed the kitchen, Elsie was wearing a dress that came just below her knees. The sleeves had been removed, leaving the raw edges of the original material showing at her shoulders. She wore an old apron over her dress with faded blue flowers in the print. The apron had huge stains where she had wiped her hands on several occasions. I looked at the brown spots on the apron and thought, *"I'll bet she was wearing that apron when she killed the chicken that Grandma ate."*

When Elsie sat down, her dress moved up above her knees. She had on old holey nylon stockings that were rolled down about half-way between her knees and her ankles. She wore black laced shoes that, by comparison, were in much worse shape than the ratty old shoes that Grandma wore as her *Gardening Shoes.* I could see the knots on her knees and the big purple blotches on her legs which Mama told me later were varicose veins. But I think the thing that fascinated me most was the *hair.* Boy, did Elsie ever have hair on her legs. I always thought Daddy had hair on his legs, but Elsie had grown a crop of leg hair that was unequaled—except perhaps by a chimp I once saw (many years later) at the Topeka Zoo.

I was fascinated by that glorious hair. I closed my left eye and sized up the length of different hairs by looking out of my right eye, through my thumb and forefinger, at individual hairs on her leg. Some of those hairs must have been well over two inches long.

While I was still contemplating what I could do with all that hair, Elsie jumped up and opened one side of the stove. As it turned out, there was an oven on that side. She reached in a pulled out a nice *room temperature* Gooseberry Pie. Once again, there was an offer of something to eat. This time Daddy got up and wiped off a dirty plate with an even dirtier looking dish towel. Both he and Grandma had slices of Gooseberry Pie. Mama was looking at me, and I didn't want to tangle with those fingernails, so I said, "I don't like Gooseberry Pie." To tell the truth, I don't think I even knew what Gooseberry Pie was at the time.

Shortly after Daddy finished his Gooseberry Pie, I fell asleep standing up while leaning against his leg. I don't know how I made it to the floor or how long I slept, but I remember Daddy stumbling as he carried me down the wobbly steps to the car. He almost fell and stepped in *dog doo*—causing him to leave the same way he had arrived—cursing, "*Sonofabitch.*"

Years later, when the *Ma and Pa Kettle* movies came out, I remember thinking, *"Elsie's place must have been used as a model for the Kettle farm."* At first, I thought they were documentaries. Ma Kettle made me think of Elsie, and though I really didn't see Gus except for one time, I think he must have borne a strong resemblance to Pa Kettle. But neither Donald nor Ronald could ever hold a candle to that good-looking Richard Long, who played Ma and Pa Kettle's oldest son—only in Hollywood.

Personal Note: It hardly seems possible, but sixty years have passed since that incident. So what have I learned as I've passed along life's highway? Well, I certainly had very little compassion for Elsie during my early life; and even until Elsie died sometime in the early 60's, I had very little feeling for her. I regret that. Grandma used to say, "Elsie's got a lot of problems to deal with—she's doing *the best she can.*"

I guess I got to the point where I believed that and put that philosophy into practice in my own life. I went to college and got my degree. I reared my children alone after my first husband and I divorced. I moved up from one job to another increasing my income, got my master's degree, and I had earned almost 40 hours beyond that before I got sidetracked. When the time came, I took care of my mother (after my father's death). I helped my kids get into college. And through it all, I managed to save enough money so I could retire and hopefully still have a few things to pass on to my children. In my heart, I really believed that I was doing *the best I could.*

In some ways, however, I am no different than Elsie. I got caught up in appearances and expectations of others. My long terms goals were set aside by immediate needs, employers, family, friends, and a whole line of acquaintances. Only now do I realize that *the best I could* was really not good enough if, somewhere along the way, you lose your dream. What about the things I wanted to do? What about the things that I really wanted to achieve for me? What about the mark I wanted to make on the world—my name carved on the tree of life—left to be seen after I am gone.

Now that I'm 65 in this year of our Lord, 2003, I'm finally ready to start working on *my dream.*

Elsie may have planned it that way, too; but she didn't live to be 65. If Elsie had a dream, it must have died with her. (Actually, I'm sure she had a dream, but from what I saw, her life couldn't have been it.) I know that both of my boys are talented and creative, but they, too, seem to be following in my footsteps. I'm proud of both of them. They are doing well with families and jobs. And, I'm sure they think they're *doing the best they can.* But while I'm sure they both equally had dreams for their lives, I don't see either of them actively working on those dreams.

If there's one thing at which I'm an expert, it's pushing aside dreams. How many times did I say: "Someday I'll work on *my* dream . . . I just don't have time now." Or, "I'm on the road traveling for the company; I can't work on my dream now."

It was always something: "I need some relaxation, so I'll just watch television instead." Or, "I have too much to do for the children now." Or, "I need just one more course at college." Or, "I have commitments to

Mom so . . . " Or, "I need to work this extra job." There was always something to prevent me from getting started on my dream.

We have to assume that we only pass this way one time. Don't do what Elsie did. Don't do what I have done. Don't wait until you're 65 to start working on your dream. Find time while you're still young enough to work toward that one thing that will make you happy. I'm not advocating that you give up your responsibilities; just recognize your priorities so that you're always taking steps toward your dream.

So, what is my dream? Well, you're looking at it. This old *bull shooter* is still talking—just not in a face-to-face mode. My dream has always been to be a writer. And I still have a lot to say! So please, keep reading! I'll be back to write the next story as soon as I finish shaving my legs.

7.

MY FIRST BEST FRIEND
(The following was written in honor of
my First Best Friend's 66th birthday.)

September 18, 2004—Today is the 66th birthday of my *first best friend*. It seems impossible that we are that old. I am seven months older than Peggy, my birth date being February 18, 1938. How did all the years go flying by so quickly? It's been a long time; yet, I can remember this dear friend and our adventures as if they happened yesterday.

———————

Most of my earliest memories are associated with the house on 5th Street. We (Mama, Daddy, and I) had been living with Grandma and Grandpa Clark in the upstairs apartment of the house that Grandpa had first purchased when he moved his family from Missouri to Horton in 1920. It was a big two-story house on East 5th Street. Mama and Daddy had converted the upstairs of Grandpa's house into an apartment when they got married in August, 1936. Shortly thereafter, Daddy bought the property on the southeast corner of 6th Street and First Avenue East. He moved two smaller houses onto the property, put them together, and spent all his spare time for about four years remodeling them. The two old houses ultimately turned out to be one very nice home for our family (my brother Darrell joining us in 1940.) But at this point in my story, Daddy was still working on our house. Being in our own home was a while down the road.

The summer after I was three, Grandma and Grandpa Clark bought the bungalow just across the street from the property where Daddy was building our new home. My grandparents' house was on the southwest corner of 6th Street and First Avenue East. Just across the street from them, and catty-corner from the house Daddy was building, was the home of the Kallos family, who were soon to become so important in my childhood. The fourth corner, for those of you keeping track, was where Bertha Sowadski lived.

At the time I first met Peggy, we had just moved into the little bungalow with Grandpa and Grandma, where we stayed *temporarily* until early spring the next year. Peggy James Kallos, as I soon found out, lived in the corner house directly across the street to the north from the bungalow. Since the Kallos house faced First Avenue East, I had a good view of their back and side yards from Grandma's front windows. Mrs. Kallos would occasionally come outside, bringing Peggy in her *Taylor Tot*, and would walk along the sidewalk. (At that time, a *Taylor Tot* was a brand name for a type of stroller.) Usually, Peggy's older sister, Stella, would be along—either helping to push the stroller or just having hold of the handle. I had graduated from the *Taylor Tot* once brother Darrell was born, so I was surprised when I first learned that Peggy was so close to my age.

I'm not sure just how or when we first started playing together, but it quickly became apparent that my mother and grandmother, who I considered extremely strict and concerned about what I did, where I was, and with whom I played, were very liberal when compared to Mrs. Kallos. She kept an eye on her four children like no one else that I have ever known. In fact, I can probably count the number of times on both hands that Peggy was allowed to come to Grandma's house or to our house during those early years. Even though invitations were given for Peggy to come play with me, it always ended up the other way. I would get a return invitation to come to the Kallos house to play, but I seldom was allowed to return the favor.

It's funny as I look back on this time; Mama always insisted that all children had to come to our house to play. She was so protective that she worried if I was out of her sight and Grandma wasn't the one watching me. I never got to go to anyone else's house except Peggy's where

Mama obviously knew that I would be watched just as much, or even more closely than when I was watched by Mama or Grandma Clark.

It is almost impossible to talk about my dear friend Peggy without also talking about her family. I guess I learned a lot through osmosis during those early years—things that I really didn't understand until years later. One of the first things I learned was that the family was Greek. I really didn't have a concept of *nationality* or *heritage* back then. Mama simply explained to me that *Greece* was where Peggy's parents were from—a place where her mother and father had been born and lived before coming to our country. She explained that I was 3/4 Irish, 1/8 German and 1/8 English. I told her I didn't understand; I was a *whole* child. Daddy would just laugh and tell me that it meant that the Kallos kids were *pedigreed,* while Darrell and I were *mongrels.* I didn't think that sounded very good, but decided that if Daddy could laugh about it, it had to be okay.

As time went on, I learned that Mr. Kallos had come over from Greece, established himself in Horton with his shoe and leather shop, and had then gone back to Greece to get Mrs. Kallos. Things were so much more formal back then. Children always gave respect to adults by calling them Mr. and Mrs. It wasn't until much later that I learned that Mr. Kallos' given name was James (Jim) and Mrs. Kallos was Crisoula. I believe that Peggy once told me that the closest translation for Crisoula was something like *Goldie.*

Peggy has two older brothers, Gregory and Donnie, and an older sister, Stella. I was always fascinated as I listened to Mrs. Kallos when she called her children. Gregory, being the oldest and a boy, had taken to wandering away from home a little more than the others. He must have known that if he was *out of calling* distance, however, he was in trouble. For the small little lady that she was, Mrs. Kallos sometimes had an extremely loud voice. About dinnertime during the summer, she would come to the south end of her big porch and call Gregory. It sounded to me like she was yelling , "Re-wad-e," but I'm sure it must have been Greek for Gregory—something like "Gre-gor-ie," with a rolling "r" sound.

Donnie's name sounded something like "De-o-ne-see," Stella was "Es-ta-the-a," and Peggy sounded like "Pee-vou-la." I soon learned also that each child carried their father's first name as their middle name— "Dem-o-stenni" (James). Gregory was Gregory James Kallos, Donnie was Donald James Kallos, Stella was Stella James Kallos and Peggy was "Pee-vou-la Dem-o-stenni Kal-o-ur-op-ol-os"—the last name being the original Greek name that was Americanized to Kallos, using the first three letters and last three letters.

Please, if you speak Greek and I have totally butchered their names, accept my apologies. I love the sound of the language, and I am compelled to try saying the Greek names and several other phrases I learned over the years.

Now, my cousin Roger, on the other hand, had absolutely no respect for names or just about anything else *important* at that time. He got a real kick out of being *disrespectful* to everybody. He really enjoyed calling Peggy, *Pee-Wooly.* I can still hear him yell, "Hey, Pee-Wooly, your Mama is callin' you."

I do believe that my cousin Roger was the model for Dennis the Menace. Just give him an opportunity, and he was disrespectful to anybody and everybody. I remember one time he told my Grandfather, the Chief of Police for Horton for over 30 years, "I'm going to grow up and be a bank robber, Grandpa, so I can shoot you." Of course, he didn't become a bank robber and he really didn't want to shoot Grandpa; but I guess Roger did the next best thing. He worked for the Internal Revenue Service for 30 years before retiring. I know people who think they get robbed annually by the IRS; don't you?

It was Mrs. Kallos who gave me a love for the Greek language. She used to sit on her porch swing and laugh as she would repeat names and phrases for me to say. I loved her accent and her classic beauty. I don't ever remember seeing her when she wasn't immaculate—every hair in place. Even though she wore housedresses like other mothers of the time, they were always clean and crisp as if they had been freshly laundered. Even the apron she wore never had a single spot on it. She had a beautiful, clear, light complexion with dark, silky hair which she wore up in a bun at the back of her neck. Her skin was so flawless that, to look at her, you could not believe that she had boys as old as they were—she looked so young. I decided that she must have been very young when she married and came to the United States. To look at her profile, it was easy for me to imagine her as the model for my Cameo brooch.

The Kallos children were the cleanest kids I ever knew. Gregory and Donnie went out riding on their bicycles and came back home still as clean as they were when they went out. They never came back sweaty or dirty, or with torn clothes like my cousins Al, Duane, and Roger did. Stella and Peggy were probably the cleanest, best-dressed little girls in town. And they never seemed to have scabs on their knees and chigger bites on their legs like mine did.

This was also at a time when mothers made a lot of the clothes that their children wore—at least my mother did so I thought that was the way everybody did. Peggy and Stella always had the most beautiful clothes. I'm not sure if some of them were store bought, but I know that many of their dresses were made by Mrs. Christ, a professional seam-stress who lived on the next block. Peggy and Stella always looked like they had stepped off the pages of a children's fashion magazine. Most of my clothes were made from flour sacks at that time, this being during World War II. I remember Mama even cut up some of Daddy's old suits to make some of my clothes.

The Kallos home had a huge front porch that ran across the entire front of the house. Kids today don't know what marvelous play houses a front porch could make. Peggy and I played for hours with my pretend *house* being in one corner of her porch and her *house* in another. We always managed to go somewhere in *pretend land* using an elevator. Since elevators were almost totally non-existent in Horton, they were magical things. The front screen door was always the elevator. Just step inside, push the knob on the screen door, and "z-z-z-z-z-z-z-t," we were off to some other fantasy destination.

Occasionally, if the weather was bad, Peggy and I got to go up to her room and play. Peggy's house was exciting to me because it had an upstairs. Our house was all on one level. I can remember climbing the stairs and when we got to the top, just to the right was this extra huge step that took us into Peggy's room. Usually I brought over at least one of my dolls, and we got to be *mommies,* as we pretended to have hus-bands and our own houses. I don't know where we were getting the models for our behavior (because it certainly didn't sound like my mother or Mrs. Kallos), but those dolls got scolded and spanked quite often, and our invisible husbands were put through terrible ordeals as we chided them for not bringing home the milk we had requested or for some other domestic trauma they had caused.

Usually, at some time during my visit with Peggy, we would be invited to come downstairs for cookies. There was a butler's pantry between the dining room and the kitchen in their house. There, on the counter, Mrs. Kallos had wonderful treats for *good children.* I always wanted to be a *good child* at her house. I especially liked the little white powdered-sugar cookies she made from a traditional Greek recipe.

The fall after I turned six, Mama and Daddy let me start to school. I say *let me* because I had wanted to start to school earlier, but they decided that they didn't want to turn loose of me the year before. Therefore, I missed kindergarten altogether and went directly into first grade. When I got there, I was disappointed to learn that Peggy was not there. Because I was Catholic, Mama and Daddy sent me to St. Leo's Grade School, but Peggy was going to Public School.

When *church* was cited as the reason, I really didn't understand why we were in different schools. Peggy and I had talked some about going to church. I went every Sunday, but at that time, Peggy and her family had to drive all the way to Kansas City to go to church. When she told me about the services, however, they sounded just like what happened on Sunday at St. Leo's. The major difference, as far as I could see, was that Peggy got to celebrate things like Easter and Christmas twice: first, at the same time that I did, and then again the next week—something about the Greek calendar made this possible. I remember asking, "Well, really? So then, do you get two sets of presents?"

I missed Peggy a lot when we started school. By the time we got home, there usually wasn't enough time to play. There was homework, piano lessons and piano practice, and helping around the house, and, well, you get the picture. Then both of us eventually made new friends. I think Peggy got a serious new friend before I did. Her name was Judy Wart. She may have been a very nice person, but I hated her guts. I felt she was responsible for taking my friend Peggy away from me. But truth be told, we had very little time for each other during the school year, and there was Judy getting what little time we had. Aah, the green eyes of envy!

We still saw each other, and got together from time to time as we got older. One time, I can't remember how old we were, probably about eleven; it was a warm summer night. Joanne King was visiting Stella, and I was over visiting Peggy. There were no adults around; Mr. and

Mrs. Kallos were gone somewhere. We had been having a grand time gossiping and sneaking treats from the kitchen. As it got a little later in the evening, we gathered at the piano in the living room, and Stella began playing the piano while we all sang. I think we may have told a few ghost stories before that, because Stella started to play *Ghost Riders in the Sky*. After several loud choruses, we all stopped suddenly when we heard an even louder sound, a bumping noise on the porch.

We all crowded around Stella as she led the way to the front door and turned on the porch light. No one was there. Then we heard a bumping sound on the south wall. We all screamed and went running to the back of the house. Then there as a bumping as if someone was trying to get into the screened-in porch at the back of the house. Stella thought the screen door was locked, but no one wanted to venture out to see. Someone said, "Did Stella lock the screen door to the front porch when she looked out?" We all went scurrying back through the dining room on our way toward the living room.

There were more sounds on the wall below the dining room windows and screens being scratched. We were all hysterical by then. Stella turned out the lights, and we got down on our knees and crawled over by the dining room table. Stella got to the phone and called somewhere to locate their parents and let them know what was happening. Then, there was even more scratching, and we were sure that someone was *cutting* the screen. Eventually, we made it back to the front door, and we all rejoiced to learn that the screen door was locked.

Still, we stayed down low, in a group, just below the windows. When we peeked up over each other to look out, we saw some guy in a white tee shirt out by a tree in the front yard. He must have seen us because he ran up the street to the north of the Kallos' property. Joanne or I asked, "Could that be Donnie?" Peggy and Stella were sure that it wasn't him. He had a plaid shirt on when he left and besides, he knew better.

A few minutes later, Mr. and Mrs. Kallos arrived to calm us all. My parents were called to come across the street to get me because there was "some crazy person scaring the girls." Just as Daddy got to the front porch, Donnie came walking in. He did have on a plaid shirt, but someway Mrs. Kallos knew instantly that he was the culprit. He got smacked on the back of the head several times before he made it through the door, and Mrs. Kallos was on a roll yelling at him in Greek.

Later, when we started high school, I was happy that Peggy and I would once again be spending time together. I remember our freshman initiation. We were told to wash our hair, but not to put it up in curlers. We were told to wear no makeup and to come dressed in an older woman's house dress and *combat boots*. I don't remember what horrible costume the guys were supposed to wear, but I have a picture somewhere that Mom took of Peggy, Reva Searles (who lived over the hill east on 6th street) and me in Mrs. Kallos' old housedresses. Reva usually wore her hair in a pony tail, and Peggy's hair seemed to just fall into place naturally with the haircut she had, but I looked like something out of a horror magazine.

All of the Kallos children were talented musicians and played in the school band. Peggy and Stella took piano lessons from Mrs. Howard Clarke, who was also my piano teacher. I used to marvel at their abilities during recitals and when they played for Chorus or for other musical groups when we were in high school. They stayed so calm and relaxed. Such confidence! Such poise! I always got rattled on those occasions.

I can't remember when, but sometime before we started high school, Mr. Kallos sold his shoe and leather shop and opened a restaurant in the heart of downtown Horton—on west 8th street. It was called *Jim's Waffle Shop*. It was one of only a few good restaurants in Horton, and it was definitely the best. Sometime shortly after the opening, Mrs. Kallos started going to work with Mr. Kallos. Soon, she was doing most of the cooking for their dinner menu. Each of the kids took his or her turn working at the Waffle Shop. I remember seeing Gregory and Donnie working there and later, as each got older, they became an integral part of the family business. I was always impressed by the *team effort.*

Of course, Gregory went away to college after graduation in 1949. He went to Kansas University (KU) in Lawrence, Kansas. My cousin Al (Junior) graduated from high school the same year, but Al went directly into the Air Force. We were all proud of Al, but going to college seemed really sophisticated. Peggy reported back to me that Gregory had joined a fraternity—Sigma Chi. How exciting to have a big brother who was a fraternity man. Sigma Chi! I had a terrible crush on Gregory at the time. I thought he was so good looking; he could have been a movie star. I sat at the window watching for hours on the several occasions when he brought some of his fraternity brothers home with him.

How cool! Peggy said they sang *Sweetheart of Sigma Chi* at her house. I asked her to sing it for me. She sang it over and over before I would let her quit. The words still come to me from time to time even today.

Finally, it came time for Stella to work at the Waffle Shop—and then later Peggy. I think they may have officially started working there *part time* when each was a freshman in high school. Stella was a junior when Peggy and I were freshmen. A number of us felt sorry for the Kallos kids, thinking that they missed out on a lot by having to work. As I look back now and see the strength of the Kallos family unit, I now recognize that this structure and their ability to work as a team, were all part of the development of their value system—the moral and ethical values set for them as they grew into adulthood. My parents were good, moral people who helped set the value system for me and my brother Darrell. The other major influence for me, of course, was my early Catholic education. But we never had that same kind of intense family bond that went with being a team—everybody working together for a common goal.

The *Horton Headlight* always published a list of the honor roll students for each quarter. I can remember reading it while I was still in grade school and seeing my cousin Al's name in there next to Gregory's name. Then Donnie's name was there. Then Stella's name and finally my name and Peggy's name were both there. Now, I know how hard I had to work to be on the Honor Roll; but when I think of the long hours that Peggy worked each day at the Waffle Shop while still maintaining her place on the Honor Roll, I marvel at her perseverance, ability and talent. She was/is a natural leader; and like her older siblings, she worked hard—earning the many honors bestowed upon her.

Peggy also found the time to take part in many school activities. Both Peggy and I were in the Junior and Senior plays. She was excellent in her parts and didn't seem to get rattled a bit. I had been in a lot of plays during my years at St. Leo's Grade School, but I still got a bad case of butterflies each and every time. Both years, Peggy got very sophisticated roles and handled them flawlessly. My junior year role was so bland that I can't even remember what it was. But I did get what I thought was the better role our senior year.

The play that year included the part of *Dorthula, the colored maid.* Unfortunately, Horton wasn't very diverse. We didn't have any *negro* students in our class! Our advisor at the time needed someone who would play the role without making a mockery of it. Not being fully aware of the underlying implications, I asked for the part. I thought it sounded like fun!

"Are you crazy?" everybody seemed to ask me; but I went ahead with it. Mom gave me a tight permanent with little bitty curls. I dyed my hair black and used a dark brown shade of theatrical makeup. I was surprised how large and beautiful it made my eyes look and how much contrast there was when I opened them up wide. Peggy laughed with me. She thought I looked *marvelous*.

After the play, the entire cast went down to the Waffle Shop for *cokes* and a bite to eat. While we were there, Mrs. Kallos came over to the booth where I was sitting and patted me on the hand. She always pronounced my name "Dee-ahn-na." "Dee-ahn-na," she said. "Don't worry about your hair. It will grow out. I'm just glad to see your skin back to its natural color." I felt only acceptance and love in her statement. She appreciated having *me* back.

I know that people felt sorry for me for taking that role, but I had the time of my life. I really was able to get into the experience of being someone else. I even got to belt out *When the Roll is Called Up Yonder* and *Swing Low, Sweet Chariot*. Gene Kletchka took my photograph and sent it in to a thespian magazine. It earned him some kind of award and was published. He gave me a copy, which I had until 1993, when it was lost during my move to Atlanta. It was in one of several boxes that the movers left setting on a dock in St. Louis when the van was overweight. The photograph totally disappeared. I have visions of the photograph hanging on one of the dock worker's walls. Yep! I'll bet I'm his pin-up girl.

Like their brother Gregory, each of the Kallos children took his or her turn at attending KU. Unlike Peggy, however, I turned down a scholarship at KU. The scholarship was in music, and by that time, I was sure that I didn't want to be a music teacher. My father thought it would be a waste of my time to go to college, so he sent me to Clark's Business School in Topeka.

Unfortunately, this is when Peggy and I really started going our separate ways. She was at KU and I was in Topeka at Clark's Business School, and later working at *Household Magazine*. After working awhile, I decided I wanted the education I had missed, but by that time I had to pay for it through money I had saved working at the magazine and by working in the Administration Building at Highland Community College. None of that was as prestigious or as sophisticated as KU, but I worked hard and I was proud of everything I accomplished on my own.

I went on to finish up my bachelor's degree at Kansas State University (KSU). Those *Aggies* weren't nearly as sophisticated as KU graduates either (although former Governor John Carlin was in my graduating class of 1962). By the time I got my bachelor's degree, Peggy had joined the work force—getting journalism experience working for local magazines in Topeka—but in positions with more clout than the secretarial positions I had after Clark's Business School.

Peggy and I were clearly on different paths from that point on. I hardly ever saw her after that. I remember one summer night coming back home to Horton and seeing Peggy across the street. I was either on a break from working in Topeka during summer vacation (to help pay my tuition), or I was home from taking an extra session at summer school. I do remember, however, that we talked about a major event that was about to take place in Peggy's life. This was when I first learned about Michael Jeweler, her then soon to be husband. He sounded like Prince Charming. It was like Peggy was destined to meet her Prince and had been groomed for this from childhood. Now it all made sense. Why bother with all the *frogs* when you knew that someday the Prince would be there. We were standing on the sidewalk in front of her house. "There he is," she said. I told her that I'd see her later, and then walked to the corner. As I crossed catty-corner to my house, I looked back to see Michael get out of his car. Wow! What a hunk!

Since moving back to the Kansas City area in 1996, I have seen Stella on television and in the newspapers a number of times. Last year, the *Kansas City Star* called her the *Matriarch of Greek Cooking in the Kansas City Area*. She has taken a major role in the Greek Festival for years. But, as I've said, she and Peggy were always so mature and confident. They always took on responsibilities and made them seem effortless. Yet, again, they performed flawlessly. That, it seems has always been a major difference between Peggy and me. Where she always excelled with grace, I always floundered around and really had to work hard just to get minor things to come out okay.

Just look at our lives since leaving Horton. Peggy went on to lead a very exciting life and has traveled to a number of places, including the Great Wall of China. She has lived in Italy (while traveling to Greece and other places in Europe), and lived many years in the Washington, D.C. area. Michael worked for the FBI, and Peggy was employed by the CIA. I don't know anyone from our class who can top that for excitement.

I was a teacher, social worker, and spent over 20 years in management at AT&T, but I'm sure my life's resume looks dull compared to the exciting life Peggy has led. She rubbed shoulders with the people who made the news every day, and my only excitement came from the strange events that seemed to follow me everywhere, such as being locked in a Minneapolis Shopping Center at night with the lights out, being trapped in an elevator of a Cincinnati hotel during a fire, and being on a plane in Oklahoma City when the wheel assembly fell off during landing. If I had made the news, with my luck, it would have been as a statistic or a casualty.

Our 50th high school reunion is coming up in May, 2006. A number of our classmates know that Peggy is back in the Midwest and hope Peggy and Michael will be there for the reunion. Some are already preparing to see Peggy again and meet Michael. Classmates are already working to get their faces off *Wanted* posters in the Horton Post Office— just in case Peggy and Michael still have ties to the CIA and FBI. Just kidding, of course! After all these years, it is nice to know that Peggy is just a short drive or a phone call away.

Peggy is and always will be my very first and dear best friend! I love you, Peggy! Happy Birthday!

8.

AN EARLY LESSON LEARNED

When I was very young, maybe only three years old or so, my cousin Roger came to our house to play with me and my toys every day. He was really good at entertaining me—especially with our toy Cowboy and Indian set. He took my furry coat, turned the sleeves inside out for tunnels, and formed mountains and valleys out of the rest of the coat. He could do a whole Roy Rogers' movie replay with those cowboys, Indians, and horses, having them race around chasing and shooting each other. He did all the voices for everybody. Of course, the Indians didn't say too much. They just mostly said "Ugh," but that was just like the movies, too. Roger even provided the music accompaniment—also using his voice. He was especially good at the *William Tell Overture.*

Before Roger started school, he was at our house for several hours every day. Then later, he was only there after school and during the summer. By that time, my little brother Darrell was no longer confined to his baby bed. He was crawling or walking all over the place. Now Mama expected me to entertain him like Roger had done for me.

As Darrell grew older, I was also expected to watch him to see that he didn't get into trouble—and continue to entertain him. Since I didn't want him messing with my dolls, I had to play with his toys, which by the time I was seven or so, really didn't interest me much. But that was the routine. I was expected to spend a good deal of my time watching and entertaining Darrell—not just occasionally, but everyday—*all the time!*

At a certain point in time, I would want to quit; but Darrell wouldn't be ready for me to stop playing. He always wanted me to keep going—to keep entertaining him. Then he'd get mad, and, of course, then I'd get mad. Then he'd throw a toy or start crying. Then Mama would immediately jump in with, "Why can't you children play nice with each other?" I was too young to know it at the time, but it was because we were *children* and five hours or more of *whatever* was already too long.

Mama would then go back to whatever she was doing, thinking that she had just settled something. Darrell always took this to mean that *he had won.* Within a short time, he would either pinch me, or throw another toy, or knock something over and kick it. Then I'd yell, "Mama, Darrell doesn't want to play nice!"

This was an instant inducement for Darrell to start yelling and go on a *destroy* tantrum. He'd yell, roll on the floor, and kick and throw his toys all over. Mama would have to stop what she was doing and come back into the room. "If you can't behave, then I'm gonna have to whip you," she'd announce. By that time, Darrell would be screaming and crying, but I'd still be listening to Mama's steps as she went to the Utility Room door, opened the door to the broom closet, and came back with the *dreaded flyswatter.* I hated that flyswatter like nothing else! A switch from the willow tree . . . maybe. The yard stick . . . okay, but that broke after a couple hits. Rolled up newspapers . . . child's play. That didn't even hurt the dog. But not the *dreaded flyswatter!*

Mama always came after me first. Maybe it was because I didn't run. She'd grab me with her left hand, and then I'd go around her in a circle trying to get away from her swing. It never happened, though. I was never able to get away. The first few swats would stun me. Then she would smack me over and over with the rubber, floppy end of the flyswatter until I would scream. I usually got it six or seven times in a row; and since she kept me in dresses, I got hit against my chubby, bare legs. It hurt! And, it left red marks for quite sometime afterward—especially from the metal spine on the flyswatter. Sometimes the marks were still there the next day.

In later years, Mama used to always tell people, "Johnnie and I never ever had to whip the kids. They were always real good and minded us." I know we never got whipped with belts, and nobody ever used their hands on us, but that flyswatter (and the *switch)* hurt a great deal, I assure you. She may not have wanted to admit it, but we were whipped and she was the one who did it. I don't remember Daddy ever giving either of us a whipping.

Of course, while Mama was ripping into my legs, Darrell stayed around to watch. He seemed to sense when she was getting ready to turn her attention to him, and he'd start crying (or as Mama called it, "blubbering"). Then he'd run away as fast as his little legs would take him, and Mama would have to chase him. Sometimes he would run through the dining room and then the doorway into the kitchen. He'd hang a left into Mama and Daddy's bedroom, continuing on through the bathroom and my bedroom. The circle would be complete when he came through my other bedroom door and back into the dining room. He'd run round and around making a complete circle through the house. Sometimes he'd reverse it if he saw that Mama had stopped and was waiting for him to complete the circle.

By the time she finally caught him, Darrell would be crying so hard that he was sobbing and having a difficult time catching his breathe. Mama always felt sorry for him. She was afraid that he would have a bad heart and thought he might die if he cried too hard. So she would put her arms around him and comfort him. "It's okay, Darrell. Don't cry so hard, honey. Mama won't whip you. It'll be okay." She'd comfort and hold him for a long time, whispering loving words. He had her just where he wanted her.

In fact, there is only one time I can remember when Darrell got *his just deserts*. When he was young, he was a *biter!* He bit me on the hand several times and gave me one really bad bite on my shoulder, where he actually broke the skin and made it bleed. That time, Mama grabbed him and bit him back—hard! Then she grabbed the pliers and threatened to pull his teeth out. You may not agree with Mama's methods, but Darrell never bit me again. There were several times he was going to bite, but he caught himself in mid-*chomp*. He would grab my arm and be just ready to bite down. Then he'd get this funny look on his face as he realized what he was about to do and what the consequences would be. It was about that time that he would let go of me and stomp a toy instead.

So what did Darrell and I learn as an early lesson from these experiences. Well, I learned that he was a lot quicker than me. He must have learned to run instinctively whenever Mama was after him. But he also learned that if he was not getting his own way when we played, all he had to do was yell or throw something and Mama would *come a runnin'*. If it was the first time he threw a fit for that play session, Mama would probably just warn us to *play nice.* He learned to do this preemptively—to keep me in line—because he knew I wouldn't run; and since I didn't want to get hit, he'd get his way. He also knew that if *things* escalated, he could cry and get away with it. Crying exonerated him. Only big sister got the whipping!

After awhile, I learned something, too. I also knew what the final outcome was going to be. And, I got tired of Mama punishing me and then just holding Darrell and comforting him while he stuck his tongue out at me over Mama's shoulder. So when he started throwing things or yelling, I'd just go ahead and hit him as hard as I could. Not just once but several times. And while Mama was getting the flyswatter, I'd thump him on the head a couple more times. Of course, Darrell would already be yelling and crying, and I'd start yelling, too. Mama would think it was just one of our usual scraps. She'd grab the flyswatter and switch me with it. But someway, it didn't hurt quite as bad knowing that I'd already given Darrell some of the punishment that I knew he deserved, but wasn't going to get. And besides, the way I looked at it, I was just giving him a little help in getting started with the crying spell I knew he was going to have anyway to get Mama's attention and pity.

I learned to recognize this behavior even in some adults I encountered in the business world. I ran into a lot of *ol' yellers* during my work life. I'd work hard or try to get a job done right, and then somebody on the team would decide they were tired or that something wasn't going right. Instead of trying to finish things, they'd decide to back out, throw a tantrum, or run to *Mama* (the boss) to complain or tattle. I always managed to get the job done, but often at my expense in having to shoulder the effort alone until *Mama* finally realized that they were making faces at me over *her* shoulder. I survived, but still, it would have been so much more pleasurable over the years if I could have just *thumped* them on their heads a few times.

By the time that I was about seven or eight, Grandma Clark stopped gathering all the grandchildren together and taking us to the Saturday afternoon matinee at the Liberty Theater. I became the responsible party for getting Darrell and myself there. Darrell no longer needed to go in the Taylor Tot since he was perfectly capable of walking.

Saturday afternoon and evening were busy times for Horton merchants. This was the time that most farmers came to town to buy groceries and tend to their business. After lunch, Mama would go to the store with Daddy to help him. This left Grandma Clark to see that Darrell and I were ready to go to the movie. After she made sure we were clean, she would walk down to the corner with us and watch us as we walked the two blocks north to 8th Street. When we got there, we crossed the street from the City Hall; and Grandma would lose track of us as we walked by the buildings west on 8th Street to Four Corners, then north on Central Avenue to Daddy's store and the additional block to the Liberty Theater.

Before leaving Grandma, I was told to hold Darrell's hand all the way. What a bummer! He always got his hands dirty during the brief trip; and besides, our hands would get sweaty if I hung on to him for too long. Usually a half block was about all I could endure.

As we walked along, it didn't take long for Darrell to start lagging behind; and I'd have to go back and drag him along. I'd usually find him in a squatting position playing with a stick, or a bug, or a piece of old gum. I'd grab hold of him and start dragging him on a bit further. Finally, he'd break loose and dawdle behind; and, once again, I'd have to take hold of him and drag him along.

There was one place where Darrell especially liked to dawdle. This was at the big plate glass window in front of the Kroger Grocery Store. For some reason, he liked to look at himself in the window. Sometimes he would make faces at himself, but the most disgusting thing he did was to walk close to the window and run his tongue along the glass—which I'm sure had not been freshly cleaned. (I always thought this *looking in the window* might be the forerunner of a high school trait he developed. During his junior year, Darrell let his hair grow extremely long on top of his head so it could be combed down to below his chin. Then he spent hours in front of the mirror combing it and waving it and poofing it, trying to get it just right, in near Elvis Presley fashion, complete with ducktails on the sides.)

Now, let's get back to our journey to the matinee at the Liberty Theater. When we got to Daddy's store, we would stop and get money for our tickets and have some left over for refreshments. I had a little red coin purse into which I'd put the two shiny quarters Daddy would give me. The movie only cost 12 cents each so that left money for a small pop and pop corn for each of us and a package of Necco candies—still leaving one cent. I didn't like the white candies or the licorice (black) ones, so I gave those to Darrell, and I got all the others. That seems only fair. Right???

After the movie, we'd usually hit Daddy up for more money. Then, we'd go down to Cook's Variety Store on West 8th Street where we could each buy two used comic books for 5 cents. Darrell always picked out really dorky comics, like *Dick Tracy* or *The Green Lantern* or some crime comic, rather than the good ones like *Little Lulu* or *Archie* or *Lassie*. After I selected my two, I usually tried to have at least one additional good one in reserve that I liked. If the opportunity presented itself, I would switch it with one of Darrell's crummy ones before we got up to the cash register to pay Mr. Cook or his son Bob. Then we would run back up to the store to wait for a ride home with Mama and Daddy when they went home to eat supper. Later, they would go back up and reopen the store in the evening until 10 PM. Grandma Clark stayed with us on those Saturday nights either at her house or, in later years, at our house watching television. She stayed until Mama and Daddy got home from work.

We kept that routine fairly religiously until I was ready to go to high school. By that time, however, Darrell tagged along without me having to hold his hand; and he had given up licking Kroger's window—thank Heaven! I also often had another girl going with me when we went to the movies. I think it started with Reva Searles or Bernetta Clarke and then Eloise Claunch was added. Of course, Eloise had the same problem that I had. She had a little brother to drag along with her. But, Jerry Claunch was the same age as Darrell, and so they became best friends and remained so throughout their high school and college years.

Having a *partner in crime* such as Jerry, the two of them found all sorts of ways to wreak havoc on the lives of Eloise and me and our other girl friends. One of their favorite ways was to continue to follow along with us when we went to the movies, or afterward when we'd walk down the street to get a *coke* or something. We, of course, were at an age where we wanted to impress *guys*. But how many guys do you think we could impress with the original "duh" boys following us around everywhere we went. Why do I call them "duh" boys? Because, at that time, their standard answer to any question you asked them was "duh." Several years after that, everybody seemed to be saying "duh," but Darrell and Jerry always claimed that they originated the term. Today, we probably would have just called them "Dumb" and "Dumber."

From early on, there was one particular thing that the "duh" boys liked to do. They would go to the very front row of the theater when we arrived and sit where they could slide way down in their seats so that even their heads didn't show. Then when the movie was on, they would crawl back up one of the aisles until they were several rows behind us— we usually sat in the center seats of the middle section about 10 or 12 rows back. Then, when they thought we had forgotten about them, they would crawl down a side aisle to the row in back of us, or in the next row behind that if there happened to be some guys sitting behind us. They really enjoyed trying to listen in on our conversations—they hoped that something *juicy* would be said that they could later use to embarrass us or that they would have the opportunity to tattle on us to our mothers.

If their listening didn't give them any ammunition, then we'd eventually hear them giggling because they thought they had put something over on us. If that didn't work, then in their *itty-bitty girl voices*, they would take turns repeating everything we said. Of course, they paid a price for their spying. There were several times Darrell and Jerry messed themselves up pretty good, coming out of the dark theater with pop stains, bubblegum, and other gross things stuck to their pants and shirts—after crawling over things that had been spilled or dropped on the theater floors. But then *curiosity* has always been a bit of a problem for Darrell.

"I've never known another child to have so much trouble protecting his hands." I don't know how many times I heard Mama and Grandma Clark say that. Mama always said it was because he was so curious. She compared him to a cat, saying that, "Curiosity killed the cat; but in Darrell's case, it gets his fingers smashed all the time." Whenever Mama opened a drawer or door, it seemed that Darrell was there immediately to stick his hand in it as it was being closed. Mama got to the point where she watched carefully before she shut any drawer or door whenever he was around. Yet, no matter how carefully he was watched, he still managed to get his fingers smashed on a regular basis.

I remember one time when we went across the street to our neighbor's house. She was an older lady named Bertha Sowadski. Bertha was trying to show Mama something and opened a drawer on a chest she had in the living room. She didn't know about having to watch Darrell. There he was standing on tiptoe trying to see everything. As he put his hands on the top edge of the drawer, thinking that she would see his hands and keep the drawer open, she shut the drawer and caught all ten fingers.

On our way home from school one day when I was in the third grade, Sister Cyprian asked me to drop off something in the church vestibule. I opened the huge wooden doors and went in to put some papers on a table just inside the door. I came back out and let the heavy doors swing shut. Of course, Darrell wasn't finished looking inside. The doors managed to catch both hands. Darrell eventually lost several fingernails over that. I felt awful because I knew that it hurt him terribly—he cried all the way home. And, I was scolded severely for not being more careful. I almost think it would have been better to have gotten a whipping instead of the horrible guilt I felt at letting my little brother get hurt. Mama said it would be a miracle if he grew up with all his fingers intact. He did, so I guess that was one miracle I witnessed.

Even though he was my little brother, I have to admit that he had some good qualities. He was always very musical and had much more natural ability than I did. I had started taking piano lessons when I was nine. Darrell started about two years later. He used my old books, but he progressed at a very rapid rate. For example, when he sat down to practice, he'd ask me to play his next assignment. Then he'd play it back to me and he almost never made any errors—although sometimes he did make the same error that I had made when I played it for him. Unfortunately, he gave up piano lessons after about two years. That was when our music teacher, Mrs. Howard Clarke, realized that he was playing by ear and said it would be a waste of money for him to continue. And that was why he had always wanted me to play his lesson for him before he practiced.

Although he never took piano lessons after that, Grandma Clark taught him to play the harmonica. Later, Mama and Daddy bought him several more harmonicas in all different sizes. He could play all of them, even the one he could put entirely into his mouth and play. Darrell also learned to play the trombone and was very good. In addition to playing in the band, he played in a brass quartet and a number of other small groups. There was no denying that, by that time, he could actually read the music. He was a junior or senior in high school when Daddy got him an electric guitar which he also learned to play in true *Elvis style*.

Darrell also had a natural rhythm. The two of us would watch *American Bandstand* when we got home from school. He would watch and then pick up the steps—then he'd teach them to me. He became a very good dancer; and though I never was as good as he was, I could dance with him better than any other partner I ever had.

Now, my little brother didn't do too well in school when he first started out. It was as though he didn't really catch on to reading and math at first. But by the time he got to the third grade, it was easy to see the *student* in him emerging. I had always been a good student in school and remained on the Honor Roll throughout high school. I was a junior when Darrell graduated from St. Leo's to Horton High. And I was equally proud of his being on the Honor Roll list in the *Horton Headlight*—since my name was always there, too.

There was something else that Darrell did that always made me proud. He was very small, maybe second or third grade when he first became a server (altar boy) at Mass. He learned all his responses in Latin and never seemed to make any mistakes. He always had his hair in place and looked so nice in the black cassock and white surplice. He continued to serve Mass throughout his years in school—even on weekends when he came home from college in Manhattan.

Darrell had been a short, plump little guy when he started high school. Then he grew about seven inches over the summer before his junior year and slimmed down quite a bit. That's when he started wearing his duck tail hair and his collars turned up. He liked to wear black, ivy-league pants and had a silky black and pink shirt with silver threads running through it. He had all the latest clothing styles—including blue suede shoes that went with another outfit. He also had *white bucks* that he wore with a number of his outfits. He was *high maintenance* at that time. I wonder if he remembers the many hours I stood at the ironing board pressing his shirts until I got them just right. He had the girls taking notice of him. Even some of the older girls who had been in my class thought he was good looking. He was!

I'm sure that there will be more I'll tell you about my little brother Darrell in my next book of life stories as I journey through my second twenty years. I really must tell you about the white, '61 Ford Starliner with red interior that he got when he was in college. But before I move on, I do want to let you know that my brother is a very special person, and I have always been proud of him—even when he was a pain in the tush!

So overall, if there was one thing I would point to and say "that's my most important *early lesson learned*," it would be this: Don't *kill* your brother when you're kids! He might just grow up to be someone you really care about.

9.

GOING RABBIT HUNTING

It was one of those cold, crisp days when your nostrils stick together as you suck in each breath. Being a Sunday, we had gone to 8 o'clock Mass. Daddy had put the chains on the tires because a new blanket of snow had covered the ground. Approximately six inches of new snow was now on top of the five to six inches we had received earlier in the week. Still, Daddy hadn't even finished his first cup of coffee when he announced, "This would be a fine day for going rabbit hunting."

I had heard these words before and had whined and cried, knowing that ultimately it would mean the demise of a rabbit. This time, I worked my way up to a howl, but it didn't seem to have any effect. Daddy was going rabbit hunting, and we were all going along with him

Mama tugged and pulled until she finally got Darrell into his silver-gray snow suit with a hood. He had just had his third birthday that past November; and when wearing his snow suit, he reminded me of one of the robots in the Saturday afternoon movie serials that Grandma took us to at the Liberty Theater. He waddled around in the snow suit just like the robot; and when tilted over, he couldn't get back on his feet by himself. It was always fun to tip him over at least once when we went out to play. Sometimes I would try to roll him down the hill in our backyard, but I found that he didn't roll too well. His suit was so stiff that it made his arms stick out too far—so he seemed to go flip-flop, flip-flop instead of rolling really smoothly.

I had just had my sixth birthday that month, February, 1944. Even though I wasn't in school yet since Mama and Daddy wouldn't let me go to kindergarten, I was expected to handle all my own problems in getting dressed to go outside. I pulled on my snow pants, and then tried to get on my boots. I think I had a pair of hand-me-down boots that had belonged to my cousin Roger. Because Daddy thought they came up higher on my legs, and would be needed in the deep snow, I got to wear *the clunky old boots*. These were different from the little, lined pull-ons that I later wore to first grade. With those, I could just kick off my boots and put on my shoes (which I carried to school in a brown paper bag).

Yes, Roger's boots were much more difficult to put on than mine. I hated them. I had to pull them on over my regular shoes. Then my snow pants had to be tucked inside them, and some kind of metal clips folded over at least in five places. Mama decided that I should wear my heavy, brown, teddy bear coat, which was a popular choice at the time. I think it was a very early attempt at making imitation fur; but the pile of the fur, which was almost an inch long, turned out to be stiff and scratchy. It made me look more like a porcupine than a teddy bear. And, of course, I mustn't forget the candy-striped stocking cap that was attached to a neck scarf that was at least six feet long. Mama wrapped the scarf around my face and neck at least three times. My mittens had gone on before my coat because Mama had sewn elastic to the cuffs of the mittens, and the elastic was threaded up through the sleeves and across my back so the mittens couldn't be lost.

I was ready to go; and Daddy had already been out to the car several times to put his rifle, shells, and other things into the trunk. He checked the chains one last time and came back into the house. Mama had blankets to take to the car, and I was already complaining because I was too hot. Daddy took hold of my hand to take me down the steps so I wouldn't slip on the ice. Only then did Darrell decide that he needed to go to the bathroom. I knew what that meant in getting Darrell undressed again so Daddy and I went out to the car to listen to the radio while Mama handled that problem by herself. Amazingly, the whole process only took her about 5 minutes, and we were on our way.

I liked the crunching sound that the chains made on the snowy streets. Daddy had been right to have put them on earlier. We passed several cars that were slipping and sliding around and not making much headway in getting to where they wanted to go. As we reached K-20, we headed west out of town past the city dump. Daddy had decided that the best place to go hunting was out to Grandma's farm, some 10 miles west of town and just on the other side of the Kickapoo Indian Reservation. Daddy drove slowly, and we arrived safely—without incident.

As soon as we arrived at the farm, Daddy drove through the gate and parked up by the farm house. He told us to wait in the car while he went up to the house. Daddy wanted to talk with the farmer who was farming the land for Grandma and notify him that we would be in the fields hunting. When he came back to the car, he said that everything was set, that this was just a precaution that every hunter needed to take to make sure that no one else was already there hunting. We got a little *safety* lecture as we drove back the quarter mile to the part of the farm where we would be hunting—near where the one room school house was located.

The little school bordered Reservation land but it had been built on a small part of Grandma's property intentionally. Why? I don't know. But, Daddy said that would probably be a good place to find rabbits because he thought some of them lived under the school. The building itself was up on concrete blocks, which allowed openings in the foundation. Some of these were large enough for small animals to get in and nest. Daddy figured that since this was Sunday, and it had snowed since school had let out on Friday, we would be going into *virgin snow* where he would be able to track the rabbits from the little footprints they made in the snow.

For me, this was all getting a little too real. Daddy parked at the side of the road and opened the back door for me to get out. It had already been decided that Darrell and Mama would just stay in the car and watch. Daddy opened the trunk and took out the rifle. He put some shells into his pocket, but didn't load the gun. "I'll just take the shells along with me until after we size up the situation," he said. "I don't want to carry a loaded gun around while you're with me. You might slip or something, and I don't want to shoot you by accident." This made me feel real confident. Daddy was going to shoot a rabbit—that is, if he didn't shoot me first.

I walked around behind the car. Daddy closed the trunk. Then he stepped into the ditch at the side of the road. The snow came up above his knees. He reached out his hand to me—to help me across to the other side. I was whining and pulling back. When I finally stepped into the ditch, the snow came up above my waist. Then I really started to cry.

Daddy said a bad word and then pushed me back up onto the road. "Okay," he growled. "I guess you can't go with me. The snow is too deep—even over here on level ground. You just stay here and watch. And don't get out into the road in case somebody drives by! You can have your mother let you into the car if you get too cold."

By that time, Daddy was out of the ditch and on the other side—ready to walk down the snow covered drive to the school. The snow hit him just below the knees there, and he had to pick up his legs really high to walk. As he took each step, the snow made that crunching sound I like so much.

As he got closer to the schoolhouse, more of Daddy's legs began to show. Daddy yelled back that the snow drifted the other way on that side. "Guess what," he yelled. "There are rabbits under the school. Here are their tracks leading away from the building."

"Daddy! Daddy!" I screamed. "Please don't kill the little bunnies!" I saw him stop to load his gun. "Please, Daddy! Don't shoot those soft little bunnies!"

"Get in the car, Deanna," he yelled back. "It's too cold out here for you anyway." He was a man on a mission now. He had found the tracks left by those rabbits, and he was going to have a rabbit dinner.

"I won't get in the car," I screamed back. I stomped my feet in the snow and cried. I had been crying off and on for so long that I could feel the tears quickly turn cold and make little burning spots on my cheeks. Mama had opened the car door and was also telling me to get back into the car.

It was then that I heard a loud cracking-like sound that seemed to echo in the air. It was followed quickly by two more cracking sounds. "Daddy has found the bunnies, and he's shooting them," I yelled. "He may even be shooting the Easter Bunny for all I know!"

It was then that I saw Daddy come scooting around the side of the school just as fast as he could. He was headed back to the car at *pert near* full gallop. And from the looks of it, he had found a way to skirt those snow drifts without ever having to touch the ground. "Get down! Get down!" he yelled.

"Deanna, what's going on?" Mama screeched. She could hear the shots and the yelling but couldn't see out of the car windows. They were all steamed up from the car heater running too high. Condensation had begun forming on the car windows.

"Get down! Get down!" Daddy continued to yell as two more shots were fired. I got down at the side of the car and was crawling toward the back door.

"Deanna, what's happening???" Mama demanded to know. She had opened the passenger door and had popped her head out, looking around. Her voice sounded like she was ready to get hysterical.

"Daddy's coming back to the car and someone's shooting at him. I think maybe the bunnies have guns, too." As I turned and crawled back toward the trunk of the car, Mama pulled her head back inside and closed her car door. "Wait for me!" I cried.

Just then, Daddy crawled up the side of the ditch and came up behind the car. He threw open the trunk lid and did something to the rifle so that several shells popped out and dropped into the trunk. Then he threw the gun in and slammed the lid down. "Didn't I tell you to get into the car?" he yelled at me. Still crawling, he grabbed me by one arm and dragged me up to the driver's side of the car, threw me inside, and then rolled me over the seat from the front into the back.

Three more shots could be heard as Daddy rolled down his window, put the car into gear, and drove down the road. He had to drive with his head out the window so he could see where he was going—since the windows were all fogged up. After we had gotten down the road a *safe distance,* Daddy stopped the car and literally shook all over. Mama asked him what had happened, and all he would say was "I don't want to talk about it."

After Daddy had regained his composure, he went back to the farm house to make sure that the farmer had not given anyone else permission to hunt on Grandma's property. The farmer said he had not. Daddy then used the farmer's phone to call the Nemaha County Sheriff and tell him what had happened. He told the sheriff that there were at least two other hunters on the opposite side of the thicket that were firing back across the field in his direction. One of the bullets had narrowly missed him, going over his head into the schoolhouse wall. The sheriff said that he would investigate and get back with Daddy the following day.

When Daddy came home for lunch the next day, I immediately asked him if he had heard from the sheriff. He said that he had, but he would wait to tell us all at the same time during lunch. "Go help your mother set the table." He added. True to his word, that was the first thing discussed as we sat down at the table eating tomato soup and grilled cheese sandwiches.

Apparently the sheriff had called and said that he had identified a couple of Indians from the Reservation who had been out hunting the previous day. By law at that time, they could hunt during any season for any wild bird or animal, and they were allowed to cross private property lines as long as they were not endangering anyone's life or property. When questioned, the Indians claimed to be unaware that they had been hunting on Grandma's farm or that my father or anyone else had been there at the same time.

So, from the sheriff's perspective, that was supposed to be the end of it. Forgotten! From Daddy's perspective, however, something had changed. The whole incident just seemed to take the wind out of his sails. He still kept several rifles and shot guns, and periodically he would take them out, take them apart, and clean them. But to my knowledge he never went rabbit hunting again, or for that matter, I don't believe he did any other hunting.

No, that one hunting trip was never forgotten. And even though Daddy never went hunting again, he became a *hunting legend* in our family. In fact, the story was told over and over again around out house and at family gatherings. That day became known as "The Day Johnnie went Rabbit Hunting and almost got *Scalped* by two Indians"—*a.k.a, Johnnie's Hare Cut Day.*

10.

WHEN I WAS A LITTLE GIRL . . .
(As told to my Grandson Timmy in 2000)

. . . my mother, my father, my little brother (your Great Uncle Darrell), and I lived in a little town in Northeast Kansas called Horton. My grandpa and grandma lived next door to us and my aunt and uncle and their four children lived up the street—just across the *alley* from us.

Now, you've probably never heard the word *alley*. Back then, when I was about your age, about six or so, all the little towns had *alleys*. They were like little access streets that were made of gravel. You know how our backyard is only separated from the house in back of us by a fence? Well, if you look up and down the street, you see the same thing for all the houses in the neighborhood here. Back when I was a child, there was a gravel road or *alley* between your property and the properties behind you. These alleys had multiple uses. Garages weren't attached to the houses like they are today. Instead, they were detached and back close to the alley. If you wanted to park your car in the garage, you had to drive up the alley and then pull the car into the garage from there.

We used the alley for other things, too. In small towns, trash companies didn't come around to pick up the trash, so everybody had trash barrels out by their alley. People would periodically burn some of their trash to keep it from becoming overwhelming. Otherwise, they would have to find some way to get it out to the city dump.

Barns, chicken houses, buildings to keep the coal for your heating stove or to do your laundry, and even the gardens were all located close to alleys. That way, things that had to be delivered, such as a load of coal, could come in from the back—leaving your front lawn so it wouldn't be bothered. Alleys also made it easy for somebody to get in to deliver feed or tend your garden.

The alley behind our house was also like a sidewalk and shortcut for me to go see my cousins who lived three doors up and across the alley. Most of the time, however, it was my cousins who came down the alley to see me—especially my cousin Roger, who was two years older than me, or my cousin Duane, who was just four years older.

Most days, my cousin Roger came down to visit and spent most of the day. He was really good at entertaining my little brother and me. He would take coats and turn them inside out and make the sleeves into tunnels. We didn't have action figures back then. All we had was plastic horses and plastic *Cowboys and Indians.* Roger was marvelous at making these little plastic figures come to life. He'd make up stories about the little plastic men fighting and chasing each other. In the summer time, we'd sometimes dress up like Cowboys and Indians and chase each other around the yard and even up the alley into other yards.

Daddy had finished building our house several years earlier, and we had several buildings that he had moved onto our property. One was a chicken house where we actually grew chickens, and I collected the eggs each morning. The other was a one room house that became our playhouse, although it was always called the *wash house* because it had been used for that purpose on the property where it had been located prior to Daddy moving it to our backyard. My grandmother used to tell me about families always having these little buildings where they'd pump and carry water and put it into big tubs and use lye soap and a washboard to do their laundry. But that's another story to tell you.

Behind the chicken house and bordering on the alley, Daddy had planted his garden for several years. But this one year was different. Daddy bought a lot directly across the alley and tore down an old house. Then he had plowed up the yard behind the house and planted his garden there.

We knew that he had something *big* in mind for the spot where the garden had been because he smoothed out the dirt and had a big load of sand dumped on the old garden plot. And we were so excited when we saw this big truck hauling a trailer behind it coming down the road.

There, stuck right up on top of the trailer, was this big, tall, double garage. There were red flags hanging out from the side of the trailer, and a truck with big orange lights was driving out in front. The driver of the truck was directing cars to pull over to the side and stop so our garage would have room to pass. When they got to the alley, they turned and came up to the place where the *old* garden plot had been. I don't know exactly how they did it, because all the kids were herded away from the site so we wouldn't get hurt; but when we went out later, there was our big, tall garage sitting on the former garden plot.

The garage was a lot taller than the average garage. Daddy had bought it from the County, and it had been used to house big bulldozers or other pieces of equipment. It didn't have garage doors like today's garages—the two doors hooked together in the center and opened out. They were so big that they were too hard for us kids to open—unless two or three of us worked together to pull them open. Within several months, Daddy would change both the height of the building and the way that the doors opened. He had the building cut down to a normal height, added a concrete floor, and put in garage doors that opened overhead. He even moved it to another spot closer to the street.

But, in the meantime, until the garage could be used as a garage, it became a new, marvelous place to play. We could go inside and yell, and our voices sounded loud and *echoed* back at us. And the damp sand was cool to sit on when it was so hot outside. And we could bring out our plastic army men and tanks or our Cowboys and Indians and make all kinds of hills and tunnels in the damp sand floor. The stories Roger told with the little plastic figures seemed to be so much better out in the sandy-floored garage. Each night when we left the garage, we took an old rake that Daddy had standing in the corner of the garage and raked and leveled out our mountains and tunnels. We felt we needed to do this because cousin Duane had said that if anyone found out we were playing there, the adults would find some reason to say it was dangerous and keep us out. So we'd rake the sand carefully, pick up all our toys, and then use the back of the rake to make sure that it was all smooth and evened out again.

One hot morning after Darrell, Roger, and I struggled to open the door, we came across an unusual sight—the sand had lots of lines and designs in it, but there were no sticks that we could find that could have made the lines and no footprints close enough to the lines and designs to have allowed someone to stand there, holding a stick, and drawing in the sand. Ah, ha! A real live mystery! One that was indeed worthy of a Nancy Drew Mystery! See, when I was a little girl, Nancy Drew books were stories written about a young girl named *Nancy Drew* who seemed to run into mysteries to solve everywhere she went. I had a whole series of books about the mysteries solved by Nancy Drew.

So there we were in that big garage with all the lines and designs in the sand. Roger was so enthralled that he didn't want to disturb the drawings by putting out the tanks and army men. He wanted to run up the alley and get Duane to look at the drawings, and he made us swear that we wouldn't touch anything until he got back. He checked to see if we had anything *crossed* to negate our swearing and *promised* (threatened) to cut my hair and give Darrell three knots on his head if we were lying. So out the door and up the alley he went—as fast as his little legs would take him.

While he was gone, I walked up to the edge and stood on tiptoe to look as far back as I could see. The drawings went all the way back into the corner. Darrell started to walk back and forth in the part of the sand that had no drawings—coming closer and closer with each step to where they started. He was acting like he was doing a balancing act and was going to fall into the sand. I thought sure that he was going to fall and mess up the drawing—then Roger would get us for sure. So, I thumped him on the head a couple times and he started crying. I don't think I hurt him; he just liked to use every possible occasion to get me in trouble with Mama.

At that point, Roger and Duane came rushing in. Duane examined the art in the sand. He stroked his chin in Sherlock Holmes style. "I think you guys are just trying to mess with me," he said. "Either you did this, Roger, or you kids (referring to Darrell and me) came out before Roger got here and did it."

Roger doubled up his little fists and shook them at us. "Did you do this?" he yelled. But we couldn't do anything to convince him—just shake our heads "No" and pray he believed us. Roger's little face got red and he got down within inches of our faces. "Liar! Liar! Pants are on fire!"

Duane pulled Roger back by the shoulder. "Okay, I believe you. So now we gotta find out who did it." Duane and Roger got down on their hands and knees and started crawling across the sand inspecting the lines. Duane sent me next door to Grandma's house to get her *big magnifying glass on a handle* so he could look at the lines real close. Time passed as he inspected every nook and cranny—every wiggle and squiggle. So many theories, but they all got shot down. Duane finally got tired and theorized that my Daddy must be setting us up, but we argued that he couldn't have done it because he didn't even know that we were coming into the garage. And we couldn't tell him or we'd probably get switched.

So we hatched a plan. We smoothed out the sand and closed the doors. We left and played outside, but always with an eye on the doors to the garage. About 5 PM that afternoon, Duane came back to see if anyone had been caught in the act of going into the garage. We assured him that no one had been there and no one had gone in. He opened the doors. As the light shown in, we were all shocked. New drawings were back in the sand. We looked all over, both inside and outside, for hidden doors or panels that would open, but nothing could be found.

A new plan evolved. We smoothed the sand again and closed the doors. Duane said that he was going to wait it out and catch the person in the act. He sent Roger to get their *bed rolls* and other camping gear. (A *bed roll* is what they called the rolled up covers they took camping out at the creek.) Duane sent me to Grandma's to get Kool-aide, peanut butter, Grandma's homemade grape jelly, and some bread to make sandwiches. Duane and Roger were camping out, and they needed nourishment to *keep their brains intact.* When I got back with the provisions, the camp site was ready.

Daddy came home from work. He parked his truck on the concrete slab across the alley where he had torn down the old house. He stopped to pull a handful of green onions from his new garden spot. Then he came over to the garage to see what we were doing. Roger said, "It's a good night to camp out, Uncle Johnnie, and if you don't mind, we'd like to camp out here by your garage."

Daddy seemed a little skeptical but said, "I guess it will be okay, but I don't want you boys sneaking up to the house during the night and scratching on the screens and scaring the kids." Daddy even called the boys in after we had had supper and gave them each an ice cream cone before they turned in for the night.

The next morning, we had to wait until Daddy left so we could open the garage doors. Once again, the drawings were there in the sand. Duane examined them closely. He thought there was a conspiracy. "Someone has been here watching us, and they went in while we were eating ice cream. They're just a lot sneakier than I thought. But at least we know that it isn't Uncle Johnnie 'cause he's the one who made our ice cream cones." Duane struck his Sherlock Holmes pose as he stroked his chin and looked over the end of his nose through Grandma's magnifying glass.

Roger grabbed the magnifying glass from him and ran to the other side of the sandy area. "What's wrong with you guys?" he inquired. "Can't you see that these aren't just writings or drawings? They're kinda like that stuff found on the walls of those tombs in the movie, *The Mummy*. You remember that don't you. They're called *'higher gilphics'* or something like that." For an eight year old, he really sounded like an authority.

Roger went on with his theory that the reason we didn't see anyone coming into the garage was because they were already there. He thought spirits were in the garage, and they were trying to communicate with us. A whole big story tumbled out of his mouth about someone being killed in the garage and now the dead person's spirit was coming back to try to communicate with us and draw a map telling where he was buried and who the killer was. Boy, were we scared by then! The hairs were standing up on our arms, and we all had goosebumps. Duane said he didn't believe that story, and he was going to catch whoever was doing it. So our surveillance continued!

We left the garage doors open all day and played just outside the garage. Mama went to work at Daddy's store that afternoon, so Darrell and I had to go next door to Grandma's house. We went out in her backyard to peek over at Roger and Duane several times, and Grandma came out several times to see what they were doing. They just said they were camping and reading comic books so Grandma thought everything was okay. When Mama called to say she and Daddy were leaving the store to come home, Darrell and I ran out to tell Roger and Duane. They smoothed the sand in the garage one final time and closed the doors.

Daddy offered the boys ice cream cones later that night, but they wouldn't leave their posts. They were committed campers that night. They even borrowed flashlights from Daddy in case they needed *to look at something after dark.* Duane brought his bow and arrows along that he had made from tree branches and twine. Roger laughed at him because he knew that they would have no effect on spirits. He simply made a cross out of wood and pulled Grandma's green onions and made a necklace of them to wear around his neck since he couldn't find any garlic.

About 7 AM that next morning, Roger knocked at our back door. He wanted to know how soon Darrell and I would be coming outside and how long before Daddy was going to work. Mama and Daddy had grown suspicious of him since he had been camped out in our yard for two days and nights; and besides, he still had the onions tied around his neck. When Daddy asked about the onions, Roger explained, "There was a full moon last night, and we didn't know if the Wolfman or Dracula might be out. My necklace was just a precaution."

Daddy finally went to work, and we literally threw open the doors to the garage. The sunlight spilled onto the sand in the corner of the garage. The sand was filled with lines, and squiggles, and what looked like partially completed drawings. We all started screaming and running around in circles bumping into each other as we finally pushed our way outside. Once again my stomach felt queasy, the hair on my arms was standing straight up, and I had goosebumps all over my body.

We argued for awhile about what we should do. Finally, it was decided that since it was our garage, Darrell and I should go in and take another look. I didn't want to do it, but Roger kept pushing me. I definitely didn't want to go inside alone. I thought that if a spirit did come after me I'd just push Darrell over so it would get him first—and that'd give me time to get away. So I took Darrell by the hand and pulled him in after me.

Darrell had picked up a tiny branch off a tree and brought it in with him. I think it was a branch off our weeping willow tree that Mama had used as a *switch* several days before. When we were inside the garage, I approached the sand carefully. I had brought one of the flashlights Daddy had loaned to the boys, and I flashed it on the lines and squiggles. Nothing seemed to make sense.

Darrell had gotten awfully quiet so I turned to see what he was do-ing. He was using the switch to sort of sweep at the sand and poke at something. Then he seemed to poke at another something. I looked closer. He was poking at those little black bugs that look like they are wearing armor. They were crawling through the sand; and when he poked them, they would roll up in little balls as defense. These were the bugs we used to call Rolley Polley Bugs. If you left them alone for a while, they would unroll and run through the sand leaving little tracks or squiggles. Darrell was only three, but he had solved the *Mystery of the Rolley Polley Bugs*. It wasn't spirits or something evil. The bugs had been the culprits all along.

Now, I suppose you might think that Roger and Duane would be glad that the mystery had been solved. Hardly! When we called the boys in and explained our theory about the bugs, Darrell and I got roughed up and even threatened before we closed those garage doors one final time. *Never* were we *ever* to tell what had happened—under pain of all kinds of wicked things happening, including cutting off the hair on all my dolls and burying them in pieces out by the creek and destroying Darrell's Hopalong Cassidy gun and holster set.

So we kept the secret. No one ever told. Well, at least not until now, but I'm 62 years old. Even though we still live by a creek, we also have a security system on our house. I guess I can take the chance now and tell you. But, whatever you do . . . don't let Duane and Roger know I told!

11.

BEING GASSED

It was a really cold night in January. I remember crawling under lots of covers in my bed and wishing that I had more. Both my bed and a smaller bed were in the room that later was to become my bedroom. I had the larger bed, and Darrell slept in the smaller youth bed. This was at a time before Mama and Daddy had added on the *sun porch addition* to the back of the house which created another bedroom for Darrell and a utility room for the washer, dryer, and large chest freezer. It hadn't been too long since I had graduated from the youth bed and Darrell got out of the baby bed. I know that my sense of timing must be wrong, but it seemed that it hadn't been too long since we moved out of Mama and Daddy's bedroom. They were so paranoid about the two of us getting hurt, dying in our sleep, or being kidnapped that they kept us in their bedroom where they could monitor our every breath and movement until we were *big kids.*

Not long before this particular night, Mama and Daddy had gotten rid of the big upright heating stove in the dining room. It had been used to heat the whole house in the winter. The whole house at that time included the L-shaped living room, dining room, and music room, two bedrooms and a bath, the kitchen and a big front porch that ran the full width (east to west) of the house. There was also a huge walk-in closet off Mama and Daddy's bedroom. A door off the kitchen led to a concrete porch, which we called the *Side Porch*. Along the back of the house was a concrete slab where Darrell's bedroom and the utility room were added later.

In the winter, the only way that the big upright heating stove was able to heat the house was by making the house *smaller* to heat. This was done by having French doors put in which shut off the living room and music room. As it started to get colder, Daddy moved his big chair into the dining room, and it became our *winter living room.* There was also a door from my parents' room into the kitchen and another from the dining room into my bedroom; so in effect, the bedrooms could be shut off during the day, as well—leaving only two rooms to be heated when needed.

But Daddy had made additional improvements to the house so we could get rid of the big old heating stove. That fall, Daddy had hired a plumber to install a floor furnace. I remember that when they came and cut the big hole in our dining room floor, I had to inspect things and saw that the hole went right down into the crawl space under our house. I remember being very uneasy about this fact for several nights until the new furnace was moved in and put into place. The hole had been temporarily covered with a large plastic sheet, and I kept worrying that rats or snakes or huge bugs were going to come out of the hole and come after me.

Finally the floor furnace was installed. Daddy and the plumber tried it out while we were at school. Darrell was in the first grade and I was in the third. I could hardly wait until it got really cold, and we got a chance to use it.

Fall made its way into winter, and I'm not sure I noticed its coming. We had gotten into our usual routine. I sat at the dining table in the evening while doing my homework. Daddy sat in his big chair with his feet up on his hassock. Darrell would sit on the floor playing with his Cowboys and Indians. Mama usually had her sewing machine open over by the windows and was either making me a new outfit or hemming Daddy's pants. We all listened to *The Shadow*, *Amos and Andy*, *George Burns and Gracie Allen*, *The Phil Harris Show*, or some other radio program. There was no television at that time. People had to be more responsible for their own entertainment.

This is what we had all been doing that fateful night in January just before Darrell and I went to bed about 9 PM. Mama and Daddy usually stayed up until 10 PM or sometime later. Mama may have gone to bed a little bit earlier that night. She had been complaining for several days about having a headache and feeling like her heart was *jumping around*. She thought that she might be coming down with the flu and kept quizzing all of us to see if any of us had flu symptoms. No one could tell her anything that seemed to satisfy her, so she finally just *let it* go.

About 1 AM, I heard a strange sound that woke me up. Daddy had a little red neon light that he had put in our room as a night light. I sat up in bed and looked over in the direction of the *sound*. I heard it again. It took me a moment or two before I realized that it was Darrell vomiting.

I started yelling, "Mama! Mama!" It seemed like it took forever to wake my parents up. Finally, they came into the bathroom between the two bedrooms, and Mama turned on the light. I had expected her to come running into the room. I thought she had just sleepwalked her way there and now seemed to be trying to hold onto the doorway. She slid down and collapsed onto the floor. Daddy was just behind her. He took hold of her and tried to pull her to her feet. Again and again, she would just grab hold of the door frame and slide back down to the floor. Daddy was getting the same result with Mama that I would have gotten if I tried to stand my Raggedy Ann Doll up against the wall and then let go of it. I think Daddy picked Mama up about three or four times, getting the same results.

All the while, Darrell was still vomiting. The last time Daddy picked Mama up, *she said something* to him as she crashed on the floor, this time falling sideways hitting her head on the bathroom sink. Daddy repeated, "Gas. It's the gas." He came over and grabbed Darrell up out of the bed, wrapping him and the vomit in the covers. "Deanna, go to the phone and call Grandma to come help us." He meant Grandma Clark who still lived just across the street from us.

I went to the phone and called Grandma. This was at a time when even a call next door required an operator to connect you—day or night. I think I woke the operator up, because she sounded as sleepy as I felt. When I told her I needed to talk to my grandma, she tried and kept ringing the phone. In the meantime, she came back to me several times to find out what was going on, but all I could tell her was we needed Grandma.

When Grandma finally answered, I just told her that we needed her, and she said that she would be right over. By then, I was starting to feel funny, too. Daddy had pulled Mama to the kitchen door that opened to the side porch and had propped the door open. I could feel the cold air blowing into the kitchen.

Darrell was wrapped up on the side porch. "Deanna, put on your coat and boots and go sit on the porch with Darrell," Daddy said. Daddy was running around from one room to another using a flashlight to guide him as he tried to open up the windows. For some reason, he was adamant, "Don't turn on any more light switches!" But air, more than light was his concern, and try as might; he couldn't get the windows open. We had wooden storms that were put on in one piece. There was really no way to prop them open without having some kind of board or stick. Giving up on these windows, I heard Daddy open the bathroom window, which was different than the others, since it cranked out. Then he opened the French doors and living room door out onto the big front porch.

By this time, I was starting to feel nauseous and went out to the side porch just as Grandma arrived. She wrapped Mama in a blanket and then guided and half dragged her outside onto the porch. Daddy had me go back into the house with him briefly to get clothes for Darrell and myself. Then Darrell and I went with Grandma over to her house. I remember it was really slick outside, and I kept slipping as I tried to walk. Grandma had put Darrell in my big, red wagon and pulled him in it across the street to her house. It was only minutes later when Daddy arrived with Mama. I don't know how he got her there because she was still very groggy and still had difficulty standing.

The next day everybody was feeling better. We even went to school. Mama was still feeling pretty shaky, but she went up to the store and kept it open while Daddy went down to the house with someone from the Gas Company. They found that the flue in the wall in the corner between the bedrooms was stopped up. Birds had been building nests in it. They cleaned it out and put a covering over it so nothing could get into it, and everything seemed to be okay after that. At least, it was for Darrell, Daddy, and me. It took Mama a little while longer. I think that was because she had been exposed to the fumes a lot longer than the rest of us. She was at home all day, while we were just exposed to the fumes at night.

When the next *Horton Headlight* came out, there was an article about our adventure. According to the gas company, we were poisoned by carbon monoxide, not natural gas. It also said that if Darrell hadn't started vomiting, and I hadn't been able to wake everybody up, we probably would've all been dead by morning.

———————

Personal Note: I guess that should be the end of the story, but I associate this event with something else. My father always had a crazy sense of humor. He always had a joke to tell—usually Pat and Mike jokes for us kids. At heart, he was a prankster, too—a big kid. He and the Hays kids were always thinking of ways to tease each other. Daddy also liked to tell stories about some of the wicked things that he did to torment his brother Joe when they were kids—the old foot in the popcorn bowl trick was notorious—and we had heard over and over about how Daddy got the nickname *Onions* when he was a boy.

Sometimes he made sarcastic or facetious remarks. He especially liked it when he was able to get one over on someone without them even knowing that he had. His mother, Grandma Campion, was that way, too. Sometimes she would make a remark and know that she had just given someone a real jab—a *zap,* we called it—but it was so much the better if they didn't acknowledge it, or if it seemed to go right over their heads.

I think it was shortly after the *gas* incident that I realized how really *neat* it was to be able to do this, to be sarcastic or make facetious remarks. Several weeks after the *gas* incident, we were all sitting around in the dining room. It was just about bed time. Mama had just started the *going to bed ritual* with Darrell and me. Darrell had already gotten into his pajamas, and I was heading that way. As I kissed Daddy *goodnight*, I noticed this horrible smell. I looked him in the eye and said, "I think the furnace is *passing gas* again." Of course, I knew what it *really* was.

Mama said, "Everything will be okay. Go on to bed now." Her face was totally serious. She didn't even *crack* a little smile.

As soon as I was out of the room, I heard her tell Daddy, "Will you *please* stop that! You smell terrible."

"Well, then stop feeding me ham and beans for supper," he responded.

I think they actually thought, that I thought, it was the furnace. I just laid in bed laughing as I thought about how much fun it was to *put one over on somebody*.

I never revealed it when Daddy or Grandma tried to put one over on someone, and I enjoyed it when I caught them doing it. I think it made me feel that I was smarter than the person they had just *zapped*. Sometimes they would *zap* me, and I would know it, and then I would feel smarter than Daddy or Grandma because I would know what they had done, and they wouldn't know that I knew.

Then, one time when I was in college, I told Daddy that *I was on to him* when he made a sarcastic remark or tried to put one over on me. He said, "Yes, you think you're so smart, but the expression on your face has always given you away. I could tell when you thought that I was *zapping* you and when you didn't, but you don't know the hundreds of times that I *zapped* you and you didn't even know it." Unfortunately, there is no way to know if he really knew or whether he was just saying that to get me. Come to think about it, I guess he got me again!

One Final Note: Over time, I watched my Daddy grow beyond *zapping* people to a position of helping people as his primary concern. Especially after his Mother, my Grandma Campion, died, *putting one over on somebody* didn't seem to matter so much anymore. Daddy developed a quiet dignity and a genuine love for the people in his life. I only hope I've followed his example. . . That doesn't mean he gave up teasing, joking, and laughter. Those were always part of who he was—the fabric of his being. Laughter is an important part of what keeps a good Irishman going!

12.

GRANDMA'S LYE SOAP

Things don't get scheduled today in the same way they were scheduled back when I was growing up. My Grandma Clark had certain things that were scheduled for each day of the week just like ritual. I can't remember what all of them were anymore, but I know the schedule didn't change. I guess I'll have to get the tea towels out of my mother's cedar chest and look at what I embroidered on them when I was about ten years old. I didn't think anything of it at the time, but I do remember that they reflected exactly what Grandma did on a weekly basis. I remember Sunday was *church* day, Monday was *laundry* day and Tuesday was *ironing* day. Still, I can't remember the rest.

Laundry Day—Grandma didn't deviate from this. Even after Mama got her electric washer and gas dryer, Grandma didn't take her up on the offer to come next door and use the *modern conveniences.* I can remember even as a child of three or four, Grandma would plug in her old washing machine with the wringer at the top and start the laundry. The old machine would churn around for a long time with the dirty clothes and flakes of Grandma's homemade lye soap—all the while making a chugging-clunking sound. Then Grandma would pull out some of the clothes that she knew had particularly bad stains and look at them. If the lye soap that she had cut up in the washer had not done a complete job, she would stop it, pull out a small washboard that she would set into the washer, and rub on those stains with the lye soap until she got them out. There was never a stain that could not be conquered by lye soap!

Children today have no idea what lye soap is. It was the *cure all* of cleanliness when I was a child. It was not only good for stains, but Grandma used it for her face and hands and said it made her skin soft and white. Strangely enough, it didn't seem to irritate my sensitive skin; and, for that matter, it was also good for keeping mosquitoes away in the summer. Mama used it to soak some of her pots and pans. If they had baked on food that was hard to get off the pan, just add a little lye soap and they were clean in no time. Mama also used a diluted form of it for cleaning our linoleum floors. She even used it to take dirt out of the carpet after Daddy or Darrell had tracked in.

So where did Grandma and Mama get this marvelous product? Grandma made it, of course. She had learned how to make it from her mother, who learned from her mother, and who knows how many generations further back this originated. I watched Grandma make it, but Mama never tried to make any lye soap as far as I know. No matter how much she used it, like on our diapers to clean them up bright and white when brother Darrell and I were babies, Mama never took to lye soap the way Grandma had. (I was also told that neither Darrell nor I ever had diaper rashes when we were babies—the lye soap killed all the germs.)

What was this marvelous lye soap and why isn't it coveted today? It could be because it really didn't look like the fancy bars of soap we buy today. The bars that Grandma made were just irregular chunks that she had mass produced. By pouring the hot liquid soap she made into rectangular pans and marking off sections before they were hard, she could estimate about how much soap she was going to get out of a batch. Then she would chip the *bars* apart after they hardened. Sometimes they broke and didn't come out looking much like bars of soap. Still, even the tiniest of chips was hoarded away to be used for cleaning in some fashion. That was what was important. There were no fancy, frivolous wrappers, no fragrant scent, and almost no color—unless you consider *yucky pinkish tan* a real color. And to say there wasn't a pleasant smell was a bit of an understatement. Lye soap was serious stuff, and you could tell just how serious by the harsh smell.

Now, I may be old, but I didn't grow up during the pioneer days. So why was Grandma still making and using lye soap? As I mentioned, she had learned to make it from her mother, who probably did need to make her own soap. Then Grandma had weathered the Depression and also felt she had a need to save. You didn't throw away anything back then. Instead, you learned to be practical and re-cycle things. Even in the 40's during World War II, many items were scarce and a lot of folks were still finding ways to save and re-cycle. My first coats were made from Grandpa Clark's old wool suits, and some of my fancy dresses were from flour sacks. Mama made our diapers from the same muslin material used to make her fancy, embroidered tea towels. I asked Mama on one occasion if she used the diapers later to make tea towels or if they were tea towels first. Mama just laughed and said, "Well, people used to comment on the embroidered designs on your diapers, so what do you think?"

So how did Grandma make lye soap? First and foremost, it was dependent on Grandma and Mama saving all their grease from cooking. Mama had a metal pot that had a spout like a teapot. She poured her grease into this pot. Under the lid, it had a little screen-like filter in it to strain out pieces of bacon or other small particles. The filtered grease was then poured into glass jars and set on a shelf above the stove along with the teapot/filter device. There it would all wait until there was *enough* grease for the next step in the process.

When both Grandma and Mama felt there was finally enough for a batch of lye soap, Grandma checked her *Farmer's Almanac* and listened to the weather report on radio station KFEQ (St. Joe) to see if the wind was going to be calm enough to build an outside fire. In addition to giving the weather report, along with the news, they also read from the *Farmer's Almanac*. This was like getting a gospel from the *Farmer's Bible*. Both of my Grandmothers and Daddy did all their garden planning based on the *Farmer's Almanac*.

After Grandma had all the ingredients and on the first *good* day, she would take my wagon out to the storage side of the chicken house and carefully lift a huge, black, cast-iron kettle into the wagon. Then she'd move it to a spot out in the open—away from the house and other buildings. There, she'd build a small pit surrounded by old bricks. She always used kindling, corn cobs and corn husks, and even a few pieces of coal in making her fires. When she had the fire going *real good*, the cast-iron kettle was placed over the fire, with the kettle being held in place by a special metal framework that Grandma had made to keep it from tipping over.

I must have been about seven when I was first allowed to watch. I had to stay back some distance away because Grandma said being around the lye was so dangerous. She always told the story about a nephew of hers who had been horribly burned by being splashed by hot lye. I had to sit on a chair on the side where the wind was coming from because Grandma was afraid that I would *breathe* the lye fumes. Grandma would lick her index finger on her right hand and hold it up to test where the wind was. It had to be ever so gentle or making the soap would be scratched for the day.

None of the Hays boys were allowed to be around when Grandma was making soap. Most of the time, they just drifted back and forth across the alley into Grandma's yard. But when she was making lye soap, even Grandma got a stern sound to her voice; and they knew that they needed to *high-tail it* out of her yard. (*High-tail it* was Grandma Terminology. It meant "as fast as possible," i.e., run *lickity split*, which was another Grandma term also meaning "as fast as possible.")

Grandma carefully poured the jars of grease into the kettle, along with the lye and water. There may have been other ingredients, but I'm not sure what they were. She had a long handled, wooden paddle that she used to stir the liquid in the kettle as it cooked. The handle was much darker than the part of the paddle that was in the cooking liquid. That part of the paddle had been bleached almost white, either from the contact with the lye or from the strength of the finished product itself—the lye soap.

I remember several times when we were making lye soap in the early fall, close to Halloween. As the kettle boiled and Grandma stirred, she laughed and chanted, "Boil, oh Cauldron! Boil and bubble! Keep old Grandma out of trouble!" Then she gave a horrible laugh just like that witch I had seen in Walt Disney's *Snow White*.

When the mixture had boiled about as long as Grandma felt it should, it thickened up enough so that it just seemed to slide off the paddle. Then, Grandma said it was ready. I asked her how she knew, but she always responded, "When you have done this as long as I have, you can just tell." Yes, she always knew. Just like she always knew when the bread dough had been kneaded enough, when the candy syrup had reached *soft ball* stage, when you needed to take a coat because it would be cold before you got home, when it was going to rain, when you were coming down with a cold, and just about a hundred other things. She always knew.

Grandma had this huge metal lid that she put on the kettle, and she used her long-handled, metal shovel to take the hot coals, etc., from the sides of the kettle. She put them in a coal bucket to cool and then put them aside to use later as fertilizer for her garden. After the mixture had cooled some, Grandma had a special dipper with a long handle that she used to pour the thickened liquid into a pan or frame until it was ready for cutting.

The next day, Grandma put on these old, thick gloves that went almost up to her elbows. Taking a long-bladed butcher knife, she cut the soap into rough rectangles. Then I got to help, but only after I had put on a pair of Daddy's thick gloves. Grandma broke the soap bars apart, and we carefully placed the bars on racks that had been set tray-like on boards covered by newspapers and some old oil-cloth table covers. Grandma then carried the racks into her screened-in back porch where they were set on shelves to finish drying. After several weeks, the new soap would be ready to use for laundry day, or any other heavy duty cleaning project, for that matter.

Grandma Clark was one of my favorite people to be around when I was growing up. Most of my early life, I saw her every day. Since she lived next door, Grandma became the ideal babysitter when Mama starting working most afternoons at Daddy's store. Grandma always had a hug and a kiss and started a practice that I have continued with my grandchildren. Grandma never wanted to pass on any germs, so she would brush the hair away from the back of my neck and give me several kisses there. She always called it *getting her sugar.* My sons and grandchildren have learned to put up with this same idiosyncrasy from me!

Grandma loved cowboy movies. When Darrell and I were too small to go to the movies alone, Grandma would push Darrell in his *Taylor Tot* and take me by the hand to walk the five blocks to the Liberty Theater on Saturday afternoons for the matinee. She knew Roy Rogers, Gene Autry, Charles Sterrett, Lash LaRue, William Boyd, John Mack Brown, Tom Mix, and all the others. After we got our first television, Grandma always came to our house after school so we could watch the cartoons and old silent movies before Mama and Daddy finally got home shortly before 7 PM.

Grandma liked to do things with her grandchildren. She taught me to embroider and do some simple crochet. We pieced together a number of quilt tops on her old treadle sewing machine the summer I was five. (I'm sure she did the same with cousin Kathleen in her time, as well.) Grandma always took time to drag out old pieces of carpeting to put on the porch railings for Roger and me to use as horses. She didn't mind my sloppy work when I helped her paint her upstairs bedrooms. And I wish now I still had her recipe for the *egg less* (no egg) chocolate cake she used to bake. She let me help her make it during and just following WWII. One time, Grandma even clipped a pair of roller skates to her shoes and taught the grandchildren how to skate. She built snowmen with us, threw snowballs with us, and when we were too small to go down the hill by ourselves, she even rode on our sleds with us. Grandma always made it a point to stay involved in our lives—whatever we happened to be doing.

Grandma was quite a cook. She always believed in hot breakfasts, including homemade bread made from *sour dough starter*, hot oatmeal, and hot tea or coffee diluted with lots of milk. She always topped the huge slices of bread with butter and either sugar or big globs of her homemade jelly—made from grapes from the rows of grapevines in her backyard. And, no Thanksgiving or Christmas dinner was ever complete without Grandma's homemade noodles—a tradition carried on down by my mother, then me, and soon, my son Dan, who will just have to learn how to make them the right way before I am gone. (Dan tends to improvise. His brother Shawn still teases him about the time he made mashed potatoes that smelled like *curried gym socks*.) Grandma was the one who taught Mama to make German Potato Salad and Wilted Lettuce with hardboiled eggs, green onions, bacon and bacon grease, and hot vinegar.

No project was too big or too small for Grandma. She made her own feather beds by stuffing chicken or duck feathers into covers she made of striped material she called *ticking*. On cold winter nights when we stayed overnight, she wrapped old metal irons without handles in layers of towels after they had been heated so that they could be placed in our beds to keep our feet warm. It was a *special treat* when we stayed overnight to see that old iron warming on the wood stove in the living room and know that it would be under the covers in bed with you, just inches from your feet, later that night. *Pleasant dreams!*

Homework was always completed when Grandma was around. She never seemed to tire of looking up words in the dictionary, listening to our spelling words, checking our math problems, practicing our cursive writing, or helping us with stupid art projects we never should have volunteered for in the first place. And, Grandma was always there with an encouraging word or just to listen to each of her grandchildren as we practiced for music lessons, recitals, or solos in concerts. She often took all the other parts when we were practicing our part for a school play.

Once in awhile, we could get her to play her *French Harp* (harmonica) like she did at dances when she was growing up, and she could still clog dance with the best of them. She had taught herself to read music and play the piano; and when encouraged to play, she could knock out her own version of *The Missouri Waltz*. In later years, this was followed (or at least almost always followed) by the question, "Now, wasn't that just as good as President Harry S. Truman does it?"

I'm really glad I have these wonderful memories of my grandmother, Rubie Aeneita Setzer Clark. She was a grand old girl. Just thinking about lye soap makes all these wonderful memories come flooding back to me. And I don't even like lye soap. I really prefer the sweet-smelling bars of soap you can buy at the store!

And while I enjoyed the benefits of mosquito-repelling soap, I always figured that any soap that can repel mosquitoes might also repel other things, and maybe people, too. But dear Grandma Clark, I thank you for all the memories and the good character traits you helped build in me. I will never forget all that you gave me and all the sacrifices you made for your grandchildren.

13.

AN IRISH TRADITION:
ST. JOHN DRIVES THE SNAKE OUT OF OUR LAND
OR
DADDY AND THE SNAKE

This life's adventure starts on a day in early June when I was about 8 years old. Now, at that time, my cousin Roger still spent a lot of time entertaining my brother Darrell and me. Early in the morning, sometimes even before we had eaten breakfast, he would run down to our house and see if we could come out to play. Several days that week, he had come down to see us. On most of those days, he had come in the side door into the kitchen just as we were finishing breakfast. Each time he had done so, he had passed the concrete steps out back leading down to our one room basement that had just been completed earlier that spring. On that one particular day, what he saw shocked him—so much so that his mouth and his little feet just couldn't seem to keep up with what his brain wanted to get inside to tell us.

As I already mentioned in previous stories, my Daddy built our house by putting two three room houses together and then making additions. These houses were set on a concrete block foundation. The front house became a large dining room and the two rooms across the front became a living room/music room. He added a large porch that ran across the full width of the house. The other three room house at the back became my bedroom, my parents' bedroom, and a large kitchen with a door and small porch leading off the kitchen. We called these the *side door* and the *side porch*.

At the time the two houses were put together, a large bathroom and walk-in closet were added, with a door for the walk-in closet off my parents' room and two doors coming into the bathroom—one from my bedroom and the other from my parents' bedroom. We moved into this house when I was about four years old.

When Darrell outgrew his baby bed in my parents' room and moved into my room, Daddy added a *sun porch* to our house. It ran the width of the house along the back and was behind my parents' bedroom and the kitchen. This enclosed room was never used as a *sun porch*. It did have lots of windows on three sides, but it was divided into two rooms. One room became my brother's bedroom and the other, behind the kitchen, was where the washer and dryer and the big deep freezer were kept. It was also where the better lawn furniture was stacked inside during the winter, and even more important, it was where the dog bed for the current dog was located over the years. My parents even put in a child's security gate at the doorway between the kitchen and the *utility* room, as it was called, so the dog could see us and feel more like a part of the family during the hours it was not allowed into the rest of the house.

Aah, but I digress . . . When Roger threw open the side door and came running into the kitchen that summer morning, he was flailing his arms and yelling about a big snake that was sunning itself out on the side ledge of the concrete steps leading to the basement. By the time Daddy got there to look; however, there was no snake in sight. Something similar had happened twice earlier that week. "Something" was outside that we "just had to come see." Each day, when nothing was there, Daddy got to tease Roger and tell him the story of the little boy that cried, "Wolf!" Roger got the message and stopped coming down quite so early.

As with the earlier days that week, this day was also sunny and warm. Daddy left for work about 9 AM. Mama had put a load of laundry in the washer. Roger had gone home dejected for awhile, but had come back again through the sun porch door. Darrell and I went outside with him, and we were running around playing in our backyard. Of course, we were actually back and forth into and out of Grandma's backyard next door where she and Grandpa had just moved into the Hoffman house.

At some point, Grandma asked me to stop playing and come with her. She and I went back over to help Mama with the laundry. We carried the load of wet clothes from the washer out the back door of our house to dry. Grandma and I worked to hang the wet clothes on her clothesline. Mama and Daddy didn't have a clothes line in our backyard.

When we were finished hanging the clothes out, Grandma returned to her gardening, and I went back to where Roger and Darrell were playing. Grandma had also been doing some weeding in her garden, which was about 20 feet wide and ran the full length of her clotheslines. Grandma was a real wizard with her hoe. Seeing her snapping those weeds out with one simple wrist action was like watching a magic trick. The three of us would stop and watch her sometimes, and she said that was okay. She also said that we were to stay away from her hoe because she kept it polished and sharp. She had a chair that she had set outside her back door and a grinding stone with a foot pedal to sharpen her hoes and knifes and other tools. When asked why she kept her hoes so sharp, she would say, "It's easier to kill weeds and any other unsavory critters that might get in my way."

It must have been about 11:30 when we ran back over to our yard to continue playing. The sun was up high—almost overhead—and was shining full on the concrete ledge by the basement steps. As we rounded the corner of the house, Roger, Darrell, and I all saw it at the same time. It was the snake!

Once again, it had been laying spread out on the ledge sunning itself; but this time, it quickly got into a coiled position and hissed at us. Darrell went running around to the front of the house in a panic; Roger started jumping up and down in place like he was going to pee his pants; and I did what I've always done best—I started shrieking.

It only took a few seconds for Mama and Grandma to come running. When they got there, both of them were shocked at the size of the snake. They didn't know what *kind* of snake it was, but both felt sure from the design on it that it was poisonous.

They quickly decided what to do. Mama said she would run in and call Daddy. Grandma told Roger to run over and get her hoe. As Roger took off, Grandma kept telling me to stop crying and go into the house. But I was too afraid to go into the house. I was afraid snakes would come out of the walls and get me. In their decision making, I had heard Grandma and Mama contemplating the possibility that the snake had come out of a crack under the house—between the basement wall and the crawl space under the house. I started imagining a whole army of snakes coming out of the walls to get me if I went inside.

Mama came back out and said Daddy was on his way. Roger came running back and gave Grandma her hoe. Then he started dancing around again like before. He was a ball of energy and totally hyperactive at this age. The rest of us just stood and waited. Soon, Daddy pulled his old Chevy truck up into the driveway and came running up the slight incline to where we were standing. Of course, he came to an abrupt stop and did a double take when he saw the snake.

The adults seemed to be sizing up the situation even while the snake hissed and bobbed his head. That was the first I was aware that a snake doesn't blink—it doesn't have eyelids like we think of them. The adults decided that it was the biggest snake they had ever seen outside of captivity. They judged it about 5 or more inches in diameter at its biggest point and guessed that it would be about 8 to 9 feet long if it wasn't coiled up. Daddy called it an "old Granddaddy snake" and said that it had to be old and smart (as snakes go) to have gotten that big.

Roger couldn't be contained any longer. With Daddy now there, he went screaming up the alley, "Snake! Snake! We got us a big old snake!" Within moments Roger and his older brother Duane were back. Darrell was down by the street standing on tiptoe looking up into the yard. "Is it still there?" he kept yelling. I was still walking back and forth making whimpering sounds and biting my fingernails.

Grandma and Daddy were discussing how they might use the hoe on the snake. Between the two of them, Grandma sounded almost eager to have a chance at the snake. Of course, you wouldn't know it to look at her. She wore a simple faded housedress. She had on some old canvas shoes with the toes cut out and her nylon stockings were rolled down around her ankles. She had her white hair pulled back and rolled into a little bun in the back—covered by a white straw hat with red flowers painted on it—plopped down on her head. And, as usual, she had on an apron. Grandma wouldn't have been fully dressed without her apron. She kept telling Daddy, "I've chopped many a snake with my hoe over the years, Johnnie. You'd better let me have a whack at it."

At first, Daddy seemed willing to take Grandma up on her offer. Upon further consideration, however, he was concerned that whoever struck at the snake would have to take a swing over the side of the concrete staircase. That person would need to put all their strength into it to kill the snake. Daddy commented quietly at though he thought the snake might understand, and he didn't want to let it in on their plans. He said, "But this is a really big snake, and I think we're only going to get one swipe at it. So I guess I'd better do it."

Grandma agreed that Daddy was stronger and would probably have the best chance of killing it. They conversed about where he should aim. Duane and Roger kept saying they would run up to the City Hall and see if they could find Grandpa to come home and shoot it with his gun. (Remember, Grandpa was Chief of Police.) But Daddy seemed to think that the hoe would be sufficient.

Everybody got real quiet. Daddy raised the hoe up over his head and made a mighty swing. "Thud!" With a dull sound, the hoe hit the snake down about two feet from its head, and it also caught one of its coils. While it didn't even make a dent in the snake, it bounced back up and the back of the hoe hit Daddy square in the middle of his forehead. Grandma grabbed the hoe just as Daddy wobbled and sunk to his knees, blood spurting from his forehead. Mama grabbed hold of Daddy's arm and seemed to guide him back up as he staggered to his right on rubber legs. Eventually, he just sort of collapsed to the ground and stayed there.

"It's trying to get away," Grandma yelled. She was trying to keep it on the ledge and kept pushing at it with the hoe, but it seemed more like she was teasing it than directing it. It hissed and thrashed about trying to get down off the ledge.

Meanwhile, Mama tried to tend to Daddy. She took his big white handkerchief out of his back pants pocket and kept trying to wipe the blood from his head. "Speak to me, Johnnie! Are you going to be all right? Should I get you a washrag and wash off your head?" she asked frantically.

Daddy took control of the handkerchief that Mama kept dabbing on his head. Although he was still a bit unsteady, he used Mama's body like a crutch to pull himself up to his feet. Grandma was still teasing the snake when Daddy took the hoe from her. This time, he maneuvered the hoe back around behind the snake and pulled it off the ledge—letting it fall into the area at the bottom of the concrete steps. Seeing the snake drop, Darrell apparently felt safe enough to come running back up to the house.

Now, there was a full length wooden door at the bottom of the stairwell. It was a nice door, not too fancy, but it had glass panes at the top to see in or out. For the snake, however, the view was not a good one. There wasn't enough space for the snake to crawl under the bottom of the door. The snake was trapped. There was only one way out. It would have to crawl up the stairs to get out, and Daddy had positioned himself at the top with the hoe.

Daddy yelled orders to my mother. "Neta, run out to the garage and get the can of gasoline for the lawnmower!" Mama headed off at a trot. Roger and Duane, hearing the word *gasoline* decided to follow. Mama had one on each side of her—the boys were keeping up with her all the way. Of course, the door to the garage was locked when they got there, so Mama sent Duane back to get keys from Daddy.

By now, Daddy was taking his turn at teasing the snake. Using the hoe, he kept pushing the snake back down into the stairwell—even while trying to fish his *keys to the garage door* out of his pants pocket for Duane. Roger ran back up to the house since there was not enough action going on at the garage. Daddy asked us to bring him some of the big round and oval rocks that surrounded our flower beds. There were *reds* and *pinks*—each about the size of an ostrich egg. Daddy started throwing these small boulders down on the snake. Roger, Darrell, and I kept delivering them to Daddy so he could heave them down on the snake. Roger was his best cheerleader. He would dance up and down as he handed Daddy the stones, all the while yelling, "Get him, Uncle Johnnie! Get him! Kill that mean ol' snake!"

As soon as Mama and Duane got back to the house with the gasoline, Daddy poured nearly the entire contents of the can, maybe a half gallon, down on the snake. By that time, the snake was under a pile of about thirty small boulders. Next, Daddy sent Mama in to get the matches. She brought out a box of wooden matches she kept by the gas stove in the kitchen. With all that gasoline, we expected a quick fireball to kill the snake. Still, Daddy had to throw down four or five lighted matches before one went "Poof!"

The next few minutes were total hysteria—just like a scene out of the Keystone Cops. Daddy must have poured a lot more gasoline down into the stairwell than any of us thought. Flames shot straight up into the air about fifteen feet. Not only were they engulfing the snake, but the wooden door was aflame, glass panes were popping out of the door, and flames were licking at the white siding under the kitchen window just above the staircase. The heat was tremendous.

Darrell ran back down toward the street making repeated howling sounds at the top of his lungs. He continued to make these sounds with each breath. Roger and Duane ran in circles, finally ending up down at the street yelling at cars to stop—I'm not sure if they thought they were going for help or if they just didn't want anyone to miss seeing how much fun we were having. Mama seemed to be in shock. She started having *pains* and went to sit down in the swing in the backyard—holding her chest and taking deep breaths. I was back to whimpering and biting my fingernails. Only Daddy and Grandma seemed to be working together to save the house.

Grandma screwed a garden hose to the faucet at the side of the house. Daddy uncoiled it and kept hosing down the house under the window. I think he had already given up the basement door as a loss. Eventually, Daddy got the fire out and started to assess the damage. He called out to Mama, "Neta, will you please take all the kids into the house and feed them or something? Get them out of here so we can clean up." So Duane, Roger, Darrell, and I all went into the house with Mama. She gave us some pop and fed us hot dogs and potato chips while Daddy and Grandma disposed of the snake.

Later, when we were allowed back into the backyard, the rocks were in place around the flower beds, the burned door had been removed, a new door from the Lumberyard was on sawhorses waiting to be painted white, and the siding and door frame had been scrubbed with Grandma's lye soap. Both only looked slightly scorched. Daddy said, "Now, it's best if we don't talk anymore about the snake. It's gone now, and it won't be bothering any of us anymore. I don't want you kids to start having nightmares about snakes." Ah, the power of suggestion! I had nightmares about snakes for years afterward.

But as with most stories, that wasn't the end. Grandma loved to tell the story of *The Day that Johnnie Almost Burned the House Down*. And

Roger, with his warped little mind, would always press Grandma to tell the rest of the story about what happened after we children went into the house: "Well, Johnnie went and got his hoe. And together with my hoe, we removed the rocks from that old snake and pulled him up to the concrete patio in the backyard. Johnnie watched him carefully for any sign of life while I went home and sharpened up my hoe even more. When I got back, we chopped him up in little pieces, and he didn't bounce the hoe off even once—but then you know, cooked snake is more tender than a *raw snake* in his skin. Then we took his pieces and mixed them up and put them in the trash barrels in Johnnie's backyard, Uncle Alfred's backyard, and in my backyard—cause you know that if you leave the pieces close together, they'll all pull together and the snake will come back to life after sundown."

Personal Note: With that kind of *Old Wives Tale* being fed to me on a daily basis, it's a wonder that I grew up as well adjusted as I am . . . To this day I can't stand to look at a snake—even on television. And I never, ever, touch the picture of a snake in a book or newspaper. It's bad enough just to have to look at one. It gives me goose bumps!

One Final Note: After I told this story to my grandson, Timmy, I was surprised to learn that he was rooting for the snake! But then, what can you expect from a child who says he wants to be a herpetologist. Ick!

14.

TERRY AND THE IRON BED

M y parents were very protective of my brother and me when we
were children. In fact, in later years Mama admitted that they
were probably overprotective. She said that she always worried so much
that something would happen to us that they never let us go anywhere
without them going along. They were always the ones to drive or take us
to ballgames, or the carnival, or whatever. Of course, they let other kids
come along with us because they didn't trust any other parent to watch
us as carefully as they did. And we were never allowed to be cared for
by babysitters. Only Grandma Clark, Mama's mother, was allowed to
watch over us if Mama or Daddy wasn't around.

My parents always opened their door for other children to come to
our house to play, but we were never allowed to go to their houses. Peggy
Kallos, my little Greek friend from across the street, was the one exception. Her parents were even more strict and watchful than my parents,
and thus, acknowledging this, my parents would, upon occasion, allow
me to go *catty-corner* across the street to play with Peggy.

Overnighters with girlfriends were popular even then. I had numerous invitations, but was never allowed to go to other girls' homes to stay
all night until I was in high school. But Mama spent time decorating my
room so it was really very pretty, and my girlfriends were invited to stay
overnight quite often. Later, when Grandma Clark lived next door and
had several bedrooms upstairs, there were several times when I had slumber parties there as a teenager. But those were Mega Slumber Parties

where six to eight girls were invited and that's another story. (See Mega Slumber Parties)

One summer, when I was about eight years old (1946), my cousin Francie, just six months my junior, kept insisting that I needed to come to *St. Joe* (St. Joseph, Missouri) for a visit. She had been to our house several times for a week and often spoke about visiting her cousin Georgia, who was also within a few months of our ages. Georgia lived in Colorado, and Francie had actually been out there and had stayed for several weeks all by herself with Georgia and her family. That sounded so grown up. Francie did not get scared or homesick. And, it sounded like she and Georgia had had such a good time.

Now, most Sunday afternoons during the summer were spent up visiting Daddy's mother, Grandma Campion, who lived on Euclid Avenue in the north part of Horton. If the weather was nice, usually Uncle James, Aunt Gertrude, Terry and Francie would make the drive over from St. Joe to Horton, about a 60 mile trip. Sometimes Uncle Joe, Aunt Agnes, and their two children (at that time), Elayne and Paul, would also visit, though they always had farther to travel whether from Kansas City, Ames (IA), or Topeka where they lived at various points in time when we were growing up.

Francie cornered Mama in Grandma Campion's *parlor* one beautiful Sunday afternoon. "Please, Aunt Aeneita," she said. "Let Deanna come back to St. Joe with us. She never gets to go anyplace. What are you trying to do, turn her into a retard?" I thought Francie probably meant *recluse*, but at eight wasn't completely sure of the correct word either.

"I think that it would be good for her, Neta," said Grandma. "Deanna needs to learn what goes on in the world. There is a world outside Horton."

I could tell by the tight look on Mama's face that she didn't want me going to St. Joe. And Grandma interjecting herself into the situation was definitely not what Mama wanted. She tried to stay out of any conflicts or discussions with Grandma. Yet, Grandma managed to get into and control more of our lives than Mama wanted anyway. Daddy was the only son to remain in Horton, and was thus, at Grandma's *beck and call.* And Grandma was never one to hold back on the *beck and call.* No, sir! I think she managed to get Daddy on the phone at least once a day every-day for a nice, heapin' helpin' of the *beck and call*—whether it was to her house to do something, or to drive her someplace, or just to have someone listen to her latest problem.

(Somehow this all sounds familiar. I'll have to ask George, my husband, who this sounds like when he gets back from running errands. Or . . .oh I know. I'll call Shawn, my oldest son. He'll know why it sounds familiar. Hmm, no answer on his cell phone. Wait, I'll just ask Dan, my other son, when he gets here. He's taking me to Home Depot.)

So, while I really wanted to go, a part of me also felt guilty when I joined in, "Come on, Mama. Let me go just this once. I never get to go anywhere." Still, I felt pretty safe begging to go. I just knew that there were all sorts of reasons why the answer would be "No." I knew even then—they didn't want me to go anywhere without them. I always had to watch over Darrell and keep him out of trouble. I had my piano lesson on Tuesday. They would be miserable without me. I didn't have a suitcase, and Mama hadn't had time to get my clothes ready to take with me to St. Joe. And, these were just a few of the excuses that flashed through my head. It was all pretty obvious.

Yes, I felt perfectly safe in begging to go. Mama was a rock! I even looked forward to the feeling of control it would give me—knowing that very soon Mama would reach out and grab my hand as I stood there whining to go. I just knew she would end it—she would pinch the skin on the top of my hand really hard (so hard that sometimes she drew blood). She would demand that I "Quit!" and I would. Yes, knowing all this was comforting. I could throw a fit, take a pinch, and then maybe later, work it for a bowl of ice cream as consolation.

So I had every confidence that I could beg and whine until *the cows came home,* and Mama would never give in. Unfortunately, I had lost touch with the other appeals that were being made, especially with the *wild card* influence of my grandmother. "Neta, you shouldn't be so over-protective. You've got to learn to let go a little." By that time, Daddy, Uncle James, Aunt Gertrude, and Terry were involved in the conversation. Terry was two years older than Francie. He was dancing around in front of Mama's chair doing a Red Skelton routine where he stuck his front teeth out and crossed his eyes. He was either the "Mean Widdle Kid" or he was "Clem Kadiddlehopper." He was promising that he would be good and see that I had a really good time. I'm sure Mama really believed him! Yeh . . . sure.

Now to his credit, Daddy backed Mama—smart man. Surprisingly, however, this time Daddy's objections finally got weaker and weaker until he just sat there almost in stunned silence. Finally, it seemed that everybody but Mama was certain that I should go to St. Joe. And then . . . she gave in! I couldn't believe it. The rock had cracked! Mama had let them beat her. She asked Daddy to take her down to the house. She was going to pack my things to go to St. Joe. I was stunned.

———————

The agreement was that I was to go back to St. Joe with Francie's family that night (Sunday). Daddy had business at Wyeth Electrical Supply on Wednesday; so Mama and Daddy would drive to St. Joe on Wednesday, take care of business, and then come out to pick me up to take me back home with them. Francie moaned and groaned because I wasn't even going to get to stay a week, and I moaned some, too, just to keep up appearances. But this time I didn't moan too loud for another reason. After all, I wasn't stupid. It didn't take but once to teach me a lesson. I never believed that I would actually be getting into their car and going to St. Joe on a Sunday night in the first place. And it had all come about because of a lot of moaning and groaning and badgering of Mama. So now I had to make the best of it until Wednesday night. Fine. I could do that, but I was darn sure that I wasn't going to be too loud with any future moaning. Otherwise, I might end up in St. Joe for two weeks— when Uncle James planned to come back to Horton again. Oh, heaven forbid, what if I ended up there all summer!

Of course it wasn't that being there was something really bad. It's just that I knew Aunt Gertrude did things differently than Mama did. And although I saw Terry and Francie quite often, I also knew that I could probably get along with Francie by herself; but Terry was an entirely different matter.

Terry was a skinny kid which made him seem extra tall for his age. Terry was also smart. He was always *figuring things out,* usually up-to-something, and often planning *no good.* Terry did such terrible things to Darrell and me.

When he came to visit Grandma, for example, Terry always wanted to play a game he had invented, *Bad Angel/Good Angel.* He got top billing as *Bad Angel.* This allowed him to make some awful faces and talk with a scary, gruff voice. It didn't matter what he called the game. I knew he was really the devil; and when he was dragging me around on the ground by my foot, I just knew he was looking for a portal to take me straight to hell. He did other evil things, too, like locking me in Grandma's outhouse after making sure there were a sufficient number of bees inside to keep me company. Yes, I'm sure he had good qualities. He was smart (and he did turn out to be a nice person as an adult); but at that time, I could only think of all the reasons why I didn't want to be in the back seat with him on my way to St. Joe. And I didn't want to live *unprotected* (without Mama) in a house with him for three days.

Surprise! After several days, I had gotten an entirely different perspective. I was having a marvelous time. Francie had a beautiful, big bedroom and a sun porch in which to play. This sun porch ran the full width of the back of the house. Francie had all her toys, dolls, and doll furniture out on the sun porch, which we entered from a door off her second floor bedroom. We played for hours on that porch. We even laid out blankets for padding, with sheets on top, and slept two nights out there. Aunt Gertrude kept Terry away when we were on the sun porch. He hadn't bothered us since the first day.

Terry had even been a help at times. We caught the bus about a block from their house and had ridden it to the end of the line and back several times. If it had only been Francie and me, we would never have been able to do it. In fact, if my parents had been there, we wouldn't have gotten to do it at all—even with Terry there. Still, we had even gone out to Krug Park, rode the carousal, and saw Lake Contrary. On one occasion, I went with Terry to deliver his newspapers which I had helped him fold. It seemed like a long way to walk, and I was really getting tired until I realized that Terry was making me carry the bag with all the newspapers, and I turned it back over to him.

Time seemed to pass quickly, and it almost seemed a surprise when Wednesday was there. I remember Francie and I were out on the sun porch when we heard a lot of noise from downstairs. This was not unusual as Terry had gotten Aunt Gertrude revved up several times each day, but this seemed somewhat different. There was this loud sound as someone ran up the stairs. Then, there was yelling, cursing, and screaming as a second person came running up the stairs. Terry's bedroom door slammed shut. Almost immediately, someone pounded on it until it came open. Then there was a swishing sound followed by a banging sound. Then there was another and yet another. This just kept going on.

Francie and I jumped up to run next door to Terry's room. Aunt Gertrude was there and had worked up quite a sweat. She kept yelling, "You come out from under there, Terry. When I get my hands on you, boy, I'm going to beat your butt raw!"

I had wondered why Terry's room was so sparsely decorated. There was only an iron bed, open coil springs, and a mattress in the room. Now I knew why. Aunt Gertrude was at the foot of the bed, which was on wheels. She would grab the bed, roll it, and fling it against the wall. Then she grabbed it again, rolled it back and forth, and flung it against another wall. She did this over and over again trying to jar Terry out from under the bed. If you put your head down by the floor and looked under the bed, you could see him hanging there, right in the middle, with his hands holding onto the open coils of the box springs while his feet were stuck up in between the coils. To him, this was all great fun. He was laughing and having a grand time. Meanwhile, Aunt Gertrude was hot, tired, red in the face, and screaming a blue streak about what Uncle James was going to do to him when he got home from work.

Francie suggested that we go back to the sun porch. She acted like she was bored. She must've known something I didn't. I wanted to stay and see Terry get his due. Still, it wasn't long after we had left that Aunt Gertrude was talking in a very quiet, calm voice. She came out of Terry's room, closed the door, and went downstairs. I was disappointed.

An hour or so later, Mama, Daddy, and Grandma Campion came to the door. Grandma came in as usual, ready to stay for dinner. But that night, Aunt Gertrude came back upstairs and was lying on the bed with a wet wash cloth on her head. She had not fixed dinner. I brought my things downstairs and said I was ready to go. But Grandma kept saying, "James will be here soon. We can't leave before James gets here." So we waited.

When Uncle James got home from work, Francie had him go up to see Aunt Gertrude before he came back down to talk with Grandma. Everybody just sat in chairs in the living room waiting for him to get back. Francie was there, but she didn't suggest that I stay there longer.

Over and over I told Mama that I wanted to go home. Still, after not pinching me when I said I wanted to come to St. Joe, now she seemed to have her *pincher* back in working order. She pinched me so hard that I could see it wouldn't be long before I had bruise marks on the tops of both hands.

Finally, Uncle James came back down the stairs. He was talking in a very soft, calm way as he explained that Aunt Gertrude was not feeling well. Grandma didn't seem to get the picture. She just kept sitting in her chair, but Daddy jumped up and said, "We need to be getting back early tonight anyway." Even at that, Grandma made Uncle James stand outside, leaning over with his head stuck in the window of the car as he was made to talk with her (sitting in the back seat) for over an hour.

So that was my one adventure staying with relatives during my childhood. I never suggested that I should go visit anyone overnight during the rest of my childhood—nor did Mama or Daddy. But, would you believe, on that drive all the way home, Grandma kept asking me, "Deanna, what did you do to get Aunt Gertrude so upset? You must have given her a terrible time. Hasn't your mother taught you how to behave?"

As I sat behind Daddy, I looked to his right at Mama in the front seat. Each time Grandma would ask one of her questions reflecting on my behavior during my visit, I could see a tightening in Mama's jaw. I remember thinking, *"Mama is doing something to lock her mouth so it won't talk."* I can't remember the number of times I saw this happen again over the years, but it always seemed to occur most frequently when we visited Grandma. Later, when I first heard the term, lockjaw, I thought of Mama. *Grandma gives Mama lockjaw.*

Personal Note: Looking back now, I believe I should have said something to defend myself. Grandma always seemed to blame me for things. I should have told everyone what had really made Aunt Gertrude so upset. But it was a different time. Children were to be *seen, and not heard* back then. I thought I was exercising discretion in not saying anything—not tattling. Still, I might have changed the whole dynamic and eased some of the underlying tension in Mama, if I only had *let the cat out of the bag* and told on Grandma's *Bad Angel*. I've always wondered if deep down she didn't know anyway. Daddy always got blamed for everything when he was a child—and even as an adult. I know she always thought I was just like my Daddy. She may have thought she was criticizing me, but I wore her criticism as a *Badge of Honor.* I thought it was a *good thing.*

15.

THE COMPROMISE

When I was in the fourth grade, Daddy decided to wait until September to take a vacation trip. Originally, he had planned to put it off until right after the Tri-County Fair. Then time had slipped by; and the next thing he knew, we were back in school. Now, by all accounts, this was going to be the most extensive trip that we had ever taken. And, as we had learned on earlier trips, Daddy usually had us leave on a Sunday morning and then come back to Horton by the following Friday night, so he could be there for business on Saturday—especially Saturday night. Well, this trip appeared to be a real doozey. Daddy actually intended to miss a Saturday. We would be gone almost two weeks.

Saturday was the big day for Horton businesses. This was when the farmers came into town. Cars were always parked up and down the streets, and sidewalks were filled with people standing and talking, or walking from one business to another. Sometimes, in the summer, this would go on until as late as midnight—even though most businesses had signs in their windows claiming that their stores closed at 10 PM.

Indeed, Daddy had planned a fine trip for us. We were going to go up through Nebraska, Wyoming, South Dakota, and North Dakota. He had so many plans for things we were going to do and see. But what could be done? We were back in school.

Well, Daddy's approach was to be straightforward and matter-of-fact. First, we had to let our teachers know that Daddy planned to take us out of school for two weeks. We were students at St. Leo's Grade School, and Sister Rose was the principal. She was the one who had to give approval. So, I took a note in that had been written by Mama. This was on the Friday just before Daddy intended for us to leave two days later on Sunday.

Mama's notes always started out the same, even if we had been home sick. "Please excuse Deanna . . . or please excuse Darrell. . ." Well, this one was a double-decker doozey. "Please excuse *Deanna and Darrell* from school from September 15 through September 26 (two full weeks of school) because we will be taking an educational vacation trip during that time."

Sister Cyprian, my teacher, had given the note to Sister Rose during recess. I knew I was in trouble when Sister Rose came charging over toward me and pulled me off the merry-go-round. "You tell your father he needs to come talk with me! You're not going anywhere! I won't excuse you, or your brother, from school." She pointed her crooked index finger at me and tapped me right on the nose. Then she turned quickly and seemed to fly up the sidewalk and stairs in her black habit and white headdress of the Benedictine nuns.

I told Daddy what Sister Rose had said when we went home for lunch that day. His only response was, "We're going to go anyway. So what is she going to do about it?" Aah, such confidence! But he had only seen Sister Rose from a distance.

That afternoon, Sister Rose patrolled the halls as we read from our *Treasure Chest Magazine.* She kept looking into the room directly at me as I sat there in the still warm September afternoon, mopping my brow and sliding around on my seat—as the sweat ran everywhere—from the top of my head to the backs of my legs. At the end of the day, Darrell and I went home. Daddy had not met with Sister Rose.

True to his word and just as Daddy had said, however, we did go. I remember stopping in Lincoln, Nebraska, at the state capitol. We climbed up into the tower above the rotunda, and went outside the dome to look at Nebraska. We were so high up! I made the mistake of looking over the side. I got nauseous and felt panicky. It was such an awful feeling. I just wanted to crawl back down; and if I couldn't crawl down right away, then I thought I might just crawl up on the ledge and jump. All I knew was I needed to get over that feeling immediately. I guess this was the first time I experienced a fear of heights.

We took our time and stopped at a lot of historical markers and mu-seums. We stopped at Kearney, Nebraska, to see some covered wagons along the Old Oregon Trail. We stopped at a rodeo in Casper, Wyoming. We spent several days in Yellowstone Park watching Old Faithful spout-ing high into the air, but the best part was having wild bears roam around the car as we drove through the park. Next, we went to see an Indian Reservation in South Dakota and then on to Mount Rushmore. We saw the Badlands and the Black Hills. I can't remember what all else we saw; I'm probably missing something important. But I know that we took the entire two weeks, and we all had a marvelous time.

We got back to Horton on Friday night of the second week—just as planned. We all went to bed exhausted. After two weeks, there must have been a lot of mail for Mama to go through and lots of bills for Daddy to pay, but everything just laid there on the dining room table where Grandma Clark had been piling it. Mama said, "I hate to think of everything waiting for us up at the store." Mama always handled all the bills and paperwork for Daddy at his store.

Mama and Daddy got up early Saturday morning. Daddy went on to work while Mama washed all the clothes from our trip. Then later, she walked up to Daddy's store to help with the Saturday business while Grandma Clark and I hung all the clothes out to dry on her clothes lines. Grandma and I folded or ironed the clothes while Darrell played with the toy Cowboys and Indians he had gotten on the trip. He hadn't even had them a week; and already, he had broken the leg on the black horse, and the tail was now missing on the brown horse. I shouldn't have cared; but with the recent close quarters of the car trip, it made me angry.

At 8 o'clock Mass on Sunday, I was reminded of what was in store for us the next day when we went back to school. We always sat in the 4th row on the right hand side of the church. Grandma Campion sat in the 5th row. The only ones who were ahead of us were Mrs. Dorie in the 3rd row and the three nuns who always sat in the 1st row. Personally, I hated sitting right up in front. I thought that there was a lot going on behind us, and we were missing out on all of it. Mama would never let us turn around to look even when there was a lot of noise back there. I missed the whole thing when Mrs. Schmidt's water broke in church, when Mr. Geiger had a heart attack, and when Mrs. Thompson fainted. And I'm sure there were other incidents that I never knew anything about.

Monday morning arrived. Daddy got us to school just in time to join the other children as they were walking from where they had lined up, there in front of the school, to go next door to the church for 8 o'clock Mass. As Darrell and I fell into line with our respective classes, we went into church and filed into the pews. I was in the third row on the left hand side of the church. I lost track of Darrell, but there was Sister Rose—sitting on the right side in the row behind the eighth graders. I saw her out of the corner of my eye; she seemed to be watching me—scrutinizing me.

After Mass, we always stayed a few minutes extra to say the rosary before going back to school to start our day. During the rosary, Sister Rose moved behind me. She reached forward and got me by my headscarf. This was at a time when women still had to cover their heads when going into a Catholic church. Sister Rose literally dragged me to the vestibule as she hung onto the scarf. I thought she was going to ruin it. It was my beautiful scarf—the one I had gotten on the trip. It had a nice white background as a canvas for some of the sites we had seen printed right on it. I can't remember what all was there, but I do know that the way I folded it there was a handsome buffalo showing at the back.

Sister Rose pulled the scarf from my head, taking some of my hair along with it. "How dare you wear such a thing in God's house?" she said. "You people have no respect, traipsing around wearing an elephant on your scarf. You're in the fourth grade! You should know better; and if you don't, then your parents should! They should know better than to send you to church dressed that way! Elephants don't belong on your clothes!"

I tried to explain to Sister Rose that it was a buffalo and not an elephant. I tried to tell her that it was my special scarf that I had just gotten while on our vacation trip, and I wanted it back. I promised I would never wear it to church again—that I would leave it at home in the top drawer of my dresser with my other treasures. But Sister Rose would have none of it. She took my scarf and folded it and put it somewhere behind the front flap on her little black and white penguin suit.

If Sister Rose was 5 foot tall, then that was stretching it. She was so petite, so delicate looking; yet, she was probably *the scariest person* I knew at the time. She was especially scary when she whipped out a ruler and smacked kids on the hands, or the shoulder, or the cheek. That was her way of saying, "Don't do that," or "Don't go there," or "Don't say that."

Bob Schecher was the recipient of Sister Rose's ruler taps on a regular basis, but it never seemed to bother him. He'd just go on with his obnoxious behavior and encourage his brothers, Chuck and Jim, to join in on the mischief. Sometimes he would even sass Sister Rose. Certainly, his bravery was to be admired, even if his actions were not.

When school let out at noon, Darrell and I left to go home for lunch. Sister Rose was standing by the front door of the school. "Tell your father I want to see him," she said. "I want him here before you come back this afternoon." Oh, what a day! And of all days for Daddy not to pick us up for lunch . . .

I ran all the way home checking to make sure that Darrell was still trailing behind me. I knew I had something terrible to tell Mama and Daddy. I kept having visions of Daddy and Sister Rose dueling with rulers. There would be a great battle—a clash of Titans! But I knew what the ultimate end would be; I could see Daddy on the floor with Sister Rose triumphant—delicately lifting her skirt, her long black stockings showing as she put one black laced shoe squarely on Daddy's chest. Sister Rose, the Victor!

When Daddy got home, I was still out of breath from running and telling Mama what had happened. She interrupted several times with questions as I tried to repeat my story for Daddy. Mama was as sure as I was that Sister Rose was not one to reckon with lightly. We knew that the scarf wasn't the issue. It was more than that. It all centered on "who was in charge." Sister Rose was in charge, and she wasn't about to let John Purcell (my Dad) get one over on her.

Daddy drove us back to school. He parked in front and walked up to the front door of the school where Sister Rose was waiting for him. Daddy followed Sister back to her classroom. Several eighth grade girls came running out of the classroom and down the hall. They said they wanted *out of there* because Sister Rose was already raising her voice the minute she and Daddy got inside the door. The other sisters didn't ring the bell for students to march into the classrooms at one o'clock. Time went by and everybody stayed outside. All playing had ceased on the playground and everybody was standing in front of the school. The Schecher boys went around to the back of the school, telling everyone that they were going to sneak up the back stairs to see what was going on.

In the shade of the trees there on the rectory grounds next door to the school, the rotund little Irish priest, Father Twomey, could be seen walking back and forth. His mouth moved slightly as he silently said his prayers—moving the rosary beads he held in his hand behind his back. His familiarity with the order of prayers allowed him to hold his beads behind his back where it was more comfortable rather than in front where his short arms would require his laying the beads on his voluminous stomach. Was it truly a coincidence that the path he walked was so close to the open windows in Sister Rose's classroom? Did he really seem to lean to the south occasionally and turn his ear toward the open window? I couldn't tell, at least not for sure.

After what seemed like an eternity, Daddy came out of the classroom and stormed down the hall. As he got to the door, you could see that he was angry. His face was flushed, and he was sweating profusely. I don't know whether this is an Irish thing or just a Purcell thing, but any intense emotion (anger, fear, severe disappointment, etc.) seems to cause us to turn *beet red* and sweat like a garden hose. As he stormed out the doors of the school, Daddy was muttering curse words to himself, but they were loud enough that Bob Schuetz started repeating everything he said.

Daddy walked over to the rectory, catching Father Twomey before he could retreat into the house. Daddy was shaking his finger at Father and then pointing back at the school. Just then, Sister Rose came to the door and rang the bell for us all to go back into our classrooms.

It was later that I learned what had happened. Sister Rose had demanded an apology from my father for taking us out of school when he didn't have her permission. Daddy refused, and they had words about it not being her business to determine what he did or didn't do with his children as long as he wasn't breaking the law and wasn't doing anything to harm us. Apparently, they also argued about the scarf and the relative *appropriateness* of my wearing it. Daddy demanded it back.

Sister Rose refused even though he told her it wasn't an elephant; it was a buffalo. He later admitted that he had used the opportunity to make a comment about her eyesight—as compared to a *bat*.

I guess they had gone head-to-head for quite a while when Sister Rose finally told him, "Fine, then you and your family are excommunicated. Your children can't go to school here, and you can't go to church here, or to any other Catholic church."

Daddy did have some words for her then, and I'm sure they were the kind you have to confess. That's when he told her, "Sister, I have had enough." Then he added a favorite phrase Aunt Gertrude had used quite often when describing her frustration over something my cousin Terry had done. "The $%*! has hit the fan!" Then he walked out. I was surprised to hear that Daddy had used this phrase because I had never heard him say this himself. His cursing seemed to always be limited to *hells* and *damns*—with the occasional *sonofabitch* if it was really bad. Clearly, Sister Rose had taken Daddy to a whole new level.

So as I said, Daddy had gone over to see Father Twomey immediately. Father kept telling him that he didn't want to get involved—that it was between Daddy and Sister Rose to work out. Daddy said that there was no working out anything with Sister Rose; and he wanted to know if Father Twomey was going to go along with Sister Rose's threat to excommunicate him since he didn't see that what had happened was an offense deserving excommunication. Father told him, "Well, you know, John, it's hard to go against something if Sister Rose decides it—especially if it involves the school." But Father assured Daddy that Sister Rose had a short memory, and within weeks the whole incident would be forgotten.

But Daddy was not about to let it go for a couple weeks. He didn't want to let it go for a day or even an hour. Father had suggested that he just keep us home for a week or so (which, ironically, had started the whole thing in the first place) and maybe, in the meantime, we should go to church over in Purcell or Hiawatha for the next couple of Sundays. Daddy told him "Hell, no! I'm not going anywhere else, and I'm certainly not going to let this story get around that my family has been excommunicated." He told Father, "We're going into the rectory and call the Bishop now. Our family has not been excommunicated since Mom (Grandma Campion) sent Joe to school down to Horton High

School. Imagine the irony! Mom got excommunicated because she *sent* my brother Joe to a public school, and now Sister Rose wants to excommunicate us so Neta and I will have to *send* our kids to a public school."

Daddy could not be convinced to give it up. He even threatened to call Grandma Campion and bring her up to the rectory to call the Bishop. Daddy said he thought Father Twomey trembled at that thought—having both Grandma Campion and Sister Rose yelling at him at the same time. Over and over Daddy professed that this wasn't a church matter, and Sister Rose was not empowered to excommunicate people. Finally, Father Twomey called the Archdiocese. Daddy said the Monsignor laughed when he heard the story. He assured Daddy that what had happened was neither a case for excommunication nor suspension from school.

The Monsignor said he would get the Bishop to call back to talk with Sister Rose within 30 minutes. Father Twomey went to the front door and called Johnny Wintersheidt into the house. Johnny was out in the yard cutting some branches off overgrown bushes. Father had Johnny run over to Sister Rose's classroom with a note, while Daddy sat in a chair in the parlor. Father Twomey sat at his desk in his office in the next room appearing to *watch* the phone.

Within a short time, Sister Rose came into the rectory. She went directly into the office. Momentarily, the phone rang. Sister Rose answered it. It must have been the Bishop on the phone. Daddy said he heard her say, "I believe I have been doing much better, Your Holiness . . . It's all a misunderstanding that has gotten out of hand . . . We have rules and people must learn to obey them . . . No, they are bright children and I don't believe they will be permanently damaged . . . Must I? . . . That too . . . Well, there will be makeup work . . . Thank you for your help. Pray for me." All of this had been said in a pleasant, gentle voice that Daddy did not recognize as Sister Rose. Yet, Daddy knew that Sister Rose and Father Twomey were the only ones in his office though, and it certainly didn't sound like Father speaking.

Shortly, Sister Rose stuck her head into the parlor. The old voice was back. "If you will come with me, Mr. Purcell, we'll get this little situation taken care of . . . now!" As Daddy followed her out the door, he looked into the office. Father Twomey was still sitting there in his chair.

He said nothing. All Father did was roll his eyes in confusion and disbelief.

Sister Rose walked ahead and Daddy followed. By that time, school had let out for the day; and all the children, along with Darrell and me, were waiting on the sidewalk out in front. We had been dismissed at the usual time about 15 minutes earlier; and even though everybody usually departed quickly, the children continued to wait around in little groups, waiting to see if "Mr. Purcell and Sister Rose are going to duke it out." I was pretty much a basket case by then because I didn't want to see Sister Rose hurt Daddy, and I certainly didn't want to see Daddy hit a nun—although I was pretty sure he could take her.

They went into Sister Rose's classroom. Bob and Jim Schecher walked the ledge from the front of the building, ducking down under one of the windows so they could listen to what was going on. Sister told Daddy she needed to talk with Darrell's teacher and mine, so she invited him to wait in one of the little desks much too small for an adult. He sat uncomfortably with his legs extended out to the side for as long as he could stand it. He knew this was just an additional attempt at humiliating him. Daddy got up and walked over and sat down on the window ledge, yelling out the window at the Schecher boys to "Get away from there!" Bob sassed him. Bob wasn't afraid of anybody.

Before going to talk with our teachers, Sister Rose walked to the front door of the school. She yelled at all the kids to go home or she would find some work for them to do. Kids scurried as far as the corners to the north and south, but continued to hang out in groups ready to come back at a moment's notice.

It was about 30 minutes before Daddy came out and had us get into the truck. He was loaded down with our school books, and he also had my scarf. He said, "The Bishop set up a compromise. Everything is okay." It wasn't until we got home that I learned what *the Compromise* was in this case. Obviously, a compromise is set up to make both parties think they have won. This is how it worked.

We were not excommunicated from church, and we were to continue going to school at St. Leo's. I got my scarf back, but I was never to wear it to school again. I was supposed to wear a *less busy* scarf that would not distract others when they were trying to pray. We were also supposed to make up *all school work* that we had missed while we were gone—something that we wanted to do anyway. Mama had sent a note with each of us that morning suggesting that if we had school work to make up that couldn't be done at school, "Please send home a list, and we will be glad to help at night until everything has been completed."

Darrell was in the second grade, and I guess they didn't want to pick on him too much. He had a real short list. The original part of my list (2 pages) included doing my regularly scheduled reading, spelling, math, social studies lessons and catching up with my catechism and bible stories. But two additional pages of assignments had been added, including writing themes, reading a book on the lives of the saints, and writing a synopsis of one page on at least 20 of them. The last two pages were written in a different handwriting that had *Sister Rose* written all over them—figuratively speaking, of course.

Once again, when Daddy looked at my assignments, he wanted to go talk with Sister Rose to get her to lessen the load. I begged him not to do it. We had already had enough of Sister Rose for a long while and besides, I didn't look at the extra assignments as a punishment. I loved reading and just loved to write—even then. I never missed an opportunity to write and write and write—about anything and everything! Sure, the extra work would be a challenge, but any alternative I could imagine could be much, much worse.

So I guess that should be the end of the story; well, not really. Daddy went with Mama into Duckwall's and came out with the ugliest scarf I have ever seen. It had a beige background with huge orange poppies on it with black centers. It was so much worse to look at than some buffalo that may or may not have resembled an elephant. Daddy made me wear that scarf to daily Mass for the next two years while Sister Rose was still principal at St. Leo's. So Daddy figured he *had won*. Of course, I never had the heart to tell him that Sister Rose would wait for me in the vestibule each day as we filed into the church. She would take my ugly, but neatly folded scarf, and instead would have me put on a black lace handkerchief that she kept in her pocket specifically for that occasion. I would wear that on my head until after Mass when my scarf was returned—with the understanding that I was never to reveal this addendum to *the Compromise*.

Aeneita Irene & John William Purcell – Wedding Picture

Rubie Aeneita & Winifred L.
Clark – Early 1930s

William & Frances A.
Campion – Wedding
Picture

(Clockwise from Left) Duane Hays, Grandma Clark, Darrell Purcell
(baby), Roger & Junior Hays, and Deanna Purcell

(Clockwise from Top) Stella & Peggy Kallos,
Darrell & Deanna Purcell

Grandma Clark, Deanna &
Darrell Purcell – Deanna's First
Communion

Francie, Aunt Gertrude
& Terry Purcell

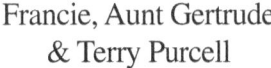

Marshal W.L. Clark – Outside Horton Library

(Clockwise from left) Al Jr. (Junior), Uncle Alfred, Roger, Duane,
Aunt DeVere and Kathleen Hays in '52

Our Home on 6th Street – Snowstorm of '54

Patsy O., Peggy, Bernetta, Eloise, Cathy, & Deanna – My Sweet 16
Birthday Party

Cousin Roger's
Graduation in '54

Grandma Clark's Home – Slumber Party Palace

Deanna, Judy, Bernetta, Reva, Peggy & Francie – Mega Slumber Party

Bernetta, Reva, Patsy B. holding Sue, Francie & Patsy S. Holding
Judy – Mega Slumber Party – Next Day

Mary Ruth & the Zombies – Trigonometry Class

Junior Class Play – Where's Purcey?

Future Homemakers of America (FHA)

Chuck, Bernetta,
Deanna & Gary – Junior Prom

Saturday Night Parties #1

Saturday Night Parties #2

Saturday Night Parties #3

Reva, Me and Bernetta – The Three Amigos

Chuck Hittle – A Special Frog

Darrell & Daddy – Behind our Home on 6th Street in '54

Deanna & Mom – Behind our Home on 6th Street in '54

Deanna & Darrell Purcell – Behind our Home on 6th Street in '55

John Darrell Purcell, 1960 – Highland Junior College

Deanna Aeneita Purcell, 1956 – High School Graduation

16.

PAT AND MIKE JOKES

My Daddy always liked a good story or joke—especially when he could tell it. Problem was, a lot of the jokes he told were *Pat and Mike* jokes, where the main characters were Irishmen recently arrived from *the Old Country*, and they weren't too bright. Daddy didn't consider this to be offensive because he was Irish, and he felt that he was simply laughing at himself and his people. Friends, including Father Fox from Atchison, actually went out of their way to take notes so they could pass their latest Pat and Mike joke on to my father for him to tell.

Today, as I hear my son repeat these same jokes to his son, I look back fondly as I remember some of these jokes. Still, I have come to realize, as my twelve year old grandson Timmy puts it, "Great Grandpa Purcell (my Dad) sure told some pretty goofy jokes." I don't know why these jokes made such an impression on me back then or why they made such an impression on Darrell, my brother—or even later, my sons and their children. Probably it was because they were a little different than the type of jokes that the other kids told even then. They are definitely different than what the kids tell as jokes today.

Let me give you an example of one of Daddy's favorites:

Pat and Mike were two Irishmen. Pat had come over from *the Old Country* several years ago, but Mike had just recently arrived. Pat had learned to speak English, but Mike still only spoke Gaelic. Now, Pat had managed to get himself a pretty good job, but because Mike couldn't speak English, they couldn't get him a decent job. But poor Pat, he couldn't afford to pay all of the expenses for both of them, so in desperation, he set out to find something—anything—for Mike to do that would let him earn some money.

Now, like most Irishmen when they come over, Pat and Mike lived in New York City. Pat had seen street musicians and other people selling items on the street corners so he got himself an idea. He got a hold of Mike, and he told Mike that he had gotten him a large metal cup and in that cup were these large yellow pencils standing up inside there. He told Mike that he was going to take him down to the street corner, and Mike was to sell these pencils to people. Mike was reluctant and said he couldn't do it *if'n* he couldn't speak English. And *it wer' a fact.* He couldn't speak English!

Well, old Pat was good at the blarney, whether in English or in Gaelic, so he just assured Mike that it wouldn't be too hard for him to do. All he had to do was learn a little English and he could teach him what he needed to know. Pat said, "Now if'n someone should come to you and start talkin', they'll probably be a' askin' you, 'How much are your pencils?' So you reply, 'Two for five cents.' You'll be a' yellin' it anyway. You just stop and politely say, 'Two for five cents.' Got that?"

Pat practiced with Mike for quite some time until he got the words just right. So, after Mike had got that down, Pat said, "Now if'n they say anything more, they'll probably be a' askin', 'Are all of 'em hard lead or are some of 'em soft?'" And so, Mike was coached to reply, "Some of 'em are and some of 'em ain't."

Mike was still worried. "What if that tweren't enough?" he asked in Gaelic. "What should I do then?" Pat told Mike that, "If'n they get their money out and they give it to you, then you should give them two pencils. But if'n they say anything more, they'll probably be a' makin' excuses and a' sayin' that that they don't really want to buy any pencils anyhow. You just say, 'Well, if'n you don't, somebody else will.'"

The next day, Pat figured Mike was ready. So he took him down to what he said was a *perty good corner* and set Mike to work. After a bit of last minute coaching, Pat noticed the time, said his *good-byes* and rushed off to his job.

So there was poor Mike—standing on the street corner yellin' out, "Two for five cents!" "Two for five cents!" At first he was pretty scared.

Then a couple of people walked by and smiled at him. He started to feel better—a little bolder. People could understand what he was sayin'.

Now, about that time, a man with a suitcase came rushing down the sidewalk. He stopped directly in front of Mike and asked, "Hey, buddy, which way to Grand Central Station?" Mike, feeling pretty good about himself, sang out, "Two for five cents!"

The man with the suitcase gave Mike a little push, looked him over carefully, and then asked, "Say, are all Irishmen as dumb as you?" Just then Mike remembered his second phrase. "Some of 'em are and some of 'em ain't," he said proudly.

Now the man was starting to get upset. Mike had been less than helpful. He said, "Ya' know, buddy, I've got a good mind to punch you right in the nose."

In most cases, Daddy just stopped there—expecting the listener to remember that poor Mike is about to respond, "Well, if'n you don't, somebody else will." Of course, the joke was that, in spite of his best efforts, Mike's bad luck had set him up to get punched in the nose.

———————

Most of the Pat and Mike jokes were like that with the listener left to figure out the little *zap* at the end. All of them, however, made fun of the Irish and their condition here in America. I think Daddy got to the point where he told so many Pat and Mike jokes that he really started to like the characters. He almost felt like they were related to him in some way—maybe distant cousins or maybe they just provided a little taste of the Irish experience, of what our ancestors might've gone through while in search of a better life.

One day, I was in Daddy's store sitting in one of the metal lawn chairs that Mama had painted and brought up there for the family (Grandma Campion, Darrell, or me) to sit on while waiting for a ride home. Two Norwegian farmers had come in; and in between the conversation about repairing their radios, Daddy had told them a couple of Pat and Mike jokes. The jokes had bombed completely. They didn't seem to identify with the Irishmen or their situation.

Daddy didn't give up, though. He started in on another Pat and Mike joke, but this time, he told it as if he were telling it about two Swedes, Sven and Olaf. I asked him later why he had used Swedes. He said Sweden was close to Norway, so he thought they might identify with the characters; but he didn't want to offend them by making the story about the two *boobs* from Norway.

Daddy started his story:

Sven and Olaf had recently arrived in the United States. They had landed at Riker's Island where they had gotten their papers in order and were then supposed to take a boat back to Manhattan (New York City). As they walked out onto the wooden dock together, Olaf got into a boat that was waiting there and had just started to sit down when the boat started moving away from the dock. To his surprise, he looked back and saw Sven still standing on the dock. Now, the boat was already about 12 to 15 feet away from the dock and pulling away fast. Olaf yelled back at Sven, "Yump, Sven! Hurry and yump! If you run perty fast, I think you can make it in two yumps." That was the end of the story.

When it had all been explained to me years before, Daddy said the joke was that if you made one jump you were in the water so couldn't possibly make a second jump. I was told that adults would all under-stand, but probably children wouldn't—at least not at first. So I thought about it awhile, and eventually it all made sense. Of course, you couldn't make a second jump if you were in the water. Even though I was only nine at the time Daddy first told this joke, I had been telling other jokes about Pat and Mike for years. I found that some kids '*got it*' and others didn't. More often than not, I'd have to explain this one and the part about not being able to jump a second time.

So here I was sitting in the chair laughing because I enjoyed Daddy's new version—especially the "yumps" and his attempt at doing a Swed-ish accent. But I noticed I didn't hear any one else laughing, so I looked out from behind the refrigerators where I was sitting in the chair. The two Norwegian farmers were just sort of looking at Daddy and then each other. No one was saying a word.

Finally, one farmer said, "Well, Yahn (that's what he called my fa-ther, John), I don't know. Those Svedish fellars are pretty strong. He yust might've been able ter make it in two yumps."

The other farmer scratched his head and then gave his opinion, "Now, if them fellars had a been Norvegians, I'm sure they could a' made it in two yumps." About that time, Daddy took up the head scratching as one of the few times he was at a loss for words. Momentarily, the Norwegian farmers concluded their business and set a time for when they would be back to pick up their radios. Daddy would have the radios repaired in a couple of days.

Interesting Note: About an hour later, I happened to be down at Luebbe's Drug Store having a cherry phosphate. The same two farmers came in. Funny, they didn't seem to have an accent when they were talking to Mr. Luebbe. Who do you think the joke was on that day?

––––––––––––––

For some reason this incident left a lasting effect on me. Daddy and I talked about it a number of times over the years. He used to say, "Experience is the best teacher, but I hope you have sense enough to learn from other people's experiences and not have to experience everything for yourself." I also learned that no matter what you do in life or how much preparation you make, there are no guarantees; you can't always predict the outcome. Life is not a *clean* science experiment, and the results of each experience are not guaranteed when dealing with the *human* element. You never know when you're going to get *a ringer*. You never know when even a small variable will totally change the outcome.

In later years, Daddy also used this story as a sort of shorthand reminder—a coded message for me—a gentle nudge. From that time until he died in 1982, if he thought I was getting myself into something that was maybe a bit beyond my abilities or commitment level, he used this story as a warning to me. I can still hear him say, "So, Deanna, you really think you'll be able to make it in two *yumps*?" My Daddy was a pretty smart guy—even if he did get taken for a ride by two Norwegian farmers.

––––––––––––––

Personal Note: Year later, while teaching in the Seaman School District in Topeka, I happened to run across several young people at a football game who had been students in one of Darrell's honors math classes at French Middle School. Darrell taught in the Topeka School District. When they found out I was *Mr. Purcell's sister*, they smiled and said, "He sure is a good teacher; we really like him! But honestly, how long has he been telling those lame Pat and Mike jokes? He's got a whole routine that he tells to each class every year." Then they started in, "Two for five cents . . . Some of 'em are and some of 'em ain't . . . I've a good mind to punch you right in the nose . . ."

17.

"HOLEY" THURSDAY

In the fall of 1947, when the new car models came out, Daddy bought a new 1948 Chevrolet Sedan. It was a pretty shade of blue/grey on the bottom and the top was a lighter blue. What a luxury this was after only knowing the silver-grey, 1938 Chevy.

Darrell turned seven in November; and the following February, I had my tenth birthday. That Easter, as usual, we all got new outfits to wear to church. As much as it always irritated the nuns, Daddy would take us out of school for the day; and we would drive to St. Joe to get our new Easter clothes.

That particular year, Mama found Darrell's new suit first. Because he had finally started to grow a little and put on some weight, it was easier to find than the year before. He had been so small the previous year when he made his First Communion and Mama had had such a hard time finding him something to wear before she had finally come across a navy blue suit with long, narrow pant legs. The new suit was similar, but a *regular*, which pleased Mama.

I remember Mama had already started sewing dresses for her and me, but we each needed a new spring coat. The one she found for herself was beige, and the one she found for me was peach-colored with a huge Peter Pan collar. With it, she got me a natural-color straw hat with a big, wide brim. It reminded me of the kind of hat that Scarlett O'Hara had worn in *Gone with the Wind.*

Later, we all had lunch together sitting on those *little round stools with red cushions* at Woolworth's. Darrell had to be corrected several times for using the counter to *push off* and swivel around. He ended up almost kicking someone as he let his legs swing out. Daddy made the comment that if we could only find Grandma Campion, who had come over with us, we could go back home early. But Mama wasn't going to let Daddy *wiggle out of it* that easily. He hadn't had a new spring suit for several years, and she wasn't going to let him get out of it that year. So, after we had finished every bite of our hot roast beef sandwiches with mashed potatoes, we headed out for some of the men's stores with Mama and Daddy.

I can't remember whether it was Einbender's or a place called Henry's, but Daddy found a beautiful blue/grey sharkskin suit. He had tried on dozens of suits before he decided on that particular one. Mama and I sat on two chairs next to a large tri-fold mirror while waiting for Daddy to try on each of the suits. Darrell had a little metal car that he was pushing around between the shopping bags while sitting on the floor next to the chairs. After what seemed like an eternity, he finally gave up. Using the bag with my coat in it as a pillow, he fell asleep. I kicked him a couple of times, but that didn't seem to rouse him.

Even though Daddy had found his suit, it still needed alterations. A guy with a measuring tape hanging over his shoulder came out from the back room. He had a piece of chalk in his hand and started making marks on Daddy's jacket and on the back of his pants. I remember the sales clerk trying to talk Daddy into getting *two pair* of trousers, but Daddy just shook his head and said that he didn't think he would need two pair. "I can't wear both of them at the same time," he said.

That following week, Daddy had to make a special trip back over to St. Joe to get his new suit. It was Easter Week and something seemed to be going on every evening—whether going to church to say the Stations of the Cross and the Rosary, or one of the many other special services that were planned for Holy Thursday, Good Friday, confession on Saturday, or finally Easter Morning—we were kept hopping around like bunnies.

It was warm that Thursday evening when we got out of church— Holy Thursday. Daddy had worn his new Easter suit for the first time, saying that he would put on a different color shirt and tie on Sunday; and it would all look new. He took off his jacket as he left the church, folded it, and put it carefully over the back of the bench seat there between him and Mama as he got in the car.

I remember we had dropped Grandma Campion off at home, and then drove by Daddy's store where he got out and checked a few things inside to make sure everything was locked up for the night. Finally, he came back, and we were on our way home. I was dying to take off my new patent leather shoes. They were rubbing against my heel. I had complained to Mama, and she said she would have Daddy stretch them when we got home, but I felt I couldn't wait.

Daddy drove down the street and turned into the alley behind the house. He proceeded into the driveway, turning the steering wheel so the car curved around gracefully in front of the garage door. The entrance was up a slight incline, so as Daddy got out of the car to open the garage door, he had put the car into *Park*. But this was still rather new to him, having a car with *automatic shift*—his old Chevy having a stick shift on the floor. Well, for some reason, the car just didn't hold in *Park*. Without a sound of warning, the car started to slowly roll backward, but then picked up speed. Daddy saw it start to roll and ran back—managing to open the car door in the process. Just as he put his foot in to put it on the brake, the door swung back on him and hit him, knocking him down on the gravel driveway. Daddy totally disappeared from view. Simultaneously, the car raised and then lowered itself—making a strange sound much as it would today if you drove over a very large speed bump. It did this not once, but more like twice—*two bumps* in very rapid succession.

I pushed over next to Darrell to try to look out the window on his side from behind Daddy's seat. Then I moved back over to Mama's side and looked out the window there. Because she had reached over and turned the wheel, the car backed out into the alley rather than going out straight down the terrace and out into the street. On further analysis, we decided that turning the wheel made the car run over both of Daddy's legs—causing the two rapid *bumps* we felt. However, it could have been much worse—if the car had backed straight out, it could have crushed Daddy's chest or even run over his head.

Mama once again put the car into *Park*. Daddy pulled himself up to a standing position there on the gravel driveway and started brushing himself off. He hobbled back to the car and drove it back to the front of the garage. This time he was very careful to make sure it was in *Park* and that it had the hand brake on. This was one of the few nights that Daddy didn't put the car in the garage but let it sit outside instead.

When we got inside the house, Mama hurriedly checked Daddy all over. Although his legs hurt really bad and later ended up covered in bruises, he didn't feel like any bones had been broken. We soon found most of the damage had occurred to the pants of his new suit. The back of his trousers was filled with small holes almost as if he had been hit in the behind with buck shot.

Daddy took the pants to Carl Boughton's Cleaners (next door to Daddy's store) to have the pants *cleaned*. He hoped that Mr. Boughton would be able to do something to mend or reweave the little holes, but Mr. Boughton said it was hopeless. Mama did her best to close and mend the little holes, but there was really no way to disguise them.

For the next few years, Daddy wore the trousers—but only when he really had to wear a suit jacket. He tried unsuccessfully to get a second pair of pants but found that they were no longer available. He soon realized that he should have bought them when he had had the chance. In business, he started to use a new phrase when talking with his customers, "Opportunity doesn't knock twice!" But at home, when he saw one of '*us kids*' passing up what he thought was a good opportunity, all he had to say was, "Remember <u>Holey</u> Thursday," and we knew exactly what he meant.

18.

BOLOGNA AND PICKLE RELISH SANDWICHES

Shortly after the first of May each year, at a time when I begin hunting and buying silk floral bushes to put on the family graves, I start thinking about Mama's *Bologna and Pickle Relish Sandwiches*. Most people probably haven't ever heard of such a thing, and probably fewer yet have tasted one, but for Mama, they were a tradition.

I went shopping at Michael's and JoAnn's Craft Stores last Saturday. Both stores were having their silk floral bushes on sale so I came back with over fifty bushes—enough for all of the family graves. My brother and I lost our mother about a month ago (March 31, 2003), just 3 ½ months short of her 92nd birthday. So even though this is the first year she will be a recipient of roses in the granite vase on her side of the headstone shared with my father, this will be the twentieth year that we have decorated Daddy's grave. Mama always reminded me to get the flowers for Daddy's grave for Memorial Day, but then I always tried to put fresh bushes on several times throughout each year.

Even before Daddy died in September, 1982, the Memorial Day tour from Topeka, through northeast Kansas and northwest Missouri, had already fallen on me as something to *attend to* as the oldest child. I, along with my two young sons, had begun the ritual sometime in the 1970's. When Daddy decided that his *girl child*, who lacked coordination and *could never remember which way to turn the steering wheel to back the car*, had somehow miraculously learned enough to be trusted with the annual trek, needless to say I was shocked. To drive the 150+

mile (one way) trip from Topeka, Kansas, through Horton and Purcell, Kansas, and then on to Kidder and back through Albany, Missouri, was a significant undertaking. Still, to be asked to do so was both an honor and a privilege. The trip was not only a labor of love; it was *quality time* with the family. Our time on the road together was spent listening to stories of the *Good Ol' Days,* while leaving flowers of multiple hues along the way.

So what do Bologna and Pickle Relish Sandwiches have to do with Memorial Day? As a child, when we made the annual Memorial Day trip (from Horton at that time), we never would have thought about making this trip without Bologna and Pickle Relish Sandwiches. Why? I'm not sure. Maybe it was because they were cheap. Or maybe it was because they were easy to pack and take. Or maybe it was just because they tasted so good on the trip. Regardless of how they became a tradition, they did.

Years ago, even before Memorial Day was officially set as Monday, we always made the trip on the Sunday before Memorial Day. I can remember Mama standing in the kitchen after she and Daddy got home from the store on Saturday night (usually about 11PM). She would have her grinder out, and it would be attached to the kitchen table. Next to her, she would have a big block of bologna which she would then cut into chunks just small enough to fit into the top of the grinder. And then, in the chunks would go, and she would grind away. I used to like to watch the little coils of bologna as they came out the other side of the grinder.

Then Mama would open a fresh jar of sweet pickles, and we'd start sticking them in the grinder. "Watch out, Deanna. Don't stick your finger in with that pickle," she'd say. "You don't want to grind your finger up, do you?" (That statement always ranked right up there with, "Don't run with a stick in your hands." And "What's wrong with you? Do you want to poke your eye out?") By this time, Mama had a towel on the floor under the grinder because the pickles were much juicier than the bologna, and their sweet juice would run down the grinder and onto the floor—leaving several sticky spots as reminders.

Mama never had a recipe. She had made Bologna and Pickle Relish Sandwiches for so long that she knew just what size chunk of bologna to use. I couldn't tell you how big that was, but it always seemed to me that the proportions were about four (4) parts bologna to one (1) part ground pickle. Then, of course, you had to add the Miracle Whip. Who knows how much of that? Just enough to make the other two ingredients stick together and give the right amount of moisture to the mixture.

So what did Mama do with the concoction then? Well, she always seemed to have a loaf of *sandwich white* Wonder Bread on hand—you know, the long ones. Carefully, she would open one end and take out all the bread. Then, she would spread a generous portion of the bologna/pickle mixture on the bread. Next, she would add another piece of bread (to make it a sandwich). And then, and this is very important, she would cut it in half diagonally. She continued to make the next sandwich, and the next, and the next until she had used up all the bread in the bag—except the heels. My younger brother Darrell and I always got some of the leftover mixture on the heels. The two of us, up way past our bedtime, would sit waiting attentively in much the same way that I have seen my three cats line up to watch me prepare a tuna sandwich.

Carefully, very carefully, Mama would put each of the sandwiches back into the bread wrapper, alternating them so that the diagonally cut sandwiches crisscrossed. You have to remember that all this started before there were sandwich baggies, or at least before we knew about them. Waxed paper by itself was just not as good as wrapping the sandwiches and putting them back into the original bread wrapper.

After they were ready, the sandwiches were stored in the refrigerator overnight. From there, they would go directly into the cooler on top of the Nehi orange and grape pop the next morning. In my early days of traveling to Missouri, a time when Grandpa and Grandma Clark went along, Daddy always went up to the ice house right after church and got a chunk of ice sized and cut just right to fit in the bottom of the cooler. That way, the pop bottles could lay on their sides on top of the ice and the sandwiches on top of them. A big bag of greasy potato chips was all that was needed to complete a tasty picnic lunch. Of course, Daddy always had a special affinity for cheese, so he would usually make a special trip to the creamery and get a half moon of Longhorn Cheese, which Mama would slice up into pieces and wrap in waxed paper to go along for Daddy *to snack on* along the way.

We always picnicked in Kidder. After we had decorated the graves at the Kidder Cemetery, it would be time for our little feast. Every year, driving down the highway on our journey, we heard about the *big band-stand* in Kidder Park, how many 4th of July events had been held there, and what a good time everybody had there when Mama was growing up. Yet, every year when we got there, it remained unpainted, having lost a few more planks in the floor, and the grass in the park seeming more like we were visiting a spot in the Kansas Prairie. During several rainy years, I would've sworn we were in Louisiana swamp lands. And as for the town . . . well, it was like something right out of a book on *Old Western Ghost Towns.*

Being a special event, Mama always made me wear frilly dresses; and even though the sandwiches were good, I sure hated to sit on the rough boards of the bandstand to eat them. On the other hand, I also hated the many chiggers that jumped on my bare legs as I walked in the tall grass.

When we got back to Horton, we would often run into my aunt, uncle, and cousins from St. Joe, who came over to Horton to visit my Daddy's mother, Grandma Campion, almost every other Sunday. Usually, after learning what our destination had been that day, my cousins Francie and Terry were merciless in their attack. "Went to Kidder, huh? . . . Kidder? . . . Let's see, Deanna. Isn't that where you go *to get splinters in your BUTT?*" My cousin Terry always teased me—glad to have something he could hold over me.

I stopped by to see my brother, Darrell, today and tried to encourage him and his wife to go along with us this year on the annual tour to decorate the graves. He quickly turned me down. But he did say, jokingly, that he'd miss the sandwiches. "That," he said, "is the only thing that I remember about the trips that was any good—*the Ham and Pickle Relish Sandwiches.*"

"Ham?" I said. "That wasn't ham."

"That wasn't ham?" he replied incredulously. "Well, if it wasn't ham, then what was it? It sure was good. I can remember standing in the kitchen watching you and Mama grind up the bologna . . . BOLOGNA! Damn! That wasn't ham. It was bologna, wasn't it?"

"Yes, of course, it was bologna," I said. "What did you think we were . . . rich?"

But I look back now, and I know we were rich . . . rich in happy memories. That has been my family's heritage and legacy . . . the wonderful memories. And now I've got one more. For now, I will never forget the look on my little brother's face as he realized at age 62, that his favorite sandwich had included bologna, and not ham.

Now isn't that rich???

19.

FATHER FOX

In the mid to late 1940's, kids in small towns all over the United States looked forward to the Saturday Afternoon Matinee at their local theaters. My brother and I, like most of the other kids in Horton, would congregate at the Liberty Theater on Central Avenue just a block north of Daddy's store. It became a Saturday afternoon tradition.

Each Saturday, with lunch finished, Mama and Daddy would rush back to Daddy's store to greet the afternoon customers. Darrell and I, with time to kill, would participate in Grandma Clark's *ritual washing of the faces and hands* and *the combing of hair*. Then, she would send us trotting up the street over the five blocks to the Liberty Theater. No matter how many times Darrell stopped to examine a leaf or a rock or to press his nose up against the glass on a store window, invariably Daddy's store would have to be the final stop before going to the theater. "We need money for the movies!" was our cry. Daddy would take two quarters out of the cash register; and then we would walk the final block (waving at Roger Swearingen in his barber shop each time we passed). Our trek complete, we scurried into the theater for four hours of blissful entertainment. At 12 cents each for tickets, we had 26 cents left over—enough for two popcorns, two drinks and one package of Necco candy (leaving one cent to spare).

Unfortunately, things didn't always go so smoothly; sometimes Daddy would be occupied with a customer when we came in for our quarters. In those instances, we were to wait quietly in the yellow-painted, metal lawn chairs that Daddy had set out behind the row of refrigerators in his appliance store. The chairs faced the front of the store so we could peek through the cracks between the refrigerators and see who was going or coming. This was where Grandma Campion, Daddy's mother, always sat when she was waiting for Daddy to take her home in his truck.

We knew better than to interrupt Daddy when he was talking to a customer. Still, it was hard to *sit still* when the big clock on the wall indicated that *by now* the *Coming Attractions* would have already been shown and the two cartoons had most likely come and gone. By all reckoning, they would be getting into Episode number XX of Buster Crabbe and his fight to save the World from the Robot Aliens! "Please, just buy it and go!" we would silently mutter as we waited *patiently* for Daddy to finish with his customer.

One Saturday, while waiting for Daddy to go to the cash register and get our pittance for the theater, I found myself migrating back to the front of the store—just to make sure that he knew we were there. As I got to the front window display, I looked out at a car parking in front of the store. Soon after, getting out of the car was my Daddy's friend, Father Fox from St. Benedict's College in Atchison.

Father Fox headed up some kind of radio station at the college; and like my Daddy, he was an amateur radio operator. Sometimes at night when we listened to the college's radio station or when Daddy was talking with his amateur radio friends, I would easily recognize Father Fox's voice. He had this big, deep, booming voice that seemed befitting his equally bountiful size. He was well over 6 feet tall and was just big all over, especially his ample belly that wasn't hidden behind his Roman Collar and ankle length cassock. Contrary to fashion suggestions, black clothing didn't seem to do anything to diminish his size.

Apparently, Father Fox also taught technical classes in radio and television repair at the college so he usually came in to use some of Daddy's equipment, get tubes or transistors, or really just to talk. As a child, I rarely liked to see one of *Daddy's friends*—especially one who liked to talk. But I actually liked to be around when Father Fox came. He was always good-natured and would tease Darrell and me—and sometimes he would give us each a nickel for *something extra* at the theater or maybe to get a comic book at Cook's Variety Store after the movies.

As usual, with big confident strides, Father Fox approached the front of the store, swinging the screen door open wide. Daddy turned as he heard the door. In his big booming voice, Father gave his usual greeting, "Ho! Ho! Ho! I'm Father Fox, and I can eat more fried chicken than any three Methodist Preachers."

Daddy took a few steps toward Father Fox and shook his hand. Then, with a big grin on his face, Daddy stepped back toward the man he had been showing a refrigerator to and said, "Father Fox, I'd like you to meet Reverend Nicklin. He's our local Methodist Minister."

With big smiles on their faces, Father Fox and Reverend Nicklin shook hands. Then Father took a step back and looked the Reverend up and down as if to size him up. He reached over and sort of felt Reverend Nicklin's arm in several places between his wrist and his elbow, and gave it a little pat. Then, in his booming voice, he exclaimed, "I'm Father Fox . . . and I *still* say that I can eat more fried chicken than three Methodist Ministers."

Everybody laughed—especially Father Fox and his big *fried chicken* belly. Daddy used the brief break in his discussion to get our quarters so Darrell and I could head off to the matinee. I noticed that Darrell seemed oblivious to what had just happened, but I was glad that, at age ten, I was in on the *joke*.

Father Fox was a big part of the Saturday Afternoon Matinee that day!

20.

WHAT ARE NARES?

The other night, I was talking with my son, Shawn, on the telephone. Toward the end of our conversation, he threw me a curve ball, "Hey, when you were telling me the other day about your sinuses, you used the word, *nares*. Where in the world did you come up with that word?"

"Nares?" I said. "They're your nasal passages—the openings to nasal cavities."

"You mean nostrils?" He sounded like a disbeliever. "Where'd you get *nares*? I've never heard anyone else use that word."

I proceeded to tell him about my visit several years earlier to an Ear, Nose, and Throat Specialist over at St. Joseph's Hospital in Kansas City. She had used the term *nares* as she described my condition. I know I told Shawn the story about the visit at the time, but this was yet another instance where he really hadn't listened to me when I first related the incident to him. I had referred to the story again about three weeks ago, using the word *nares* in my description, but he acted like he had never heard the story. So here it was, three weeks later, and he was still bothered by the word *nares*. I decided he should listen to the story once again. When I had finished, his response was guarded. "You'd better write that story down," he said. "But you might want to eliminate the word *nares*. I'm not sure it exists."

So here I am, several days later (March, 2005), getting ready to write the story. On a whim, I picked up the dictionary to look up *nares*. I couldn't find it, so I went on the Internet and put *nares* into Google.

Several other things (names of stores) showed up, but nothing referencing parts of the nose as being *nares*. So I asked myself, "Am I losing it?" I'm only 67 years old, and I know that the word *nares* exists. Besides, Shawn can't be right. I tried accessing one thing and then another—hoping the Internet will help me prove that I haven't totally lost it. Nothing!

Finally, I did a little meditation routine; I could tell that my blood pressure had gone up. If I didn't calm down soon, I might slip into a panic attack. I closed my eyes and began to hum to myself as I let my head bob up and down. "Where? Where? Where?" I chanted to myself as I meditated.

Suddenly it came to me—Biology—Respiratory System of a Frog. So I quickly searched for an Internet location where a frog is being dissected. Sure enough. The diagrams showed *external nares* and *internal nares*. Then I went to human anatomy and found *internal nares* listed again, showing the internal nasal passages and sinus cavities. Yes, sir, I may be 67 years old, but I still know a *nare* when I see one.

In early 2002, I was diagnosed with Asthma and other respiratory problems. I also have Sleep Apnea. Dr. Williams, the respiratory therapist that I was seeing at the time, sent me to see Dr. Roh (an Ear, Nose and Throat Specialist) at her office in St. Joseph's Medical Center. It wasn't long after she first looked inside my nose that she stopped, looked me in the eye, and said, "What on earth happened to you?"

When I asked her why she would ask, she said my *nares* and sinus cavities were a mass of scar tissue on top of scar tissue; and, of course, there were no nose hairs to filter germs or dust, etc. She said that the scar tissue had almost completely closed the passages, so when I would have an asthma attack or a cold and the scar tissue would swelled up, I was probably pretty close to suffocating. She asked if I had panic attacks when I couldn't breathe. From my perspective, she was describing *exactly what happens* when my nose gets *plugged up* and I have an asthma attack.

Dr. Roh said she could tell from the scars that this had been there a long time, but she wanted to know if I could remember how I got all of this scar tissue in the first place. I told her that I didn't know that I had *scar tissue*, but I did remember a time in my life when it probably had started.

I told Dr. Roh that when I was fourteen, I woke up one day and my face seemed to be paralyzed on one side. I compared my looks to what had happened to my mother when she had a stroke. My mouth had drooped on one side. The skin on my cheek and nose on that one side felt prickly. My eye on that side drooped, and I couldn't close it. I couldn't wrinkle my forehead, and I couldn't smile on that one side. I looked like I had a severe case of *bed face,* only it wasn't getting any better.

Mom and Daddy rushed me to see Dr. McCorkle. He said I had Bell's palsy. His only reassurance was that *sometimes the symptoms finally decrease or just go away by themselves.* He gave my parents an ointment for my eye and asked Mom to put a gauze patch over my eye at night to keep it closed.

We followed the prescription, but after awhile, the eye started to droop further and tears would run down my cheek all the time. Grandma Clark did a lot of muttering and grouching to herself and spent hours putting warm compresses on that side of my face. I spent hours in front of the mirror prodding and poking—trying to coax my mouth or my eye to respond, but they just wouldn't do it.

The kids at school began to notice and started to make fun of me. I remember we were practicing for the annual St. Patrick's Day Pageant at school, and I had a lead part. I had a difficult time talking and pronouncing the words and got tired of wiping the '*slobbers* from my chin. Soon, it was apparent that I would have to give up this juicy part to Viola Askren. I felt persecuted. I hated everyone and everything. I wanted to drop out of school. And even when I wasn't crying, my one eye kept tearing— almost as a constant reminder.

After about ten days, Mom took me back to the doctor. This time, Dr. McCorkle suggested that I go see Dr. Rucker in Sabetha. He was an Ear, Nose and Throat Specialist.

Dr. Rucker was a cocky little guy. After a short examination, he said he knew exactly what to do since he'd had other patients with the same condition who he'd cured. Mom and Daddy agreed with Dr. Rucker's evaluation and further suggestion that I needed to have the 13 treatments he prescribed. I was given the first treatment before I even left his office that day.

For the other 12 treatments, I caught a Continental Trailways bus at the bus stop a half block south of Daddy's store. I caught this bus every Saturday morning at about 10 AM for the next 12 Saturdays and rode it all the way to Sabetha (after a brief stop in Hiawatha). From the bus stop in Sabetha, I walked the several blocks to Dr. Rucker's office. I got there about 12:30 for a 1 PM appointment. Then I walked back to the bus stop and caught a return bus back to Horton that left there about 1:45, arriving in Horton around 4 PM. My whole Saturday was shot! By the time I got home, I felt exhausted from trying to hide my disfigurement from the world all day.

I spent the entire bus ride in my seat with a clean, white hankie folded and held over my eye. Mom had gotten me some new plastic, silver-framed sunglasses with sparkles in the plastic frames, but I couldn't wear them without my eye tearing up. So, I wore them when I wasn't on the bus—going to Sabetha and returning home. I know that, in all likelihood, no one even noticed, but it's practically impossible to convince a 14 year old of that.

Looking back, I am amazed that I was allowed to make this trip on my own. Mom and Daddy must have felt it was safe, but I don't believe it would be safe to allow a 14 year-old girl to make that same trip alone today. Of course, there probably isn't a bus from Horton to Sabetha anymore anyway.

So, what did Dr. Rucker do for the 13 treatments? He had me sit in a chair that was very much like a dental chair. He raised it up higher and had me lay my head back slightly on a head rest. On the counter against the wall of his examination room, he had a silver container which he opened and dipped what looked like a cotton Q-tip on a metal wire into whatever was in the container. Then he inserted the Q-tip several inches into one of my nostrils. Instantly, it felt like the whole top of my head was going to blow off.

After several minutes, he took the Q-tip out and inserted a second one into the nostril on the other side. Same reaction! You know how it feels when you eat ice cream too fast and you get that terrible pain in you head? That's how this felt; only it was about 100 times more intense than any *brain freeze* I've ever felt.

I asked Dr. Rucker about this and he told me that while he knew it was painful, I would need to *endure the pain* because it was going to open up my sinus cavities and get rid of my Bell's palsy. After thirteen treatments, I seemed to have improved some, but my face was still partially paralyzed. Dr. Rucker said we would try it again in six months if I didn't see significant improvement by then.

I worked hard in front of the mirror to try to rehabilitate myself, and Grandma Clark still kept up the heat pack treatments. By the end of that summer, when I was getting ready to go into my freshman year at Horton High School, my condition had improved a great deal. Gradually, over the years, it seemed to disappear altogether; but problems from the treatments given by Dr. Rucker originated with and continued from that time forward. Looking back now, we just didn't think about it long enough to really pinpoint it and say, "This is the root cause of my problem."

When I had finished telling Dr. Roh the story, she asked, "Is he still alive?"

"Who?" I wanted to know.

"That Dr. Rucker. Is he still alive?" she inquired.

I told her that I had heard he had died sometime in 1961 or 1962, about the time I was going to college at Kansas State University. She immediately responded, "He died of cancer, didn't he?"

I confirmed that I thought he had indeed died of cancer, but wondered how she had known.

She started telling me a little story. She said that while she was in medical school, those persons whose specialty was Ear, Nose and Throat had learned about a treatment, given in the 1950's and early 60's, that had been originated by a doctor at John Hopkins Hospital. It was supposed to be the latest and greatest treatment of the time, but then a lot of the doctors who were using this treatment started dying of cancer. That was because the *medicine* in the container was *live radiation*. Dr. Rucker's treatment was radiation therapy. And that, apparently, was what was being put up my nose. So it shouldn't be any wonder that my *nares* (nasal passages) and my sinuses are nothing but a mass of scar tissue.

Dr. Roh said that, unfortunately, nothing can be done to correct the problem, but I should consider myself lucky so far. Over 30% of the people who have been documented as having had these treatments have since developed thyroid or pituitary cancer, cancer of the larynx, or brain tumors. Furthermore, while I only got 13 treatments, Dr. Rucker, by the time he died, had probably exposed himself to live radiation so many times that he probably *lit up at night like a Christmas Tree.*

Personal Note: Now admittedly, this is all a little bit scary when I look back on it now. I just had another bad cold. It always seems to put me into respiratory distress, which in turn, gives me panic attacks. It's not fun; but I live with it. And, over all, things are pretty much back to normal again—until the next cold, or flu, or asthma attack.

There is, of course, an *up side* to my condition. I also have high blood pressure and diabetes. One of the medications used in my treatment is a diuretic. I usually end up getting up and going to the bathroom a half dozen times or more every night. But unlike other people, I don't have to leave a light on or carry a flashlight with me. I simply flair my *nares,* turn my head in the direction of the bathroom, and there always seems to be enough light to find my way. *Eat your heart out, Rudolph!*

One other point: I mentioned to Shawn that *'nares'* is a real word found in Biology. His response, "And *'nostrils'* is a real word found in the vocabulary of most people who speak English." Sometimes he can be a real pain in the *nares!*

21.

THE FIRST CHILD IS ALWAYS NAMED PURCEY

Even though the town of Horton had a population of less than 3,000, there were still two grade schools. Most of the children went to the Horton Grade School, which was on the lower level of the big school building between 11th and 12th Streets on First Avenue East. The junior high and high school were on the second and third floors.

The other grade school, St. Leo's Grade School, was located another block to the north, next to the Catholic Church. That is where I went to school for the first eight grades. As was the usual practice, when we graduated from the eighth grade, we transferred to Horton High School. Along with several others who had gone to Catholic school with me, come the fall of 1952, we transferred to Horton High. Those others included Robert Schuetz, Harold Morris, Charles Schecher, and Camilla Quinto. There were three others that graduated from the eighth grade with us, but they went elsewhere. Joe and George Edmonds went to Maur Hill in Atchison and Charles Hulsey went to school in Leavenworth.

Those early days at a new school were not easy—not even at a small town school. Being thirteen or fourteen years old is a difficult time in the growing up process anyway; but the first few days in a new school, a totally different environment than a classroom where three grades are blended together and taught by a Benedictine nun, was total culture shock. Gone were the days when everybody lined up to enter the building and go into the classrooms. Suddenly the environment included kids who push, shove, and hassle each other. The sounds were different: slamming lockers, yelling, screaming, and even an occasional curse word.

I'm sure I wasn't the only one who was teased by upper classmen, but I certainly didn't know how to respond to them when they flipped my skirt and tried to snap my bra. How helpless a new freshman can feel in not knowing where to go for help—especially when you think the administration is shutting their eyes to all this. Maybe the other girls could casually laugh this off or maybe it wasn't happening to them, but I didn't know where I fit in anyway. I didn't know where to turn. I felt like a total misfit.

I tried to make the best of things, to become a part of the classroom environment. I tried to be friendly and talk to the other kids, but it was a strain. I never quite felt a part of any class or group. Maybe I was naive. Maybe I didn't laugh at dirty jokes the way other kids did. Maybe I didn't have a boyfriend or an exciting past to talk about the way some of the other girls did. But I was a good student, and I got along with all the teachers—all, that is, except Miss M., the most exotic, classiest new teacher that year.

[For those of you wondering, Miss M. is still alive. I am using her last initial only because while she did have a negative effect on me, I bear her no grudges at this point. I do, however, want to share and comment on my experience in the hope that it will affect the way other new teachers treat their students in the future.]

Miss M. was a standout in her convertible. It established her as being *cool*. All of her students decided they wanted to be just like her. She must have been aware of her status and popularity. Her attention and acceptance was something sought after by those in her classes. But for some reason, she decided I was unworthy and untouchable.

Miss M. seemed to take pleasure in pointing out my deficiencies. "Stand up straight—don't slouch." "You wear the most unattractive clothes." "Class, take a look at Deanna. She is a perfect example of someone who has a ruddy complexion." (Actually, I didn't have a ruddy complexion; I simply blushed constantly because she was always embarrassing me.) "Class, Deanna should never, never wear red." And to this day, I almost never wear red—right, wrong, or indifferent.

I don't know why Miss M. took such pleasure in picking on me. I was a very quiet, well-behaved student. I tried never to bother or embarrass anyone. Besides, I was still trying to get over the devastation to my ego from having Bell's palsy less than a year earlier. But, Miss M. always seemed to *be there* with a critical remark. So, as a result, I took the one required year of *home economics* and, once completed, I never stepped through the home economics classroom door again, at least not while Miss M. was there.

From the way Miss M. acted, it seemed like she was trying hard to be a movie star. But, along with her big red lips and orange pancake makeup that always seemed to come off on her turned-up collars, she reminded me more of a circus clown. Now, I would never have been able to tell her that, however. Plus, I undoubtedly would have gotten kicked out of school for any comment I might have made back to her. It was a different time back then, and we were supposed to respect our teachers—regardless.

Does that sound bitter and super critical? Well, fifty some years later, I may be doing the same thing that I have criticized Miss M. of doing. I probably should give her the benefit of the doubt. She may not have meant to be unkind. Maybe it was just because she was young and a new teacher. Maybe her words really were meant to be helpful, but they were simply said without tact at the wrong time and in the wrong place. Still, they hurt. She never seemed to pick on the really popular girls. It was always just me, Peggy King, and occasionally Donna Koll who seemed to feel the brunt of her remarks. It's hard not to feel the pain even now.

There was only one classroom during my freshman year where I felt relaxed and at peace. This was the classroom of Betty Eiseminger, my English/Language Arts teacher. Miss Eiseminger was always my respite from the chaos I found at Horton High School. She was someone who recognized my worth and praised my abilities. I found solace in her classroom each day. Maybe it was because I used words like *solace* even then.

Now, the guys from my St. Leo's class didn't seem to have the same problem adjusting. Bob Schuetz was an athlete. He went out for football so it wasn't long before he was accepted into Horton High Society. Harold Morris was no longer called Harold. He was Hal or Homer. It wasn't long before he was accepted, even becoming a star on the track team. Charles (Chuck) Schecher had an older brother, Bob, who at that time was a terrible bully; Chuck seemed to be accepted into the new social setting by default. Camilla Quinto, on the other hand, could rely on her older sister Thomasa to pave the way in a much more subtle way. Still, to my knowledge, no one gave her a hard time. In fact, it seemed at times that all of my old classmates had gone over to the other side, and I was left to stand my ground alone.

Overall, there was one good thing about High School. I liked most of my classes, and I enjoyed meeting the other new freshmen. I knew a few, like Bernetta Clarke, Peggy Kallos, and Reva Searles because they lived close to my house in the south part of town; and we had played together as young children. There were twenty or so others who I knew by name, but I had never had the opportunity to know anything else about them other than their names.

I have mentioned that Chuck Schecher's brother, Bob, was a terrible bully. It seemed that no matter how I tried to avoid him, he was always there with a mean or nasty remark or something else to torment me. He liked to embarrass me. And I knew that, for that year, I would always have at least one hour where he *could* torture me if he didn't get his digs in before or after school or between classes. He happened to be in my third period study hall.

Other people knew that *study hall* meant a time to study or do your homework. For Bob, it was a time to play, bother people, irritate Mrs. Steele (the study hall teacher) and call her names. We supposedly had assigned seats. Bob sat across the room next to Leon Knudson. However, having an assigned seat did not anchor Bob to it. He was constantly working the room, making loud, rude remarks, throwing balls of paper, throwing spit wads, walking down aisles and hitting people on the back of the head. (This was when Bob was in high school. I hope these same behaviors didn't continue into the work place or carry on over these past 50 years.)

Sooner or later, however, Bob always seemed to get around to me. On one particular day about two months into the school year, Bob had been badgering me unmercifully. He had confronted me in front of the school before classes, in the hall by my locker between classes, and even in front of Miss M., who actually thought he and his remarks were cute.

After all, he was well over 6 feet tall and really was very good looking. By the time we got to study hall, I was beaten—I was ready to ask my parents to send me to live with the nuns at Mt. St. Scholastica in Atchison.

Bob started in again from across the room. The study hall teacher heard him but ignored him. Kay Heim and Delbert Sams sat one row over toward the front of the room. They looked back occasionally when Bob started his barrage of name calling and teasing.

At that point, a young man with glasses who sat one row over and in front of me yelled over at Bob, "Hey, why don't you leave *Purcey* alone? She's not doing anything to bother you." A few other words were exchanged, but I really didn't hear them. I was still focusing on *Purcey*. I had a nickname! And it wasn't anything bad like what Bob had used. *Purcey*—that was nice. It didn't hurt at all.

Dan Hybskmann was the young man who gave me my nickname—the person who I felt had just validated my existence that day. I don't remember ever having any regular classes with Dan Hybskmann during our high school years, but we did talk occasionally and soon he had everybody else in school calling me *Purcey*. He was the first one to make me feel a part of our class and our school.

Several years later, my cousin Terry (Purcell) was riding with us to our house from Grandma Campion's house. We had turned the corner onto 15th street when we passed Dan's house. Dan was outside and yelled, "Hi, *Purcey*," and waved.

I turned to Terry and told him proudly that *Purcey* was my nickname. Terry's response, given in his best British accent was, "My dear, didn't you know? The first child is always named *Purcey*." I guess he too had been called *Purcey* for several years. Later, my brother Darrell was also called *Purcey* when he got to high school.

Personal Note: When we were in college, I rode back and forth to and from Manhattan with Dan several times, but we've probably only talked with each other less than a dozen times since the early 60's. He still calls me *Purcey*. Over the years, I have always remembered him as my *knight in black rimmed glasses*; and when it was time to pick a name for my second son, the only name that seemed right for me was "Daniel."

Thank you, Dan Hybskmann. I will always remember your kindness to a scared and lonely girl. Nicknaming me *Purcey* gave me the acceptance I needed. We never know how one simple act of kindness can affect a life.

———————

One Final Note: Some people may think I was still too hard on Miss M. To them and Miss M., I apologize. However, when I was an Education student at KSU, I told my story in one of the Educational Psychology classes one day. It turned out to be the seed for discussion for our classes on two separate days. I had the opportunity to learn that other students had also had similar experiences, and they still carried the emotional scars and negative feelings along with them, too. As a group, we arrived at a decision. We all decided that when we would be in our classrooms, we would do our utmost to build up the fragile egos of our students—not tear them down. I took this with me, and for the 12 years I taught school, I always tried to be aware of the power of words and use them in a positive way instead of as something negative. I also found this attitude helpful to me later as a Human Resource Manager for a major telecommunications company.

22.

BEAUTIFUL BONNIE ANN

As soon as I was old enough to join the Brownies, I did. I had been reading a magazine called *Polly Pigtails*. It was about the Brownies and scouting. Even though there was no Brownie troop at St. Leo's, where I went to elementary school, Mama asked a lot of questions and found a troop led by Mrs. Kinkade. All the other girls went to the public school, but like Mrs. Kinkade's daughter Ann, all were just about my age—about nine if my memory serves me correctly.

I really enjoyed the Brownies since, at any one time, I might have the camaraderie of eight or ten girls my own age sharing an activity. At St. Leo's, there were only 8 of us in the same class: six boys (Bob Schuetz, Harold Morris, Charles Hulsey, Charles Schecher, and the Edmonds twins, Joe and George) and two girls (Camilla Quinto and me). In years to come, I was also grateful for this time in the Brownies because it allowed me the opportunity to get to know Ann Kinkade.

Ann Kinkade was a very attractive and athletic young girl—even at the time she was a Brownie. You could tell, even then, that she was destined to be a leader. Although she was intelligent and had other natural talents and abilities, she never made anyone feel inadequate. Whenever there were teams to be chosen, she was chosen first; but she was always such a nice person that she gave everybody a chance and never tolerated others being abused. Mistakes never meant failure; they were simply errors—soon forgotten.

When I graduated from the 8th grade and went to Horton High my freshman year, I had the opportunity to get to know Ann as a fellow classmate. We were in several classes together and her leadership qualities stood out both in the classroom and in activities both before and after school hours. Ann had grown into a beautiful, maturing young woman. She challenged later stereotypes; she was a blonde with a brain, and she used it. She was also good at sports, and she and Patsy Baker were always team captains for most P.E. activities. She was on the Honor Roll and was poised and self confident in taking leadership roles in class and outside activities. In what was an unprecedented event, in February of our freshman year, Ann was elected Valentine Queen in a vote by the entire student body. Her cousin, Tommy Swearingen, who was a year older than us and also very popular, was elected King.

I well remember this honor given Ann because I was on a committee to make the crowns for the Valentine's Day Dance. Some way, the other people on the committee seemed to disappear. I remember working on the crowns with Mom for about a week and just getting them finished the night before the dance. The crowns were modeled after the crowns for the King and Queen of England and were gold with a red satin lining. We sewed faux pearls and jewels on them. They were really quite beautiful.

Ann Kinkade showed such promise. How wonderful it must have been to be beautiful, smart, and yet so nice. Yes, she was that unique combination—sweet and beautiful—making her loved by all who knew her.

But that promise shown by Ann was lost to us. Ann was taken from us in a car wreck. The whole school mourned. The whole town mourned. If she had only had more time, I have no doubt that the state, the country, or even the world, would have mourned her loss—given the chance to know her. Anyone who did know her would say the same.

How did this terrible travesty come to pass? Well, you have to remember that this was the 50's in a small northeastern Kansas town. Vehicle safety wasn't the concern it has become today. There weren't any airbags. Cars didn't even have seatbelts, so even the most minor of accidents could, in an instant, be fatal.

Ann had gotten her license at 14—she was able to drive to and from school and on errands for her parents. It was the summer after our freshman year. She and her younger sister, Nancy, had gone one mile north of town to a dairy to buy milk. On the way back, she went off the road and ran into a ditch. Ann was killed instantly when her neck was broken. And, although Nancy's injuries to her leg were serious, the more devastating injury was the broken heart she sustained when she learned she had lost her beloved sister.

How could such a terrible thing happen? Why did it happen? There are some things I don't think that we will ever know. I just know that a beautiful, sensitive person was lost to us that day. For many of us, the loss of Ann was the first time we realized that death wasn't just for grandparents or other *old* people. We learned that it could happen to any of us, too! Being a teenager did not give us immunity to death!

─────────────

Given a chance, however, I prefer to remember an earlier time. I prefer to remember that happy, fun-loving group of girls in Mrs. Kinkade's Brownie Troop. And while I can't name everyone who was in that Brownie troop with us, it was obvious that Ann mirrored her mother as a real leader. I think Ann's cousin Patsy Swearingen, Judy Wart, Carol Thompson, Patsy Ogden, Tootie Mink, Karen Miller, and about six or so others were also a part of the troop at one time or another. No doubt about it though, Ann was always the standout in any crowd.

I remember how Ann always knew all the little Brownie songs. She was the one who taught me "Itsy Bitsy Spider." She wasn't just a *goodie-goodie two shoes*, though. She was a normal kid.

It wasn't until my two boys were about ten and six that I realized all kids seem to go through a period when they enjoy things that are gross. I sometimes worry, with the advent of video games, whether *grossness* will eventually go too far.

But, as I started to say, even goods kids enjoyed *gross* things during their childhood. In addition to the nice sweet little Brownie songs we would sing, Ann also taught me one that was sung to the tune of *My Bonnie Lies over the Ocean*. Below are the words to *My Bonnie*—included as a reminder to help you remember the tune.

Verse—

My Bonnie lies over the Ocean.
My Bonnie lies over the Sea.
My Bonnie lies over the Ocean.
Oh, bring back my Bonnie to me.

Chorus—

Bring back. Bring back.
Oh, bring back my Bonnie to me. To me
Bring back. Bring back.
Oh, bring back my Bonnie to me.

Of course, many of you may have already guessed which gross song it was that Ann taught me. If you haven't figured it out yet, it goes something like this:

Verse—

My mother has tu-ber-cu-losis.
My sister has only one lung.
They sit and spit blood in a bucket.
And dry it and chew it for gum.

Chorus—

Den-tine! Den-tine!*
They dry it and chew it for gum. Yum! Yum!
Den-tine! Den-tine!
They dry it and chew it for gum.

As gross as it is, I'm pretty sure that in our innocence, we failed to realize how truly gross it was when we were learning it. It just seemed funny at the time. But once in awhile, the tune, *My Bonnie*, pops into my head; and I sing the gross version (or maybe just hum if someone else is around). It brings back memories of a beautiful, laughing girl and simpler times. Goodbye, Bonnie Ann. You'll always be alive in my memory.

———————

*My apologies to the gum manufacturer. You really have a fine product—one I have used and enjoyed from time to time throughout my life. The choice to put red dye in the gum was not mine, however—nor is the song.

Personal Note: Ann was born on February 14, 1938, Valentine's Day. At the time I was growing up, she was the only person I knew whose birthday was so close to mine—February 18. Years later, I found out that my classmate and friend, Jerry Brown, was born on February 16. I wish we could go back and have a grand old birthday party!

23.

SLIDING AROUND FOUR CORNERS

The main cross street intersection of Horton then and even now is called "Four Corners." Everything came together at this intersection of 8th Street and Central Avenue East. Jim's Waffle Shop, Duckwall's, Cook's Variety Store, The *Horton Headlight*, Eubelaker's Jewelry Store, the Horton Clinic, a hardware store and two drug stores were all down 8th Street to the west of Four Corners. Several grocery stores, the Garment Factory, the Pool Hall, a bank, Judy Wart's Dad's dry goods/clothing store, and Winterscheidt's Dress Shop were to the east on 8th Street from Four Corners. My Dad's shop (Purcell Radio & Electric), Gampper's, Heim's Bakery, the telephone office, the Chevy dealership, the funeral home, Roger Swearingen's barber shop, the Liberty Theater and several other businesses were up the street to the north of the intersection. Not much still remained to the south of the intersection, with the exception of the Foster Ford dealership, Walker's Feed Store, and Rousey's Lumber Yard.

Four Corners was the crossroads to everything in Horton. And in later years, or at least for a time during my high school years, a large Christmas tree was set up there and decorated at Christmas time. But the particular year that I am thinking about, the winter of my sophomore year in high school, there was no Christmas tree at the intersection.

I know every old person who looks back on their childhood always has some dumb story to tell that starts out, "When I was in school, it snowed so much that it came up to my knees (or my hips), and I had to walk ten miles everyday to school." Well, I can't account for the tall tales of others, but I remember the winter of my sophomore year. It snowed so much that they let school out for several days because people were virtually immobilized by the volume of snow and high drifts. In most places, the snow was up over my knees, and it was even higher in places where it had drifted—like next to the porch where Darrell actually jumped off the rails and the snow came up past his waist.

By the second day, the city and county snow plows had made great headway. Most of the main streets had been partially plowed and most of the snow had been transported to the city park. However, there was so much snow that they started pushing it from four directions in the downtown area and had made this huge mound of snow in the center of Four Corners. This was just too much to pass up by kids who didn't have to go to school. Bob Schuetz, Hal Morris, Sue Haas, Bill Tulk and Jerry Brown, along with his younger brother Mike, were already there when Bernetta Clarke, Reva Searles, and I got there. Several of them had made a path to climb up one side of the huge mound. On the other side, although very steep, the snow had started to glaze over from people sitting on their tushes and sliding down at *breakneck* speed.

When Bernetta, Reva, and I arrived, both Bernetta and Reva immediately went to the top and slid down with the others. I refrained. I was a chicken. This didn't look like something I wanted to do. I was afraid that I might get hurt. Then the boys decided that they wanted to roll someone down the hill, and they started pushing and pulling Sue, trying to get her to go down on their terms. Everybody was laughing and yelling, but I think I yelled something like, "Be careful. You might hurt her."

Well, that was all it took. Suddenly, everyone was aware that I was there but not participating. The boys came after me as a unit. I was half dragged, half carried up the backside of the huge mound of snow. It looked even higher from the top. I was fighting them and screaming the whole while. They weren't quiet either—all the while yelling and laughing. Several of the merchants came to their doors to see what was going on. I kept screaming and the others kept yelling and laughing. My father even came out his door almost a block away, stood watching for a minute, and then waved and went back into the store.

There was no mercy given. I was plopped down on the ice that was forming and was given a shove. The sound of my screeching seemed to echo back from the brick buildings. Then it stopped. I had gotten to the bottom and was still alive. I sat there momentarily. As I got up, the boys came down behind me. The girls were all standing on the sidewalk just looking. I thought it was over. I had survived. Then Bob called out, "Ya' know, I think we can make her go down faster if we send her down face first."

I tried to get away, but found myself being dragged back up the mound. I was still yelling and trying to pull away, but these were *guys on a mission.* They were not to be deterred. Within moments, I was sliding down the ice face first.

But that wasn't the end of it. Next they tried to get me to pull my arms in tight next to my sides so they could roll me down the hill sidewise. I obviously didn't listen to their great engineering plans because I started to bump my face and tumble off the regular slide area as I rolled down the hill. I don't know if I ever stopped screaming. I do know that I was still screaming when I got to the bottom that third time. I also knew that I was starting to feel bruised—and really needed to stop.

I had had more than enough, but the guys were still talking about more. They were talking about packing me in snow and rolling me down the hill as a giant snowball—I think they must have seen it in a cartoon. With that, I started running up the street to my Dad's store. I must have finally stopped screaming; I could hear the sound of their boots as they followed me up as far as Gampper's Store.

As I burst through the front door, Daddy came from the back of the shop. "What's going on?" he asked.

"They're trying to kill me," I responded. "Why didn't you come help me when I was yelling at you? You just waved and came back into the store."

"I thought you were just having a good time," he said.

When I talked with the other kids the next day, they, too, were surprised. They were having a good time, so they just assumed that I was having a good time, too. As with most memories that stick out in my mind, two lessons were learned that day. First, sometimes a person has to pay a high price for popularity. I was certainly *popular* that day, but I wasn't ready to pay the price—I didn't want to forever be known as "the girl who broke her neck sliding around Four Corners." And second, you can never truly know what it's like to be in someone else's skin, so everyone needs to be observant—to try to pick up the signs that you are contributing to another person's discomfort.

Yes, from time to time, we all may experience unusual changes in our personalities or unexpected quirks in our personal philosophy may appear without warning. Suddenly we find ourselves doing something *out of character*. This is especially true when a group of people get together—*mob mentality*. It may appear at unusual times, such as sliding down the glazed-over side of an icy mound!

———————

Several years ago, I told this story to 13 year-old Marla, my husband's granddaughter. At the time, the story was being told to her as a lesson, though I'm not sure who, in the end, got the lesson.

I had learned that on a visit to relatives who live close to Branson, Missouri, young Marla and some neighborhood children had gone out one evening doing what I was told was the *latest fun activity for bored teenagers*. They had gone *Cow Tipping*. This involved quietly slipping up on a sleeping cow found standing in a field. Supposedly, by just two or three of the teenagers giving the cow a gentle push at the same time, the cow would fall over. They thought this was funny!

I was appalled. First, I was worried that the kids would get hurt out at night doing this. Second, I also couldn't believe that there wasn't something unlawful about this activity. Third, I couldn't imagine this as being a very pleasant experience for the cows, and I was concerned that one of them might be injured during the process.

I had told my story about the boys pushing me down the ice slide hoping that Marla would see that it hadn't been a pleasant experience for me. I hoped that she would make the connection that it also wouldn't be a pleasant experience for the cow. After I had finished my story, I asked her if she thought that she should now reconsider her actions. She shook her head "yes," looked at my walker, and then stated, "Yeh . . . I think we missed out on a lot of fun. We shouldn't have been looking for cows. We should have been out *Tipping Grandmas*."

Later that evening, I told my husband George that I thought Marla was disrespectful about *Tipping Grandmas*. "She sure has you pegged," he said. "You didn't believe that story Marla told, did you? You can't tip a cow . . . that's just an urban legend! Shawn and Danny (my sons) are right. You sure are gullible!"

So that's where it is and was. That's yet another reason why my books have the title, *Gullible's Travels*. Apparently, "all my boys" know how gullible I can be.

24.

DRIVING LESSONS

Granted, I had been hassling my father to give me driving lessons. I wanted to get my driver's license. After all, I had had my 16th birthday in February; and my friend Eloise was already allowed to drive her parents' car. Rita Torkelson had her own car and had been driving it to school since she was 14. But then, according to my parents, Rita lived out in the country so she needed to be able to drive. I'm not sure why they thought it was okay for Eloise. When I cited her as an example, they reminded me of Ann Kinkade, who had been killed while driving during the summer after our freshman year.

It wasn't just Daddy who was opposed to my driving. I'm sure Mom was some influence. She had never driven and always had to wait for Daddy to take her places. I think she even liked it that way. I believe the thought of driving made her nervous. She felt that it was unnecessary for me to learn to drive because if I did take the car out for some reason, there would just be another worry for her during the time I was gone. I know it bothered her even when I rode in the car with Eloise—even though Eloise was a licensed driver. For them, it was still a man's world. They certainly didn't feel the same way about my brother driving. He was only 15 when Daddy started teaching him to drive. I didn't know it at the time, but Darrell would have a license and his own car long before me.

One warm fall night in 1954, Daddy had driven out by Kennekuk, a little area south of Horton. The road was gravel and straight most of the way. Daddy was driving really slowly because he had gotten a new car that had just come out, a 1955 Turquoise and White Chevy—now a classic. The reason for his really slow driving—he didn't want any rocks to kick up and damage the finish on the new car.

"Come on, Daddy," I begged from the backseat. "Why don't you let me drive a little? There aren't any other cars and the road is pretty much straight."

Daddy gave several reasons, but he always ended up with the one, "You won't even know which way to turn the steering wheel. You're the only kid I know that couldn't figure out which way to turn the tongue on a wagon when you were backing up."

"Yeh . . . yeh . . . yeh! I've heard that one for years," I responded. "But I'm not trying to back up now. I want to go straight down this road. Just let me drive for a little while." I think I was probably whining by then. Surprisingly, it worked that night. Daddy stopped the car, got out, and walked around to the passenger seat. Mom got out (said a prayer) and then got in the back. I got out and then stepped into the driver's seat—positioning myself behind the steering wheel. Ah, the feel of it. The glorious feeling of power!

Daddy suggested that I reach down under the seat and pull the seat forward because, "your legs are too short, so you're too far away from the steering wheel." After getting properly positioned, I pressed down on the gas. It gunned the car, but we went nowhere. Very sternly, Daddy said, "Don't you think you should put it in gear?"

"Yes, sir," I replied. Then I remembered that I needed to step on the brake and move the little arm to the "D" position for *Drive*. Yes, I had been watching licensed drivers very closely, and I was so thankful that Daddy had purchased this new 1955 Turquoise Chevy. It had so much more class than the plain blue 1951 model Daddy had previously. Like the '51 Chevy, this new car had automatic transmission—not like his old truck where you had to know something about a *clutch* and how to *shift gears.* Daddy had let me drive the truck home from the store one evening several months earlier, but I didn't do a very good job though. It seemed as if we hopped or jerked the entire four blocks home. For some reason, he never would let me drive the '51 Chevy.

After the "D" was properly positioned, I stepped down on the gas. Gravel went flying out from under the back tires. "That's no way to start," Daddy said. "Don't kick up all that gravel. Put on the brakes and start out slowly. Do it again."

"Yes, Sir," I responded. I stopped the car, and this time, I made a slow and easy start. We were moving again.

Daddy seemed to approve. He was nodding his head up and down. I was so pleased that I had done something right. "Don't get it over 25 MPH. Just go down the road and try to keep it straight in your lane. Look on down the road and notice where the tracks are in the gravel. Try to keep yourself there."

Wow! I was really pleased with myself. We must have gone several whole miles or more by now. I was doing great, and Daddy didn't even seem as tense anymore. I could just see it now. It wouldn't be long before I'd be able to take the car out by myself when I was driving. I knew I looked good—really good—behind the wheel of this superbly fine automobile. It had sex appeal written all over it. None of the kids I knew or the boys that I was particularly fond of had such a fine car. I just loved the combination of Turquoise and White on the car. And the fins— wow, what class!

Daddy jarred me out of the deep contemplative state I was in. "It's starting to get dark, Deanna. Put the lights on."

"I don't know how," I said. "How do I do that? Let me stop so you can show me where they are."

"No, you don't need to do that. Just reach over there to the left of the wheel and take hold of that knob. Pull it out," he said.

But I was afraid to take my eyes off the road. I was afraid that I would get out of the track. "Where is it?" I said. "I can't drive and find it at the same time."

"It's just right up there to your left," Daddy assured me. "Keep you right hand on the wheel and reach up there with your left hand and pull on the knob—pull it out."

I tried to do what Daddy said, but when I pulled on the knob, I guess I didn't do what he wanted. "No," he said. "You didn't pull it out far enough. All you did was put on the parking lights. Pull it all the way out."

Okay, so I tried to give it another tug. This time it came out further and turned on the headlights, but the knob also came out, and off—so that I ended up with the knob and a metal attachment there in my hand.

I knew that was wrong. I knew that wasn't what he meant when he said "pull it all the way out." But there I was, just like Grandma used to say, "I was . . . just like an egg sucking dog caught with egg yolk on his mouth." I had that darned knob in my hand, but what was I supposed to do with it?

Of course, Daddy knew by the sound it made that *something* had broken. He had me pull over, and he was out of the car and around to the driver's side in a flash. All the while, he was cussing up a blue streak. I didn't even have time to inventory what words I knew or didn't know. I was in shock. The next thing I knew, Daddy was driving, Mom was back in the front seat, and I felt lucky to have gotten one leg and my butt into the car before Daddy took off down the road. The driving lesson was over. We were on our way back home. Daddy was definitely going a lot faster than 25 MPH. The gravel was kicking up fast and furious under the car, but Daddy didn't seem to be concerned about that anymore.

The next day, Daddy took the car to the Chevy dealer. They found that a screw had come out of the little metal arm connecting the switch. They replaced it and said that it could have happened when anyone had pulled on it—even Daddy. But, of course, he didn't tell me that part of the story for years. I think it was because, after that, he never wanted to give me another driving lesson.

———

Personal Note: Horton didn't have driver's education classes. I had to learn to drive by begging boyfriends to teach me and let me practice using their cars. I finally had to shame Daddy into letting me use his car to take my driver's test. I was 22 years old and knew I had to use a car to get to the school where I was going to do my practice teaching. And besides, I would need to be able to drive when I had my first teaching contract.

Over the years the full story was never told. Only the Keystone Cops or comical version was told. ". . . so then Deanna pulled it out. Yes, she pulled it *all the way out*! 'Here it is, Daddy,' she said as she handed him the knob." To this day, many of my family members still laugh about the day Deanna got her first driving lesson. I try to laugh with them—at least most of the time. Ha ha.

25.

MEGA SLUMBER PARTIES

Even though Mom and Daddy didn't like the idea of my going to slumber parties at other girls' homes, they never hesitated to allow me to have overnight guests at my house—usually Reva, Bernetta, or Eloise. While I was still in high school, the only place I was allowed to go for a slumber party was Eloise's house or a few times to Bernetta's. Eloise usually had several girls stay with her at the same time. She lived in an older, remodeled home at the corner of 10th and Central. Her bedroom was huge; and with pillows and covers on the floor, we could spread out all over the place. There wasn't any carpeting on the floor, so if we happened to get *crunched up* cookies or potato chips on the floor, all we had to do was grab a broom and sweep up.

When someone stayed overnight at my house, it would be only one girl at a time. That was because my bedroom was so small. Oh, there was plenty of room for my double bed, triple dresser and chest, but that only left walk-around room since the only other corner contained a large floor to ceiling built in wardrobe that had been put in by Al and Leonard Winklebauer when I was about twelve. Like a number of homes back in that time period, houses were built without closets so this built-in wardrobe was wonderful for holding my dresses, hats for church, and shoes, with side drawers for gloves, neck scarves, etc. I was really very appreciative of having it—except, of course, that it did eliminate any possibility of having a place to put down mats to sleep on the floor.

Only once did I have several girls at my house where we spread out and put down covers on the living room floor. I believe there were four of us. However, the next day Daddy said, "Never again." I think we did too much talking, giggling, and running to the kitchen. Since Mom and Daddy's bedroom was just next to the kitchen, it was all that giggling and running back and forth that had kept Daddy awake. Otherwise, Daddy was always very good about putting up with my girl friends when he took us to ball games and other school functions. But another "*all nighter*" where we didn't sleep, and he didn't get any sleep, well that was just too much to ask of him.

Grandma Clark came to the rescue. She and Grandpa had moved to the Hoffman house next door to us when I was about seven. They had worried about Darrell and me and the Hays children crossing the street to get to their house. 1st Avenue East was really 159 Highway and some drivers went down the street pretty fast as they headed out of town. When they moved into the house next door, one of the interesting features of the house was that the only way you could get into the unfinished attic upstairs was to climb the outside stairway on the east side of the house.

Now, one of the things that Grandpa had done several years before he died in 1952 was to hire someone to put the stairs on the inside of the house going up from the living room. After Grandpa died, however, the attic stayed unfinished for quite some time. Then Grandma decided to finish it off herself. The attic had studs around the outside walls and some wallboard up in the front section where the new stairs went up, but the back part was totally unfinished. At one time, I think the Hoffmans may have rented out a room in that front section, just inside the door from the stairs outside. But honestly, I don't know where that person would have gone to the bathroom though. There was just one bathroom in the house, and that was downstairs—just off the kitchen.

Grandma was never one to be deterred from a project that she wanted to do. She had always been pretty good with a hammer, and we used to accuse her of carrying her little hammer and her hoe around with her in her apron pocket. So one day, she just decided to finish off the upstairs. She had Daddy bring her some 2x4's and a couple of pieces of wall board at a time. Over a period of time, she turned the attic into a study room and two bedrooms. She even had a place for a closet and a bathroom, but didn't get to finish them off.

After she got the wallboard up and taped the seams, she painted the rooms. She had used up all her money on the wallboard, so she decided to use left over paint from some of Mom's painting projects. I remember one of the bedrooms had two pink walls from leftover paint in my bedroom and two blue walls from leftover paint in Mom and Daddy's room. One room was a pale yellow from leftover paint in our kitchen mixed with some white that Mom had used on the ceiling.

Sometime along the way, Grandma had hired a carpenter to come in and install new windows. She was really getting things to where I thought they were starting to look pretty good. Then one day when we thought she had been up there working for awhile, we noticed that none of us had seen or heard from her all day. So Mom sent Darrell and me over several times to try and find her. We went into the house since it was never locked, and we called to her. There was no answer and, for that matter, no sign that she had been there for quite a while. So, we went back home and told Mom that Grandma must be over at Aunt DeVere's house.

Later, when we still couldn't find her, Mom went over to Aunt DeVere's and was told that she hadn't seen her all day either. Mom began to panic. She went back to Grandma's house and called and called for her—yet, there was still no answer. Finally, Mom heard this feeble bumping sound coming from upstairs. She climbed to the top of the stairs and only then did she hear Grandma calling out, "Help! Help!"

Mom rushed into the back bedroom where Grandma had been painting. Apparently, Grandma had tried to open the new windows to let the paint smell out. Unfortunately, though the windows were in place, the hardware had not been put on yet. For some reason, the sash on one window didn't want to hold to the point where Grandma had tried to push it up. The window came crashing down. As Grandma grabbed at it to try to keep it from falling, her fingers on both hands got caught under the window sash. Grandma was stuck. There was no way that she could get the leverage she needed to push the window back up, and thus, no way for her to get loose. She had heard all of us call to her each of the times we had come in, but she was so exhausted from trying to get out that she couldn't call back loud enough for us to hear her.

Grandma survived, but once she finished her painting, she didn't try any more major projects by herself. Thus, the bathroom and closet never got finished.

Still, with tragedy avoided, the upstairs became a marvelous place for teenage girls to hang out. Grandma went ahead with the other part of her plans. She furnished the bedrooms frugally with several iron beds and accompanying feather mattresses she stuffed in ticking (feathers supplied without complaint by some of the chickens that she raised in pens in her backyard). After she added several dressers she already owned, put up a few *whatnot* shelves in the corners, and dug out some old pictures to hang, that was really all that the place needed. It was habitable.

Best of all, Grandma's *upstairs* was always available at a minute's notice for overnight guests and slumber parties. And Grandma was cool. Unlike Mom or Daddy, she never got upset with noise—no matter what the volume got to be. I'm not sure how she was able to put up with all of us (because we got pretty rowdy sometimes), but she did, and we loved her for it.

One of the best slumber parties was when my cousin Francie Purcell was going to have her 16th birthday in August, 1954. She had come over to stay with me for the week; and like teenage girls can do, we started planning an elaborate party. Party meant people. So we contacted a number of girls asking them to come to a *slumber party* at Grandma Clark's house. It went off without a hitch. The following girls were there: Peggy Kallos, Patsy Baker, Sue Haas, Patsy Swearingen, Bernetta Clarke, Judy Wart, Reva Searles, Francie, and me.

Mom and Daddy furnished all the snacks. We stuffed ourselves on potato chips and dip, bologna and pickle relish sandwiches, candy bars, and let's not forget the ice cream and birthday cake. Early in the evening, Grandma got out her harmonica and played it for us while we sang. She told us about when she had played it for dances back when she was young and lived on a farm in Missouri. This was when she was about sixteen and a number of years before she married my grandfather. She even played a song where she did a kind of *clogging* dance to it while still playing. She was in her sixties at that time, but she could really dance even then.

Later, we were all over the place. We were inside the house and outside the house, up and down the street goofing off, and finally at 2:30 in the morning, Patsy Baker and Sue Haas walked the two blocks to town to see if anything was going on. Since we were in Horton, we knew there wasn't; but it was something to do. Peggy told them to be careful as they would have to walk by her house and she was sure that someone would be watching to see that we weren't out and about, getting into trouble. They did some special slinking and maneuvering from tree to tree and eventually got by the Kallos house unnoticed.

The rest of us went outside, chased each other for awhile, told ghost stories, counted stars, and waited for Patsy and Sue to get back. We were having so much fun, I don't think we realized how much noise we were making; at one point, Mrs. Magathan came to her door and turned on the porch light. When Patsy and Sue returned, panting and sweaty, they talked about ducking down when two cars passed them and then about having to run down several alleys to get back to Grandma's house. I think they were probably lying though. I don't think there were any cars out at that time of night. No one was out! Well, *nobody but us chickens*—just a bunch of girls having a little harmless fun. Oh, but it was a glorious night and a marvelous slumber party!

———————

Personal Note: Of course, that was just one of several slumber parties that I had at Grandma's house. This one in particular stands out in my memory because of Francie's birthday and also because of Grandma herself. Grandma was so patient and sweet. She never raised her voice, but only scolded us in a gentle way if we needed it. She was really *there* for us. I had just started to appreciate her on a new level. Slumber parties were fun—but so was Grandma Clark!

26.

DRIVING WEEGIE'S CAR

During the summer following my sophomore year in high school, I worked at Jim's Waffle Shop for a short time—starting several weeks before and continuing through the Tri-County Fair and the start of the new school year. It was then that I learned that it was a hangout for young guys who *would drive* in from some of the surrounding towns in search of girls. While I only worked there a short time, I soon met boys from Everest, Powhattan, Willis, Hiawatha, Whiting, Muscotah, and Netawaka.

After school started, I still tried to work at the restaurant in the afternoon and evening after school and on weekends; but I found that I was falling behind in my studies. Being on the Honor Roll had already been established as a tradition my freshman year. Therefore, I decided to give up working at the Waffle Shop—all the while marveling that my friend, Peggy Kallos, daughter of the owner, was able to work there and still keep up with her grades.

Of course, having learned about all the cute boys who came in, I coerced my friends, Bernetta Clarke and Eloise Claunch, to stop in for a *coke* before going home on nights that we went to the library to study. Very few of the guys from the other towns mentioned came to Horton regularly on a school night, but Ralph Rosenhoover and Vernon George (Weegie) from Everest could always be counted on to be there by 8:30 PM just about every night. They were *older boys*. Both of them were out of school. Ralph worked at the hardware store in Everest, but I'm not sure what Weegie did. It must have been a pretty good job though, and a good source of income, because Weegie always had money. Most generally, any girls who would sit with him and Ralph in the second booth would get their *cokes* paid for and could just as easily get a burger, or fries, or a sweet roll if they wanted one.

Neither of these guys was a super great looker, but both were superbly nice. Times were different then, and I don't recall ever being afraid of these guys or having the thought that there might be a problem spending time together if, say, you got into Weegie's car and rode around with him and Ralph. Sometimes there would even be a couple of other guys with them, and maybe there would be as many as four or five girls. All of us would get into Weegie's car and ride around for awhile—listening to music and honking at other cars we passed—all the while laughing and having a really good time. Horton only had the one restaurant open at night and, other than the Liberty Theater and the Library, there really wasn't much for kids there to do. And besides, all of this was innocent fun. That's all any of us was looking for anyway...*a little fun.*

Well, occasionally something did happen where the *fun* turned *stupid.* Let me tell you about my part in this *little adventure . . .*

―――――――――

I believe Weegie's car was a dark blue, 1952 Chevy or Oldsmobile, but it would have been in the fall of 1954 or possibly the spring of 1955 when this incident occurred. I had already had my one driving lesson in Daddy's car, which by all accounts, had been an utter failure. Sometime soon after that, I had told Weegie about it and had then begged him relentlessly to let me drive his car. Eloise had already had a chance to drive his car on a number of occasions; but then, she already had a driver's license. Even Sugie (short for Sugar) Burke had driven his car, and she was several years younger than me.

Finally, one night when we met up at the Waffle Shop, I asked Weegie yet again if he would teach me to drive his car. That night, he finally agreed. He let me drive all around town while sitting next to me in the front seat and even better, with a couple of girls along who could attest to the fact that I had indeed been driving—perhaps it was Bernetta and Sugie enjoying *the tour* while sitting in the backseat with Ralph.

I was proud of my driving because I *clearly* was doing a marvelous job. Weegie said that I probably just needed some highway practice because I obviously wasn't having any difficulty *dodging* parked cars in Horton. He suggested that we drive the seven miles over to Everest. Unfortunately, it was already after nine-thirty, so the other girls opted to go on home. I knew that I really should go on home, too, since Mom and Daddy didn't like me to stay out after ten on a school night; but this was an opportunity that might not ever come again. So, I decided to drive the seven miles to Everest with Weegie and Ralph. Both of them promised we'd be back shortly after 10 PM.

I drove slowly all the way since I didn't have the experience to drive faster. I managed to do well keeping on my side of the road and not weaving too much. When we got to Everest, we saw David Miller and stopped to talk with him for awhile. By the time I thought to look at my watch, I saw that it was almost 11 PM and knew that I was in trouble. I pointed out the time to the boys, and we jumped in the car. Weegie assured me that we would be back in Horton *in about 15 minutes* as he flew south down the road from Everest to the main highway (K-20) that would take us back to Horton.

Without warning, maybe he hit a bump or a rock, or maybe it was the vibration from the road, anyway, his headlights dimmed, flickered a few times, and then went out. Weegie pulled over, grabbed a flashlight, and raised the hood of the car. He and Ralph started looking at various things. Finally, Weegie came to the side of the car and said that the headlights were "Gone!" and I was going to have to drive. He said that if I was going to get home, he would need to sit on one fender and Ralph would sit on the other—each of them using flashlights to see that I didn't go off the road.

What a scary prospect. But because I couldn't think of anything better and because I didn't want to be one of the two needed to sit on the fender, I agreed. And that is exactly what happened. I drove all the way back to Horton at about ten miles per hour with Weegie or Ralph yelling back at me, "A little more to the right!" Or "A little more to the left!" "Careful . . . slow down!" "Pull back left—you're going off the road!"

Now, not one car passed us from either direction the whole way. People often accused the little towns of Horton and Everest of *rolling up the streets* and closing every thing up after 10 PM. At least at that time in history, it was pretty much true. I guess our *little adventure* pretty much proved it.

Eventually, the guys got me home safely—but I had to face Mom and Daddy when I got there. By that time, it was after midnight. They had called Bennie Clarke. They woke him up to find out from Bernetta where I was. They weren't happy with the answer.

When I got home and told Mom and Daddy the rest of what had happened, Daddy said, "*That* is *the dumbest thing* I have ever heard—so I guess it has to be true. But . . . I don't want you to get in the car, or have anything to do with either of those boys again. Anyone that dumb shouldn't be allowed to drive a car."

———————————

Personal Note: I thought Daddy was talking about the boys, but I suppose he included me in that last thought. It was pretty stupid. And I guess that's at least part of why I was 22 before Daddy would let me use his car to take my driver's test—and, even then, he did so reluctantly.

I never did find out how or when Weegie and Ralph got back to Everest, but even Weegie refused to let me drive his car after that. I guess it was something Daddy said.

27.

THE FETAL PIG

I can't remember if it was my sophomore or junior year that I took
Biology. My teacher was a tall, chisel-featured, blond named Mr.
Sensintaffar. Although he was in his mid-twenties, I believe it was his
first year of teaching. He had somehow already attained a German of-
ficer stance and outlook in the classroom. He demanded *control* at all
times. He was there to teach us. There was no laughter. There was no
fooling around. We were in school to learn, and he was there to see that
we did. I'm sure he had a first name, but in his strict aloofness, we never
learned it. He will forever remain "Mr. Sensintaffar" to his former students.

Mr. and Mrs. Sensintaffar went to our church. At that time, I played
the organ for the choir; and when looking down from the pews in the
choir loft, I could see Mr. and Mrs. Sensintaffar come in on Sunday
mornings with their three little children. Mrs. Sensintaffar walked in
first with the baby in her arms. She was followed by a boy and a girl
about two and three. Mr. Sensintaffar was last.

Mrs. Sensintaffar dressed alternately each Sunday in one of two prin-
cess-style dresses—one blue and one a pale peach color. She always
wore a black pill-box hat with veil. The children were dressed neatly in
clothes of the season. Mr. Sensintaffar must have had only one suit, a
navy gabardine with multiple pairs of pants. Not only did he wear the
navy gabardine to Sunday Mass, it was navy gabardine slacks that he
wore to school each day along with a white, long-sleeved shirt and red

bow tie. The white shirt was always very carefully starched and ironed with cuffs folded under in a crisp fold so that no cuffs showed and so his sleeves came midway between his wrist and elbow. (The only other place that I have seen anyone fold their cuffs this way was the engineering staff when I worked at Western Electric years later.)

The Sensintaffars always arrived at the same time each Sunday. Mrs. Sensintaffar knew her role. She must have counted the pews from the back—eight, nine, genuflect, step aside. The boy child went into the pew followed by his mother and the baby. Then the girl child and Mr. Sensintaffar entered the pew.

The adult Sensintaffars never looked to the right or the left but knelt on the padded kneelers for the first 5 minutes or so with heads lowered and deeply involved in prayer. Even at two and three, the children knew all the proper times to stand, or sit, or kneel. Only when Mr. and Mrs. Sensintaffar took the baby and went up for communion did the children look around and cautiously move together to giggle or pinch each other. By the time their parents returned, they were back in their spots with halos intact. The whole process seemed to me to be the model of efficiency and as close to *perfect* as humanly possible.

———————

Now, I tell you that story to tell you this . . . Even today the smell of formaldehyde seems to penetrate my nose as I remember the *fetal* or unborn pig that was my very own to dissect and diagram the various systems—respiratory, circulatory, digestive . . . I had gotten behind in my work. *(Side thought: This phrase always brings to mind one of my Daddy's crazy jokes. "Did you hear about the lady who got a little behind in her work? . . . She sat in a tub of applesauce she was making.")* I hadn't done all the cutting and tracking of the systems. I hadn't done all my diagrams and labels for my lab book. I hadn't taken all the measurements. I had been a bit absent-minded . . . distracted. Imagine that!

Mr. Sensintaffar, being the nice, friendly guy that he was (I'm being facetious, of course.), had let me, and several others who were equally as behind, stay after class at the end of the school day to get all caught up. I was an "A" student who was always on the honor roll so I was frustrated at myself for my reluctance in not moving ahead with the fetal pig.

Most of the other kids who stayed were goof-offs who spent their time in class doing surgery and dissections that had nothing to do with the assignment.

Mr. Sensintaffar had stepped out of the room. Several kids moved to the chemistry lab next door where they turned on a radio stored on the top shelf of a bookcase. It wasn't long before they could be heard dancing to the strains of Bill Hailey and the Comets. Soon after that, Mr. Sensintaffar stepped back into the room and told us we had all *lost our opportunity* by not tending to our work. He said everybody was to clean up and leave. I protested saying that I had accomplished a great deal by not having joined in with the others. I showed him my diagrams and said I only had one thing left to complete. I had not yet measured the long intestine of the fetal pig.

Mr. Sensintaffar relented, "Okay, finish up quickly though."

I began again, but stopped . . . the intestine was all *crinkly and wavy*—leaving me at a loss. "How am I supposed to measure something like that?" I said, pointing to the intestine.

Mr. Sensintaffar handed me a wooden yardstick. "With this," he said.

I took the yardstick from his hand but continued to look at the intestine. Now, how would I measure it if it wasn't crinkled, I thought. So I decided to think about it like a flat ribbon. I'd hold it down with my left thumb on one end laid against the yardstick. Then I'd smooth the ribbon running my right thumb to guide the ribbon across the yardstick until I got to the end. Voila! I'd have my measurement.

So, I tried it. The intestine felt strange and somewhat sticky as I laid it against the yardstick and held it with my left thumb. Mr. Sensintaffar was still standing to my right—watching me. I felt like he was becoming impatient, so I quickly positioned my right thumb and slid it along to the right—attempting to smooth out the crinkly intestine against the yardstick.

Now, from my perspective, it all happened very fast. I was concentrating on the accuracy of my measurement. I had gotten almost to the end of the intestine, being sure to stretch it out tightly against the yardstick. Suddenly, I noticed the loose end of the crinkly intestine on the other side of my right thumb. As I had moved my hand along the yardstick, smoothing out the intestine, the loose end had been moving, twisting, wiggling, and turning wildly. And, much to my chagrin, from the open end of the intestine, a dark brownish liquid had been squirting out—making a circular, swirling spiral design all over Mr. Sensintaffar's crisp, white shirt. There, in unmistakable *brown and white*, I learned a valuable lesson in biology—even unborn fetal pigs have fecal matter in their intestines.

I stopped short. Without thinking, I grabbed a lab sponge and tried to wipe some of the nasty brown liquid off Mr. Sensintaffar's shirt. But, of course, all it did was smear it around. The students who had not yet left started laughing and making howling sounds. Amazingly, without losing a bit of composure, Mr. Sensintaffar simply said, "You may *all* leave now. I'll close up here."

I, along with the others, gathered my things and scurried to get out quickly. As we hurried down the halls, nearly running from the building, the kids started congratulating me on taking some of the starch out of *Mr. Stuffed Shirt*. I tried to tell them it was all an accident that I didn't know was going to happen; but they didn't believe me! All I got back was, "C'mon, you're on the honor roll. We know you know about things like that. It was all a part of your plan. Right?"

By the next morning, I had become a folk hero. Everybody in school knew about the incident. The more I pled ignorance and denied know-ing what would happen, the bigger the laughs and congratulations. But for my part, I just wanted to run back home and never come out again. I figured I'd be off the honor roll forever. Maybe Mr. Barnard, our princi-pal, would even kick me out of school.

———————

My knees trembled as I walked up the stairs to the second floor science lab that next day. There, as always, was Mr. Sensintaffar in his navy gabardine slacks, white crisp shirt, and red bow tie. But this time there was a slight difference. As I walked into the room, he looked me straight in the eye, acknowledging my presence. Then, slowly and de-liberately, he reached over, took a long, black, rubber lab apron off a hook, and started to put it on. The kids howled with laughter; and for the first time, we all saw Mr. Sensintaffar smile.

———————

Personal Note: I learned one other thing in biology. Sensintaffars have teeth.

28.

ENTERTAINMENT, DANCING IN THE AISLES, AND PARTIES

I guess I have always been a bit naïve and gullible, but I didn't know it at the time. I know now, looking back, that when I was in high school and then moved on into the world, I was surprised to learn that many young people didn't feel the same way I felt about life. But I didn't recognize this as my being anything but well-adjusted. I had a good life, and I appreciated it.

When I was growing up in Horton, I felt a real pride in living there—in growing up there. Most of all, however, I felt that I had the very best father and mother that any kid could ever have. I felt Daddy was the smartest person in the world—not necessarily as a result of book learning—but because he was so wise about handling situations at home and in the business world. And Mom, well she was the best cook, a fine artist, and an excellent seamstress. There wasn't any meal she couldn't prepare, any *thing* she couldn't draw, or any dress, suit, or coat she couldn't sew on her sewing machine. Between the two of them, I had a wealth of knowledge just waiting for me to *tap* in response to any problem I might encounter.

Sure, I wanted to drive like all the other kids, but I didn't realize that the way Daddy was handling the situation might be interpreted as mistreatment. He loved me; he wanted me to be safe. Who knew I was being discriminated against, or at least, overprotected? If Darrell knew, he didn't say.

Besides, to pacify me for not letting me drive, Daddy just volunteered to take me and my friends to ballgames, music events, out of town shopping—just about everywhere. Wherever or whenever we wanted to go, he was always willing to load up a bunch of us in his car or truck and take us there. It was a sweet deal!

And it's not like I needed to drive to make friends. Mom and Daddy had already started another tradition long before I got to high school. Our home had always been open to other kids. It didn't matter what time of the day or night—breakfast, lunch, dinner, evening, or even overnight. Whatever made me happy was okay with Mom and Daddy.

I can give you an example of the *open door policy* established by my parents while Darrell and I were still in grade school. We were either *the first family* or *one of the very first families* in Horton to own a television set. This may have been facilitated by Daddy owning an appliance store, *Purcell Radio and Electric*. I can remember vividly that day when Daddy brought home that first TV. I'm sure it was late 1949 or early 1950—within a matter of days, or at most a couple of weeks, WDAF-TV started broadcasting in Kansas City.

Daddy was so excited when he went to Kansas City and picked up the big oval-screened television. Darrell and I were excited, too. Daddy had this great big mirror on a stand that he set up in front of the television so he could check out the picture while making adjustments from the back. We would watch carefully, but all that seemed to come through was *snow*. Occasionally, it would appear that something moved, and Darrell and I would yell, "I think there's something there! I think I see something moving!" But most of the time, all we got was a distorted station logo and a few snowy pictures during their limited broadcast day.

Daddy went to Kansas City, St. Joe, and Topeka and talked with everybody he could find who would talk to him about television. As I mentioned, I believe that WDAF was the first television station to broadcast close enough for us to pick up anything—although they were broadcasting at a power level much lower than today—and, of course, there wasn't anything like cable or satellite dishes to carry the signal. Shortly after that, KFEQ-TV in St. Joe went *on the air*, followed by WIBW-TV in Topeka in 1952.

Daddy soon learned that he was not going to be able to pick up the stations well without putting up an antenna. So he got the best antenna available and put it up on the roof of the house. The antenna was connected to the TV using a long pair of flat wires that ran down the house, through the crawlspace under the house, and then up into the living room. This helped some; we were able to pick up a consistent *snowy* picture that improved sometimes according to the weather and the way the antenna was turned. Daddy spent a lot of time on the roof, adjusting and turning the antenna, until he figured out a way to turn it from the ground.

Of course, Daddy wasn't about to settle for an inferior picture. He had visited some of the television stations and saw the towers that they put up to broadcast their programs. He decided that that was definitely the way to go. Checking with a company that supplied metal tower equipment, Daddy purchased some, had it welded together, attached an antenna to the top part, and then set it upright on the east side of the house. I'm not sure how tall it was, but it must have been at least 50 to 60 feet tall. After a little more time adjusting the new tower antenna, Daddy got it positioned to where we could pick up WDAF, KFEQ, and WIBW. And, as other stations were added in Kansas City and Topeka, we were able to pick up those stations as well. Having television added a whole new dimension to our lives—although there wasn't a great variety of new programming available.

One of the first programs we watched was *Howdy Doody,* but to be honest, I just couldn't quite warm up to Clarabell the Clown. (I think it is interesting that Bob Keeshan, who later gained fame as Captain Kangaroo, was the first Clarabell.) At 12 years old, it was a bit immature for me even at that time. Still, considering the lack of good programming for my age, I must have absorbed more than I thought. I can still remember the opening song that the Peanut Gallery sang when *Buffalo Bob* Smith asked, "What time is it?" The response was, "It's Howdy Doody Time!" Immediately following that was the song:

> It's Howdy Doody Time.
> It's Howdy Doody Time.
> Bob Smith and Howdy, too
> Say "Howdy Do" to you.
>
> Let's give a rousing cheer!
> Cause Howdy Doody's here.

It's time to start the show,
So kids—it's time—let's go."

I don't recall *Howdy Doody* having a serious competitor until 1953 when *Kukla, Fran, and Ollie* came on one of the area stations. I rather took a shine to that big mouth Ollie. He was this nutty dragon puppet who got to deliver the punch line to most of their jokes—usually at his own expense. Whoever did the voice was the *real* nut. It was hilarious!

Sometime around 1952, we would get home from school just in time to watch a forerunner to *Dick Clark's American Bandstand,* which came on several years later. This was a program hosted by another guy out of Philadelphia and was called *Bob Horn's Bandstand.* You won't find that fact on a Trivial Pursuit card.

The early stations spent a lot of time broadcasting old time movies and cowboy shows. Grandma Clark loved these and always came over after school to *babysit us* so she could watch. She, of course, had seen most of the silent movies and cowboy shows before, and she helped us to learn the names and understand the humor. I look back on these moments as really fun times spent with Grandma. This is when Darrell and I first became acquainted with *Laurel and Hardy*, the *Our Gang* group, and *Buster Keaton.*

I especially liked the Saturday night lineup with *The Texaco Star Theatre* starring Milton Berle and *Your Show of Show* with Sid Caesar and Imogene Coca. Carl Reiner was also a regular on that show. There was also a show called *Your Hit Parade* starring Snooky Lanson, but it had a regular cast of singers, including Rosemary Clooney and Bill Hayes. (Yes, George Clooney's aunt and the same Bill Hayes who was later a soap opera star on *Days of Our Lives*.) They did a Top Ten Countdown of the popular songs for that week.

During the evening, there were a number of game show programs, such as *Name that Tune*, and serious *playhouse* performances with well-known actors like Robert Montgomery doing the opening. I think one was called the *Kraft Television Theater.* Grandma always came over to stay with us on Saturday night while Mom and Daddy were up to the store. Sunday night had the *Jack Benny Show,* and in 1951, we all fell in love with that irrepressible redhead, Lucille Ball, as the star of *I Love Lucy.*

Television changed our family and brought us new friends. The Thomas kids across the street used to come home from school just as quickly as possible and *hope* that they didn't miss us—since they went to the Horton Grade School and we went to St. Leo's. As soon as they checked in with their mother, they were on our porch beating on the front door. David and Tommy would lie down on the floor in front of the television when they were watching. I had to constantly remind them, "Get your head down." Gloria and Charlene, their sisters, came over sometimes, but not as much as the boys.

When Mom and Daddy got home at 6:30 or 7:00, Daddy would remind them, "Don't you boys have to go home for supper?" Well, apparently, sometimes they did and sometimes they didn't. I can remember a number of times when Daddy just gave up and brought a plate in to them, too.

During the summer, the rhythm of things changed somewhat. It was light out later, and Borgney Thomas (the kids' mom) would come out on the porch and call them home to eat during the news and before Mom and Daddy got home. Then they would be back watching television before Mom and Daddy got home. If the available programs weren't too interesting, they would go out and play in our yard while we ate. If they were interesting, they would simply stay in the living room gazing intently at the TV. Sometimes they even stayed in the house watching TV when Mom and Daddy called Darrell and me outside to help mow and rake the grass.

Daddy had a unique way of telling the kids that the evening of watching TV or playing at out house was over. "Come get your ice cream cone!" For a number of years, even before television, Daddy had purchased 5 gallon drums of ice cream from a Creamery Truck that delivered to the Locker Plant next door to his store. In the summer he would get two or three 5 gallon drums each week. He would also keep a generous supply of cones on hand. Every night at about 8 o'clock, Daddy would make double and triple-decker ice cream cones for any kid who came to the side door of our house. Some of them came back for seconds. My cousin Kathleen would often come over with Grandma Clark about that time. She liked the ice cream cones—as did Grandma.

Ice cream cones for the neighborhood kids was a practice Daddy had started even before I started school and long before we knew about television. At first it was just Darrell and me and the Hays kids, but later, all the neighborhood kids came by at least part of the time. Daddy continued this practice on into my high school years. Sometimes, he made more than a dozen cones a night to pass out to kids.

I remember one time when we went on vacation to Colorado but had forgotten to tell the Thomas kids we were going. When we got back, David Thomas let the cat out of the bag. "Why didn't you tell us you were going?" he asked. "Grandma Clark wouldn't let us in to watch television with her until after the third day, but she never fixed us an ice cream cone all week!"

During the summer following my sophomore and junior years at high school, I whined quite a bit about Mom and Daddy not letting me go swimming. I mentioned that they would never let me go swimming at the Horton Swimming Pool—a holdover of their fear about Polio. So they finally took pity on me and started a routine of taking a truck load of kids to Mission Lake along with bologna and pickle relish sandwiches, potato chips, cookies or cupcakes, and lots of cold soda pop. Usually, we would take a badminton set and sometimes a crochet set. Later, Bill Tulk and Patsy Baker also took a number of kids out in their older cars. Mom and Daddy fed them all—whoever wanted to come—usually a couple of Sunday afternoons a month.

I must have been a royal pain. I know that Mom accused me of being the *Social Director*—always looking for something to do. That was because there really wasn't anything to do in Horton. There had been a skating rink years earlier, but that was gone. There was the Liberty Movie Theater, but that had only one movie per week and then a separate matinee for kids on Saturday. If you had seen that one movie, what were you going to do? Of course, there was the Library, but some of the boys wouldn't be caught dead going into the Library and a lot of other kids didn't read books like I did in the summer. There was no Teen Town for us to get together and dance. There was Jim's Waffle Shop, but Mr. Kallos was running a business, and you can only suck on that straw so many times and the glass gets empty. And we were much too old to sit on the wooden floor of Cook's Variety Store and read all the comic books. So what was left; what were we to do?

It was the summer after my junior year when the natives got restless. Girls and boys were getting tired of walking up and down the street.

Riding in cars could only take you so far when making the U-turn a block west of Four Corners and then making another U-turn at 10th and Central in front of Eloise Claunch's house. "Yup! Still there," I'd say. "Go around again?" she'd say.

It was a Friday night when Daddy stopped Eloise in the long procession of cars. "Get out of there, Deanna," he said. "You need to get in the car with us now. It's time to go home." Griping under my breath, I reluctantly got into the car with Mom and Daddy. He didn't go directly home, however. Instead he stopped by his store to *check* everything as he did every night. While he was inside, Eloise pulled her car up next to us, as did several other cars. I, along with kids from the other cars, got out and started talking. More and more cars arrived. Finally, there must have been 25 to 30 kids in front of the store.

Seeing all those kids must have inspired Daddy somehow that night. He turned the lights on in the store and out front. Then he called several boys to come in and help him. About 5 or 6 went in. As we watched, Daddy had them help him push the refrigerators, and washers and dryers back from the center of the store—making a large open area there on the wooden floor. Then he dragged out his huge amplifiers. The city borrowed them each year for the Tri-County Fair. Daddy hooked one up inside and set the other one outside. Then he attached one of his microphones. Within minutes, kids were *spinning 45's* (45 rpm records) on the *hi fi* record player and taking turns acting as the DJ. We were dancing to some really good music—all thanks to Daddy's early version of *surround sound."*

It must have been about 9 o'clock when we started, and we kept it up until about 11 PM. There were probably about 30 kids there at one point. Mr. Fairbanks came over to see what was going on and told Daddy, "John, you're a lot braver than I am." While he was there, his stepson, Jerry Brown, and Loyal (Rick) Torkelson came by, but although Jerry got out and joined in, Loyal must have thought we were too immature and went on.

Now, I know those huge speakers made a lot of noise, but that was all part of the fun. I can't speak for others, but I had a terrific time. Daddy said that the next day, he had several people comment on the Friday night activities. Glenn Hybskmann came by the store and commented that he had heard the music all the way up to his house on West

15th Street. He congratulated my Dad for trying to do something *nice for the kids.*

Later, Rollie Wallingford, who was now Chief of Police (he had been a deputy for my grandfather), came by and told my Dad that there had been several complaints, and he would have to cite my dad for being a public nuisance if he did it again. Rollie was very apologetic about it, but said that the complaints had gone directly to Mayor Askren.

Daddy promised to cut down on the noise, but repeated that night's events on the next two Friday nights. Daddy lowered the volume and kept the speakers on inside the store only. The Saturday after the third time, Rollie came in again. He said the mayor told him that Daddy would have to stop since he wasn't licensed to provide a dance hall. So ended our *Teen Town* at Daddy's store.

Almost immediately, I tried to come up with something else to keep us occupied and off the streets. In the fall of 1955, during the first few months of our senior year, I had parties at my house on Saturday nights. Whoever wanted to come was invited. I have photos and know that Bob Schuetz, Sue Haas, Carol Thompson, Joanne Banning, Patsy Baker, Jim Banning, Bill Tulk, Ralph Spence, and Harold Morris were regulars. Bernetta Clarke, Chuck Schecher, Peggy Kallos, Jerry Brown, Dan Hybskmann, Sandy Tinsley, Jerry McGuffin, Joe Edmonds, Sugie Burke, and several others were there at least once. Mom made chocolate chip cookies; and we had potato chips and dip, sandwiches, veggies, pop, and other snacks. My parents always politely footed the bill for the hungry masses.

Sometime before Christmas, a number of the kids discovered *The Hilltop*, a dance hall/beer joint in Atchison. I'm not sure whether there was supposed to be a minimum age for admittance, but several people older than us were always available to take my classmates to Atchison and get them in. My parents would never let me go there when I was in high school, and they didn't really want me to go, even several years later, when I was in college. Therefore, that's one experience I never had. My parties were obviously too tame, so *The Hilltop* won out and my parties came to an unceremonious end.

My parents had not allowed me to *date* until I was sixteen. By that time, I was disappointed because most of the guys I knew were *just friends* where a number of us hung out together, but no formal dates. I did go to the Junior Prom with Gary Bottorff and went to the Senior Prom with George Tollefson. Both of these guys were very nice, sweet young men.

Sometime during my junior and senior years, I did have an occasional date with several guys from some of the surrounding towns. I remember dating several guys from Whiting, Powhattan, and Everest. But dating back then must have been much different than today. I remember these guys as being as bashful and awkward as I felt.

Interestingly, I seemed to have a knack for coming across guys who were in the service—or maybe after dating me, they decided to join the service. I always seemed to meet them just several days before they had to report to boot camp or a new base. They invariably wanted someone to write to them—to keep them in touch with home. I remember I wrote to a *George* from Everest (not my husband George) for about a year—going through mail call periods of feast and famine. He had asked me to write every day, but sometimes I wouldn't hear from him for weeks at a time. Then, I would suddenly start getting letters from him every day for about 30 or 60 days. I found out later that the increase in mail frequency was because he was in the stockade, where he didn't have anything else to do but write letters. It took me almost a year to wise up. By that time, I had 5 long distance relationships going on at one time, 5 class rings, and no one to go out with on a Saturday night. Still, in hindsight, I'm not sure who was *conning* whom.

During my senior year, I started dating *Bob* (no, not Bob Schecher) who had just returned from the Army. He had completed 3 years and was back to farm with his father in Effingham. What a good looking guy! So mature and focused. He knew just what he wanted to do with his life. He was 23 years old and he wanted to find a girl and get married. Right off, he scared Mom and Daddy to death. They were afraid I would quit school and get married to this nice, stable, down-to-earth guy. Not to worry, however. Bob would ask to take me to the Saturday night or Sunday night movie and then show up wearing flannel shirts with the sleeves rolled up and his red long-sleeved underwear showing from his wrist to his elbow. For some reason, I looked at his outfit and his muddy boots and started picturing us living in Elsie's house. Bye, bye, Bobby! I was so fickle back then.

Shortly after this, I had several dates with Ronnie Thonen and Mike Shannon from Muscotah. They were both terrifically nice young men. Through them, I met Charles Hittle. By that spring, I was engaged to him so didn't really concern myself with *trivial matters* like not getting to *The Hilltop*. I plan to tell you more about Chuck in Book Two. For now, let me just say he was tall and very nice looking with dark auburn hair and a nice smile. He definitely turned out to be one of the *frogs I kissed*—possibly even a toad.

Personal Note: Mom and Daddy did their utmost to give me a good childhood and protect me from the *evil* world outside. Maybe they did too much. Maybe that is why I always look for the good in people and find it difficult to believe when I get scammed. Maybe that is why to this day I am naïve and gullible. But protect me they did, and I saw very little of the bad, *the evil of this world*. That is about to change. I am about to go out into the world where my parents cannot protect me. I am about to be *enlightened.*

29.

TOP PRIORITY—GETTING EVEN

My Grandmother Campion, Daddy's mother, was nothing like my picture of what a grandmother should be. She was nothing like the gentle, caring, comfortable grandmothers that are the subject of poems. She was nothing like my Grandmother Clark, who babysat her grandchildren on a regular basis and sometimes had all six of us at her house at one time. Grandma Campion did wear an apron, but she didn't have a nice comfortable lap to sit on. That lap only seemed to be reserved for *Snooks* or *Betsy* or whoever her current dog happened to be. Grandma was not a warm and cuddly person. She was not a hugger, or a kisser, or a patter. There was an aloofness that she seemed to exhibit—almost a coldness. I did not penetrate this hard shell until I was going to college, and I was only allowed in at that time for a brief moment. I look back now, and I see that this was an unfortunate loss for both of us. But, rather than dwelling on that loss, I want to tell you about some of my memories, good and bad, of Grandma Campion.

Grandma ruled the roost from her perch in the northern part of Horton. She had control of her three sons from the time of their childhood on into their adult lives. Uncle James and Uncle Joe managed to leave Horton, but being in St. Joe and Topeka respectively, they were still within calling, or rather *beckoning* distance, and were expected to make regular trips to Horton to talk farm business or take care of their mother's needs.

Uncle James' family usually came to Horton on Sundays every two to three weeks, and Uncle Joe usually brought his family to Horton every 4 to 6 weeks while living in Topeka.

It was Daddy who was really saddled with the majority of the responsibility. We lived right there in Horton, and Grandma was constantly calling him and wanting him to *drop everything* at his store to take care of her business. This ranged all the way from "go to the grocery store and get me a bottle of milk" to "close your store and take me to one of my farms." During the spring and summer months, Daddy averaged one trip a week to Grandma's farms.

Heaven forbid if anything was done to irritate or upset Grandma Campion. She was the world's best at *getting even.* Sometimes she would warn you that she intended to get even, but, at other times, she would just catalog it away—waiting for an opportunity to get even at some later date. If she needed to, she would wait years to get even. But, needless to say, at some time/some place in the future, she would find a way to get her pound of flesh.

Because of the responsibility Daddy felt toward Grandma, he and Mom were never allowed to go out of town to the wholesale houses in St. Joe or Topeka without taking Grandma along. It didn't matter that Daddy just wanted to buy more merchandise for his store. Grandma always had other plans and went along. Of course, going to Kansas City was a different story. Grandma Campion didn't have a son to see in Kansas City, so Daddy had a *loophole* to exploit when he needed it.

Most of the time, Darrell and I would be in school when they took these trips. At noon, we would walk home as usual and Grandma Clark would have prepared our lunch. Then we would go to her house after school and wait for hours until Mom and Daddy would finally get home. Grandma Campion usually went along under the pretense of *shopping* downtown (which she did); but the real reason these trips took so long was she always insisted on going by to see James or Joe afterward. It didn't matter if everyone was done shopping by 1 PM, Grandma made Daddy wait until James or Joe got home from work so she could go to their home and *talk and talk and talk.*

Many times, Grandma would call Daddy on the phone late at night and tell him she had to go over to St. Joe to talk something over with James. She'd keep badgering him until he would finally take her that next day. Then when James got off work, Grandma would *talk and talk and talk* until it might be midnight or 1 AM before they finally got home. Darrell and I would be waiting by the window at Grandma Clark's house, watching for them to get home so we could go to bed—peacefully— knowing they had made it back safely.

Mom often told the story about the one and only time they went to St. Joe without taking Grandma. Daddy had been talking to Bill and Bertha Yates, and they wanted to buy a lot of new appliances and furniture for their house. Daddy offered to take them to several places in St. Joe and get what they wanted. On the designated day, Daddy, Mom, Bill and Bertha went to St. Joe to Wyeth Hardware and several other places. They bought what they wanted and then all went out to dinner. Before returning, Daddy also stopped at American Electric to buy some radio and appliance parts. For Daddy, this last stop would have been like a young child who gets to visit Santa's Workshop—and without his mother!

That's where Mom would end her story, but that's not the whole story. The next time Mom, Daddy, and Grandma went to St. Joe, Darrell and I were along. Grandma insisted on going out to see James per the usual practice. Well, we weren't through the door to his house more than 5 minutes when James asked why Grandma had not come along on the last trip Mom and Daddy had made to St. Joe. He even named the date. Apparently, someone over at American Electric had run into James and had told him that his brother had come by the store. Hearing this news, Grandma was angry. When she heard Bill and Bertha Yates had come in *her place,* Grandma was livid! She yelled at Daddy like there was no tomorrow (for him). She said that he had *no right* to take "those people" to St. Joe without taking her. Finally, when she had finished berating him, she told Daddy, "All right, old boy, I'll get even with you!"

Now I don't know when or where the *getting even* with my father took place, but I'm *sure as the sun rises in the East* positive it happened. And even though her threat was clearly directed at Daddy, I'm sure Grandma included Mom in it as well.

———————

Grandma always managed to *dump* as much as she could on my mother. Whenever there was to be a big dinner of any kind, whether holiday or special event, Grandma always managed to rope my mother into preparing the meal. I remember when I was about 6 or 7 years old, our relatives, Dr. Bill English, his wife Evelyn, and son Billie Dan from Texarkana, Texas, came into town to visit Evelyn's sister, Mrs. Eubelaker at Everest. Grandma called Mom to say that *someone* needed to have them over for dinner because the English family had been so good to Daddy back in late 1927 and 1928 when he went to Texas to work. As Grandma continued to talk, Mom learned that the dinner had already been scheduled at our house for that night, and Mom was expected to prepare it. Oh, and by the way, Joe and Agnes were also in town; they would be bringing Grandma down to dinner. Mom had about five hours to plan a menu, buy food, and prepare a meal for 12 people.

I can only remember one time that Grandma's plan didn't work out. And I'm sure there was payback of some kind for that *failure* as well. I remember it was a Sunday that also happened to be New Year's Eve. Grandma's brother, Will Crick, and his wife, Lena, lived somewhere down around Effingham. It was their 50th Wedding Anniversary. Will and Lena had planned a reception at their house for that afternoon. Now, Grandma had been after Mom and Daddy to take her to the reception for several weeks. She had been told that they would take her, but that they had something else planned for that evening so they would need to go early and get back just before dark. Grandma had agreed to this arrangement—at least verbally she had agreed.

Then on the designated day, Grandma called just about the time my parents were planning to leave. She said that she had been on the phone with James and that he, Gertrude and the kids were coming over. Grandma had decided to wait and go with them instead. Mom and Daddy reminded Grandma that they had another commitment that evening, and they needed to go on ahead so they could get back early. Grandma Campion asked if Darrell and I were going, and Daddy told her, "No." He told her that we were going to Grandma Clark's house until they got back.

Mom and Daddy went on ahead to Uncle Will and Aunt Lena's. Darrell and I went over to Grandma Clark's house. Roger, Duane, and Kathleen were there to play with—so we were set.

About an hour and a half later (around 2 PM), there was a knock on Grandma's door. When Grandma Clark opened the door, there stood Terry and Francie. Uncle James was just driving off with Aunt Gertrude and Grandma Campion. We found out later that Grandma had told James that "Johnnie doesn't think the reception is a place for the children, so he thinks they should be left at home with Neta's mother (Grandma Clark)."

Grandma Clark was shocked, but of course, there was no way to turn the kids away. She was working to prepare some food for the dinner that was planned for six o'clock that evening at my Uncle Alfred's house. He was making Oyster Stew for our New Year's Eve get together. Mom had already made a Jell-O fruit salad and an applesauce cake to take. In addition to the stew, Grandma was also preparing several other food contributions to help make the evening *special.*

The reception was only supposed to be from 1 until 4 PM. Apparently, Mom and Daddy got there around 1:30, but Grandma, James, and Gertrude didn't get there until around 3 PM. My parents asked about Terry and Francie and were told that they had been dropped off for my Grandma Clark to babysit them. Hearing this news, Mom and Daddy said their "goodbyes" and left before 4 PM—telling Grandma again that they had to get back because they were invited out to dinner at the Hays' home. Aunt Gertrude later told us that Grandma Campion had been discounting Mom's story, "Oh, she's just telling us that. Everybody always goes to Neta's for holiday dinners, so we'll just wait until they have time to get started, and then we'll stop by and eat with them when you go in to pick up the kids." Grandma thought she had it all figured out.

At almost 6 PM, nobody had arrived to pick up Francie and Terry. With no place else for them to go, we took them with us and went up to Uncle Alfred's house. Aunt DeVere stomped around a little bit because *those kids* were there when they weren't invited. Mom apologized, but it didn't seem to help. Dinner was delayed as Mom and Aunt DeVere became more and more agitated.

I never did like Oyster Stew, so that wasn't what I felt I was missing. In fact, I was starting to feel a little queasy from all the little oyster-shaped crackers that Roger and I had been sneaking from the bowl at the corner of the table. No, I wanted to dip into the vegetable tray and the deserts, but they were either in the refrigerator or sitting out on the cabinet on the back porch—staying cool.

Darrell had found some left-over Christmas candy and was munching on mint drops covered with chocolate. Kathleen had unwrapped a candy cane from off the tree and was as happy as a lark. Roger, having abandoned me to the crackers, was now standing with Duane in the living room by the front windows. The two of them were now in the midst of a verbal battle with Terry and Francie. Terry had made the comment, "Is this all you have to play with?" For Roger, those were *fightin' words!* Duane didn't think they needed to explain anything to anybody when Francie jumped into the war of words, behind Terry. Those two, Terry and Francie, could hold their own with any verbal combatant—regardless of age or size. Junior got tired of the waiting and all the noise, so he left to go *someplace quieter* in the house. Grandpa Clark sat in the big arm chair trying to give the impression that he was listening to a program on the radio—but he may have been cat-napping.

At about 7:15, Uncle James pulled up in front of the Hays' house. All three adults, Uncle James, Aunt Gertrude, and Grandma, got out of the car and started up to the front door. I had been looking out the front window and announced their arrival to the adults inside. "They're here!" Daddy grabbed Terry and Francie and helped them into their coats as quickly as he could—ushering them out into the vestibule just as the doorbell rang. Daddy opened the door and virtually pushed Terry and Francie out onto the porch. I was hanging out the door from the living room into the vestibule—waiting for the *fireworks* to begin. Mom had come to the door because she didn't know if Daddy would stand up to his mother. She said, "I'm sorry, but I can't invite you in to dinner; this is not my house and not my dinner party." Grandma had no other recourse other than to retreat back to the car. But you could tell by the look on her face, she was *not happy!*

Aunt Gertrude told the story for years following. She said Grandma got into the car swearing to *get even* with Neta for setting her up. Aunt Gertrude said that they went back up to Grandma's house, and it was clear that Grandma had only planned on one thing, Mom being *the pigeon to* prepare the meal that night. Grandma didn't have any food in the house except for a package of frozen wieners and a loaf of bread. Aunt Gertrude would later say she enjoyed those wieners more than *any banquet she ever attended* because she just loved the thought that someone just might be getting one over on my grandmother.

Although I'm sure it was purely unintentional on my Mom's part, there was a certain sense of *justice* associated with that occasion. In life, however, that isn't always true. Sometimes irony isn't very funny.

———————

Uncle James died on December 10, 1956. Terry was a junior at KU, and I believe Francie was going to college in St. Joe. I was just finishing up my secretarial course at Clark's Business School in Topeka. My parents had taken Grandma over to St. Joe to help make the funeral arrangements. Mom said that on the way back from St. Joe, Grandma had told her, "I expect we are going to have to have a dinner for those coming from St. Joe to the cemetery." While services were to be held in St. Joe, Uncle James was to be buried at St. Leo's Cemetery in Horton. Grandma said that she didn't have a large enough house and that she had to go to the farm the following day, so she wouldn't have time to prepare a meal. "Neta, you'll just have to do it." Mom said that Grandma talked like she would at least be helping her out some, by making a number of dishes for the dinner.

I rode the bus back up from Topeka the next day. When I got there, I walked up the street from the bus station to Daddy's store. Mom was watching the store while Daddy had taken Grandma to one of the Effingham farms. Mom was almost in a panic. She said that she had been cooking all morning but had not gotten everything done. She asked me to go help Grandma Clark who was at our house doing some vacuuming and dusting. She asked me to clean the bathroom, fold the clothes in the dryer, and, if I had time, bake a cake.

As usual, Grandma Campion had done a lot of talking, and it was late when she and Daddy got back to town. Mom had closed and locked up the store at 5 PM and came home. I had been able to get everything done that she and Grandma had asked, but I still remember hearing her in the kitchen after I had gone to bed. She couldn't sleep so she was still cooking.

We got up early the next morning to go to the funeral in St. Joe. After the Mass, a large number of people drove to Horton for the graveside services. When these services were over, Grandma Campion announced that relatives and friends were to come down to Neta's house for a buffet lunch. We rushed back to get to the house to try to get things set up.

When we got home, we were glad to see Grandma Clark was already there to help get us started.

It wasn't long before the house was full of people—many of whom I didn't know and I'm sure my parents didn't know them either. Mom had prepared and sliced two large hams. She had made a huge bowl of her great potato salad and both baked beans and green beans made with bacon and onions. She had prepared two kinds of Jell-O fruit salad, and she made three dozen dinner rolls. Daddy had gotten a big block of longhorn cheese which was cut into slices. There was a relish tray of carrots, olives, and celery; and there were two huge bowls of potato chips and corn chips. For desserts, Mom had made two pans of frosted brownies, and I had baked and frosted that cake. Mom thought that, with the several dishes Grandma had said she was going to prepare, that would be enough.

At the graveside services, when Mom had asked Grandma if she needed to have Daddy take her up to her house to get the food she was bringing, she said she had left *it* in the back of our car—one measly loaf of bread that was partially soggy from being taken out of her freezer. The only other person to bring any food was Aunt Agnes, Uncle Joe's wife, who brought a roast chicken that unfortunately had shriveled a bit after being taken out of the oven.

When we had rushed down to the house to start setting out the buffet, Grandma said she wanted to talk with some of the people there at the cemetery. She said that she would ride with her niece, Elsie, and come down as soon as she had time to talk to a few people who wouldn't be coming to the house for dinner.

As I mentioned, mourners and well-wishers started arriving immediately, as soon as we got back to the house. In fact, several cars were actually parked in front of the house when we arrived. It seemed almost instantaneous that people were sitting or standing and talking all over the inside of the house—spilling out onto the front porch, sitting on the porch rails and swings. . . most of this latter crowd were smokers. Neither Mom nor Daddy smoked, and they really didn't like people to smoke inside our house.

Aunt Gertrude and family had arrived. She was feeling pretty bad, and you could see that she was somewhat unsteady. Mom had her go into their bedroom to lie down; my bedroom was already piled high with coats.

A brother and wife of my other grandmother, Grandma Clark, lived in St. Joe. They, my Uncle Glenn and Aunt Hazel Setzer, had gone to the funeral in St. Joe and then come on to Horton for the graveside services. They knew my Uncle James and even though not related, they had planned their day out of respect for Uncle James and Daddy. They were some of the later ones to arrive from the cemetery.

Most people were milling around, hesitant to eat because Grandma Campion had not yet arrived. Uncle Glenn told my Daddy that we should go ahead and have everyone eat because he had heard Grandma tell someone that, "Today is Merchant's Drawing Day and they're having a big cash prize," so she and Elsie were going to go downtown first to see if their names were called.

Everybody was told to get started eating. Within a relatively short period of time, a large portion of food had been consumed with gusto. Over the next couple hours, people started to drift away, leaving only Mom, me, Grandma Clark, Aunt Hazel and Uncle Glenn. Aunt Gertrude and family had gone back to St. Joe. Uncle Joe and family had gone up to the Winklebauers. Darrell had left to go up to Jerry Claunch's house. Daddy had gone up to the store—since he had not been there much for several days. He had missed the Merchant's Drawing even though he was supposed to be one of the host merchants. Grandma and Elsie had never shown up at the house.

Grandma Clark and Aunt Hazel helped clear off what was left on the buffet in the dining room, and together we washed and dried the dishes and silver. Mom carefully counted all her good silver and put it in its mahogany chest as she always did. The Jell-O salads and cake were gone—as was the baked beans and the green beans.

What little there was in the way of leftovers was carefully wrapped and put into the refrigerator. Mom wrapped the remaining few slices of ham in wax paper, put a rubber band around them, and put them in the refrigerator. The remaining potato chips were dumped back into their original bag and these too were closed with a rubber band. (Mom always saved rubber bands on the kitchen door knob.) About twenty slices of Longhorn cheese remained. It was carefully laid out on a Styrofoam tray and put into the refrigerator. Mom also put the remaining potato salad into two empty cottage cheese containers which then went with the rest of the perishables into the refrigerator. There were only 2 rolls remaining out of the 3 dozen she had made and 3 or 4 slices of bread from the loaf of bread Grandma had sent. These were put back into the original Rainbow bread wrapper with yet another rubber band around the top. The bag was left on the table, along with the three remaining brownies, which were wrapped before leaving them on the table. (Mom always believed in re-using things that were there, and only throwing away things when they are no longer useful. Yes, there was always a pile of aluminum pie pans, egg cartons, and white Styrofoam meat trays—just waiting in the utility room to be used for just such an occasion.)

Grandma Clark offered to stay and help clean up in the living room, but Mom said she was exhausted and needed to lay down for awhile. Grandma, Uncle Glenn, Aunt Hazel, and I went next door to Grandma's house to visit—hoping that Mom would get some rest. About an hour later, around 5 PM, when Grandma and I walked out to the car with Glenn and Hazel as they were leaving, we spotted Grandma Campion and Elsie getting into Elsie's car. They were each carrying one of those large, clear plastic bags with handles and large flowers printed on the sides. That was a type of bag that was popular at that time. I remember the type of bag because it allowed me to see that each of them had their own cottage cheese containers and other wrapped items stuffed into her bag.

As soon as Glenn and Hazel left, Grandma and I went back into our house. Mom was still lying on the bed. "Did you know that Grandma and Elsie were here," I asked.

"I know," Mom said. "They tiptoed over to the doorway and looked in, but I just stayed here quiet as a 'possum. I heard them get into the refrigerator. Did they get themselves something to eat?"

"Yeh, I think so," was the only reply I could muster.

Mom got off the bed and came into the kitchen as we began to take inventory. The ham was gone. The potato salad was gone. The potato chips were gone. The tray we had used to lay out the Longhorn cheese was sitting on the table next to the roll of waxed paper—empty. All of the cheese had mysteriously disappeared. The bread and rolls were gone. And there wasn't even one little crumb of the brownies that had been left on the table. "What are *we* gonna *eat*?" Mom lamented.

On further inspection, a can of crushed pineapple, two packages of oleo, and some Jell-O from previous meals were all missing. There was also a third cottage cheese container that actually contained cottage cheese—that was missing. A refrigerator that had been jam-packed several hours earlier was now almost bare.

Mom walked into the living room and plopped down in Daddy's chair. She never sat in Daddy's chair! She laid her head back on the chair and closed her eyes. "Old Witch," she said. "She stole our supper!"

Mom kept most of this to herself for years. It took a series of seemingly unrelated events to bring it all back up again . . .

When the Dr. Seuss books came out, Mom read many of them to her grandchildren: Stacey, Jona, Shawn, and Dan, at the time. When she read the story of *The Grinch That Stole Christmas* to them, she commented about how the story was very much like the time when Grandma Campion came and cleared out our refrigerator. Then the year the story came out as a TV special, Mom watched intently with the kids. She started getting really excited when they got to the part about the Grinch not leaving a crumb big enough for a mouse. "That's her! That's her!" she'd exclaim.

"Not *her*, Grandma! The Grinch is a boy so it can't be her," Shawn admonished.

"Not in Horton," Mom replied. "Not in Horton."

Each year after that, usually starting at Thanksgiving Dinner, Mom would retell the story about Grandma taking all the food. And when she sat down with the grandchildren to watch the special again, she would get very animated, loudly proclaiming, "See that look on the Grinch. I know that look. That's the same look I saw over and over again on Grandma Campion's face." Then she would tell the story all over once again—ending with, "All she contributed was a loaf of bread, and she didn't even leave us a crumb to eat for our supper!"

Personal Note: I realize that the above stories don't paint my Grandmother Campion in a very good light. She had some admirable qualities; such as, being honest in all business dealings, always honoring a pledge or a promise, being a hard worker all her life, and in her own way loving her children. She also had some other qualities that made it almost impossible to warm up to her.

When I was almost twenty-one, I learned some things about her and her childhood that helped me understand her. Therefore, I came to accept her and even love her to an extent. I can't excuse her for some of the things she did, but I accept the fact that she was the product of what had happened to her, and she was what she was because that is what she had learned to do in order to survive. But that is another story, one I'll save for Book Two. I guess you'll just have to wait for my second 20 years to find out more about Grandma Campion.

30.

A CHRISTMAS TRADITION

It seems that my family never wasted an opportunity to get together. And there were certain traditions established for every holiday—things that were done religiously—almost as rituals every year. Some of these events seem to run together, year after year, to where it becomes difficult to remember if I was five, or ten, or even twenty when *something* occurred. But I don't look upon that as being anything bad. Having family traditions for events is something safe for a child, something to look back on, and sometimes, something to carry forward as I have done with my children, and now my grandchildren.

Christmas was always my favorite holiday. For the eight years that I was a young student at St. Leo's Grade School, the Christmas Season always started just after Thanksgiving—when the nuns began planning our annual Christmas play. That was always a major event, keeping the children busy learning songs of the season, practicing parts for the plays (given out specifically for each of the classrooms), and learning solo parts (if you were one of the lucky ones). For my mother, this usually meant making me wings to be an angel or sewing up some other kind of special costume for me to wear. Oh, and Darrell needed a costume, too—a shepherd, a tree, or a rock, I think; something easy! A bag of potatoes . . . maybe? No, that was St. Patrick's Day. Superman? Now, that's another story. It comes in Book Two. But I digress . . .

Father Jerome Twomey was the jolly old priest in Horton from the time I started school until after I had graduated from college. He was a transplant from Ireland, arriving in the United States as a young priest, and coming to the Midwest because he had a sister, Rose O'Donnell, who lived in the Kansas City area. At Father's insistence, the whole school always put on performances at Christmas and again at St. Patrick's Day, which, of course, a good Irishman couldn't let pass—not without hosting "a banquet ever so grand as to properly celebrate St. Paddy's Day!"

In the first grade, I got to be an angel with a solo number singing *Away in a Manger.* From that point on, I was hooked. I always had a major role in each production, and I even looked forward in anticipation to the next program. As for the last minute jitters, the butterflies in the stomach, and the feelings of stage fright I experienced, well, they just went along with the territory.

Father Twomey always had a major role, too—especially at the Christmas program where he dressed up like Santa Claus. At approximately 5' 2", he had the perfect body for it and didn't need any padding. He had a deep voice and a laugh that sounded just like what Santa *should* sound like. His white hair, pale complexion and rosy pink cheeks also lent themselves well to the role. And above all else, he truly had the Christmas Spirit—singing all the Christmas Carols with gusto in his beautiful Irish brogue.

Father loved handing out presents and bags of candy to the children, but he especially loved listening to their Christmas wishes as they were whispered into his ear. It was reputed that those whispered words did not go unheeded. Often children whose parents did not have the means by which to satisfy their wishes, later found that by Christmas Eve, *Santa* really had heard and responded. Yes, it helped to be Catholic in Horton if you wanted an audience with Santa, but all children were welcome. A large number of protestant children seemed to show up each year at our Christmas Program, and they, too, received little presents, bags of candy, and a chance to whisper in Santa's ear. Father Twomey may have had his quirks, but he was a good man and a good priest.

Christmas morning always started out the same way—with Mass. Although we heard a lot about Midnight Mass, we never got to go when we were children. Mom and Daddy never thought we would be able to stay awake until it was over. I think I was in high school and singing in the choir before I went to a Midnight Mass for the first time.

As I started to tell you, Christmas morning always started with us going to 6 AM Mass. We usually got up about 5 AM to have time to dress and take a peek at what Santa Claus had left for us. What a chore it was for us to leave the house at about 5:30 AM and not play with our new toys from Santa. Of course, given our early morning schedule, I don't think Mom and Daddy ever got much sleep on Christmas Eve. Daddy usually spent most of the night helping Santa put our toys together after we went to bed, and Mom sometimes wrapped presents until well after midnight.

Mom usually saw to it that we were bathed and had our dress clothes laid out the night before. But, of course, jumping out of bed and into those clothes was the last thing we wanted to do. We wanted to turn the light on in the living room and see what Santa had left us. Usually it was in two piles—each on opposite ends of the couch or one on Daddy's big chair and one on the couch. There was never any difficulty in determining which pile belonged to me. Santa left unwrapped presents, and Darrell didn't get dolls and other girl's stuff. He got the stinky old *boy toys*.

Santa also left lots of candy and nuts on the dining table. I especially liked the chocolate stars and peanut clusters. Like a magnet, I was always drawn to that table. I'd jump out of bed and be there in a flash! My hands would reach out instinctively to pick up a star or a cluster. I'd have it almost into my mouth when I would hear Mom yell at me from her bedroom, "Deanna! Remember . . . you can't eat anything since you are going to Communion." This was at a time when, as a Catholic, you had to be fasting from Midnight the night before to go to Communion the next morning. It wasn't so bad if you went to a 6 or 8 AM Mass, but Mom said it was probably pretty rough on the *old drunks* who couldn't make it to Mass until 11 o'clock.

So there I was—a statue with a piece of candy in my hand. How did Mom know? Did she have radar? Darn it all; it wouldn't have been a sin if I had eaten it because I had forgotten. But I couldn't eat it now, could I? That would be a sin. And I didn't want to commit a sin on Christmas. Still, Baby Jesus wouldn't care if I just took a little lick, would he? Do you suppose Mom ever figured out that some of those distorted stars and clusters looked that way because I had taken several little licks? Nah!

It always felt good to go out into the crisp Christmas morning air. Since it was so early, it was almost invariably cold enough that my nostrils stuck together when I sucked in my first few breaths after going outside. If there was any snow, then it made that crunching sound as the first people walked across it in the morning. I liked walking around the side of the house to the back and looking down by our detached garage to see the headlights shine against the garage door as Daddy sat waiting nervously while warming up the car. Occasionally, it would be snowing softly, and it would look so beautiful and clean as it came down in front of the headlights. It seemed to be an early predictor of the gentle beauty that would be there for the rest of the day.

There was only one damper on the day ahead—Grandma Campion. Although 6 AM Mass was a Low Mass and only lasted about 35 minutes, it was always at least 7:30 before we would get back home. We had to stop by and pick up Grandma Campion and take her with us to Mass— every Sunday and Holy Day. The *picking up* didn't take that long, but getting her back out of the car and into her house always seemed to take forever. Dropping her off was a major ordeal. Even though she knew that we were going to see her again later that day, she always seemed to have something that was so urgent that she needed to talk with Daddy about it *now*.

By the time we got home, Mom and Daddy almost had to harness us—we were so anxious to get in the house to play with our Christmas toys and eat enough of that candy to make ourselves sick. We traditionally didn't open our wrapped presents until Christmas afternoon—after our big dinner. But our presents from Santa were *fair game* from the moment we got back after Mass.

Mom always put the turkey on to roast while Daddy prepared a big Christmas breakfast. This was when he invariably cooked too much bacon, made a huge stack of buttered toast, and fried up a batch of *yucky eggs* in the leftover bacon grease. *Nobody wanted to eat.* We were full of candy and nuts! But we had to sit diligently at the table for awhile and pretend to *jab* at things. It's a wonder Darrell and I didn't barf just thinking about all that chocolate mixing with the bacon grease and globs of oleo on the toast. I'm feeling a bit nauseous even now.

Our early holiday dinners were held at Grandma Clark's; but by the time I was 7 or 8, Mom and Daddy started hosting most of them at our house. Mostly this was because our house, especially our dining room, was bigger. Mom always put an extra leaf or two in her table, but sometimes there still wasn't enough room. Then *we kids* had to eat in the kitchen. Most years there were at least 6-8 adults and 6 children. No holiday would ever have been complete without the Hays family and Uncle Alfred's mixed green or Jell-O salads.

Most of the rest of the meal was the same, year after year. Two big roasting hens were on the menu for many years until Mom starting getting a 20 to 22 lb. turkey. First Grandma Clark, and then later Mom, would prepare homemade noodles the day before and leave them setting out on the kitchen table to dry overnight. The noodles would be cooked the next day by dropping them into a pot of boiling, diluted turkey drippings. This is a practice that I have continued down through the years. My kids and their families look forward to *Grandma's Homemade Noodles*—although most of them don't know that this tradition started out with my great grandmother, Pauline Whitton Setzer.

Thanksgiving and Christmas Dinners also included stuffing made with dry bread, celery, onion, boiled eggs, lots of sage and more of those diluted turkey drippings. Lots of fluffy mashed potatoes, homemade cranberry sauce, candied sweet potatoes, homemade dinner rolls, a casserole, and some kind of vegetable dish were all a part of the menu. Of course, if you couldn't wait, there was usually a cheese and a vegetable tray, complete with dip to munch on before dinner.

By the time everybody had consumed their portion of all that, we were all stuffed. The Hays boys always left the table full and then went outside for awhile to run around the block several times. They thought that it helped to get things moving in their stomachs—to jar things down a bit so they could come back in and have second helpings or dessert. Mom always made a large selection of both pumpkin and pecan pies. We didn't have *Cool Whip* back then. Mom always whipped her own cream. Freshly whipped cream on pies was so much better than any topping you can buy today.

Christmas always included Grandma and Grandpa Clark, the Hays family and us. Sometimes Uncle Glenn and Aunt Hazel and their three girls came over. At other times Mom's brother and his wife, Uncle Everett and Aunt Virgil came up from Kansas City. Several times it was a blended Clark, Hays, and Purcell family Christmas with Grandma Campion coming down to the house along with Uncle James and Uncle Joe and their families. On one occasion there were as many as 15 adults and 13 kids—28, a record. But it didn't matter. There was always a lot of food to feed a lot of people.

I remember one funny incident. Junior (Al Hays, Jr.—known to us simply as *Junior* when we were growing up) had gotten big enough that he thought he should sit at the adult table—which he did. When he had finished his dinner, however, he decided he wanted to go outside with his younger brothers when it came time to *shake down* their meal. The boys spent about 20 minutes running around outside and then came back in for dessert. Roger and Duane headed off to the kitchen while Junior went back to his seat at the adult table. As he sat down, he looked around at the adults digging into their desserts. Then he looked down at the dirty plate in front of him. "Who left this messy old plate?" he inquired very loudly and in a scolding voice. It was *his* plate—left sitting there about 20 minutes earlier.

As an *adult*, Junior was expected to clean up after himself when he finished. He hadn't. Aunt Virgil and my Dad never let him forget it. Even after he was grown and had gone off to the Air Force (and even later), whenever he attended a family get together, someone always reminded him, "Hey, who left this messy old plate?"

Christmas was also a time for fun and games. When I wrote about my Grandfather Clark, I told you the story about how he would *Hokey Pokey* candy, nuts, apples, and oranges from Santa Claus in the weeks before Christmas. This was something that he had started with his children when they were small—then later shared with his grandchildren. He would go into a closet or a nearby room and the kids would hear a lot of bumping and scuffling while he talked to Santa Claus. He'd say, "Hokey, Pokey, Diddle Dee Dum. If you've got any candy, give me some!" Then he'd come back into the room with candy or nuts in his hands for the children.

Another family tradition that started way back with my great grandmother, Emily Roberts Clark, was the *Christmas Gift* tradition. The rules were pretty simple. On Christmas morning, say "Christmas Gift!" to everyone you see (before they wake up enough to say it to you). If you say it first, then they owe you a Christmas Gift—usually some of their candy, nuts, or other treats. It was a harmless little game

Mom told the story about the time that her brothers, Everett and Forrest, got up just after midnight so they could get to say it first. Later, when they moved to Horton, she remembered her father standing at the bottom of the staircase and yelling up the stairs to all of the children, "Christmas Gift, everyone!" Mom said that her Grandma Clark, the one who had originated the practice, was still playing the game while living with Grandpa Clark's family in Horton before she died. By then, she was hard of hearing and always kept the door locked to her room. But she waited on Christmas morning, and when she knew that everyone else had gathered at the breakfast table, she would quietly unlock the door, open it and yell, "Christmas Gift, everyone!" They always had treats set aside for her because they knew she would win.

Unfortunately, a good idea *in the wrong hands* can become a bad idea. What Great Grandma Clark started out for Christmas *only* got expanded by my sons to where it became *New Year's Gift, Thanksgiving Gift, Easter Gift,* and so on. By the time we got back around to *Christmas Gift,* that year, well, the tradition almost died.

In recent years, technology changed the game. I found that I would get calls from both of my sons on Christmas morning. The first thing out of their mouths after I said "Hello" was "Christmas Gift." Thank Heavens for Caller I.D! Now I can see who is calling and greet them properly with "Christmas Gift." Several years before the advent of Caller I.D., the phone rang early one Christmas morning. Not to be outdone yet another year, I yelled into the phone, "Christmas Gift!" From the other end of the line came a young man's voice, "Boy, do I have the wrong number," and then he hung up. To my surprise, it wasn't Shawn or Dan.

Although Mom knew that the practice of getting someone's *Christmas Gift* originated with Great Grandma Clark, she didn't know where Great Grandma Clark got the idea. No one in Horton seemed to know of the practice. When I tried to *Christmas Gift* some of my girlfriends when I was growing up, they thought I was crazy. In 1987, Mom called me all excited. She had just received her copy of the December issue of *Redbook Magazine.* In it was a short story written by Kelly Cherry about a young girl named Sassy. Sassy learns a painful lesson because of a game. I quote, "We had a game, the children did. All our schoolmates, too. If someone said 'Christmas gift' before you did, you had to share your gifts with them." The author of the story was from the South and the setting was in Tennessee. Great Grandma Clark was from Tennessee. Therefore, we surmised that *Christmas Gift* must be a southern tradition celebrated in some parts of the South.

Personal Note: I wish I could tell you that after this, my first eighteen to twenty years of life, that I, like Sassy, learned some important lesson that would forever impact my life. My sons would probably tell me that I most definitely did—I was just not aware of what that lesson was when I was 18, or 19, or 20.

If anything, it was the recognition of the importance of and the deep love for *Family*. I deeply love my sons and have always told them so. Sometimes, I think that maybe I have embarrassed them with my openness in saying, "I love you." But, tough it out, boys! That is just the way your mother is. You are a part of that, and that is a part of you; in the same way that all the others who came before you are now a part of you.

I see a little bit of cousin Roger in both of my sons as I see them telling stories and entertaining their children. Sometimes, I see my brother, their Uncle Darrell, when I look at them—Dan more so than Shawn. Mom and Daddy often said Shawn looked like his father. Physically so, maybe. But I've always seen him as being a lot like me. There's also a good portion of his Grandpa, my Daddy, in him. Also like me, it's possible there's just a little too much Grandma Campion inside him—just looking for a chance to get out and get even. Like his father, Shawn is artistic; but that is also like his Grandma, my Mom. Dan is artistic as well. They both got a double dose.

Dan is like my cousin Terry. He, too, grew up to be a fine young man with a little bit of the devil in him. When he was a little boy, he'd often break things—like all the clocks he came across and my father's watch. I'm sure he had good intentions, just wanting to take things apart and see how they worked. But at a certain point, things just seemed to come apart on him, unraveled like the fetal pig came apart on me—or rather—on my teacher.

Now Dan fixes things—like his Grandpa fixed radios and appliances for nearly 40 years. Like Daddy, Dan is good at it. Some might also say that, unfortunately, like his Grandpa, he also likes to tell weird jokes.

Other people have said he has a unique sense of humor and it is. But then again, when considered in the full context, maybe it's not so different after all. And although Shawn tried to remain more controlled at all times, he gets a little goofy at times, too. So where, other than from Grandpa, did they get this quality of weirdness or goofiness? Well, maybe from me—not every other old lady spends her time writing weird, goofy stories after she retires and looks upon it as achieving a dream.

I'm a Grandma now; both my boys have children. When I see Shawn or Danny (he prefers Dan now that he's a adult, but to me he'll always be Danny) interacting with their children, I see Grandpa Clark, their great grandfather, my grandchildren's great great grandfather, telling stories and playing made up games with them just like he did with us.

As I write this, it's Christmas time—December 27, 2005. It's been a difficult year for many people: The tsunami in Southeast Asia was just a year ago and we've been through a record number of hurricanes—with Katrina and Rita delivering a 1-2 punch to our Gulf States and poor New Orleans. I'm sure a lot of people are more than ready for 2005 to go. I'm not. I don't wish away time anymore. There's something good in all of it—even the worst of our tragedies. It's the people and the way they come together.

Bad times seem to unify people in support of each other. They bring out strength of character, goodness, a decency that's always been there—you just may not have recognized it. Unfortunately, it seems we need calamity, strife, and struggle to test our mettle. As Americans, it's true that we often like to think we're unique in our ability to respond to these *tough times*. We are unique, but maybe not as *different* as we might think. When considered in the full context, we're all Our Father's children. We're all family—even if some of our traditions are somewhat different. Love one another.

And by the way . . . Christmas Gift, everyone! Christmas Gift!

About the Author

Deanna Purcell Pendleton was born and spent her early life in Horton, Kansas. She has her Bachelor's and Master's Degrees from Kansas State University (KSU), as well as numerous graduate hours at KSU and other universities. Having been a "chronic" worker since age 16, past jobs have included clerk, secretary, teacher, social worker, communications consultant, trainer/course developer, instructional technologist, and human resource manager. Deanna retired along with the new millennium after 21 years working for a major telecommunications company. After making the decision to pursue her dream of writing, she began compiling *Gullible's Travels* from individual life stories she had written. This is her first book.